The **TOP 100** PLAYER BATS *in* BASEBALL HISTORY

★ ★ ★ ★ ★ ★ ★ ★ ★ ★ ★ ★ ★ ★

Legendary Lumber

The TOP 100 PLAYER BATS in BASEBALL HISTORY

★ ★ ★ ★ ★ ★ ★ ★ ★ ★ ★ ★ ★ ★

Legendary Lumber

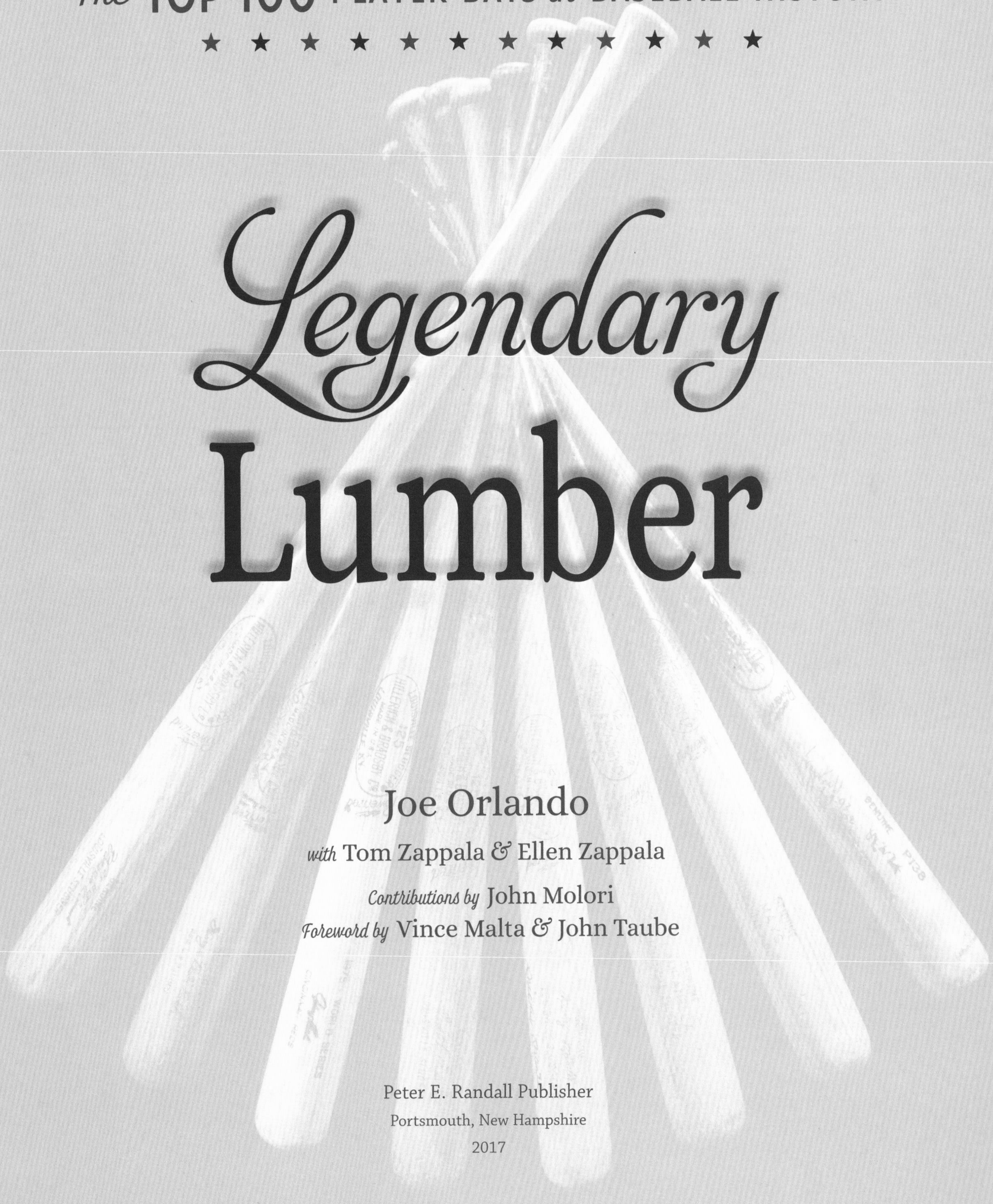

Joe Orlando

with Tom Zappala & Ellen Zappala

Contributions by John Molori

Foreword by Vince Malta & John Taube

Peter E. Randall Publisher
Portsmouth, New Hampshire
2017

ISBN: 978-1-937721-41-1

Library of Congress Control Number: 2017901939

Produced by Peter E. Randall Publisher
Box 4726, Portsmouth, New Hampshire 03802
www.perpublisher.com

Book design: Grace Peirce

Photography credit: © Images Anthony Dube/White Point Imaging 2016
www.whitepointimaging.com

Various player images provided by Memory Lane, Inc.
www.memorylaneinc.com

Additional images provided by Heritage Auctions
www.ha.com

Other images provided by renowned photo expert Henry Yee

Various player images by Getty Images and Icon Sportswire

Additional copies available from: www.amazon.com

Printed in China

To my father and mentor, Joseph James,
and my son and little inspiration, Joseph Patrick

Contents

★ ★ ★ ★ ★ ★ ★ ★ ★ ★ ★ ★ ★ ★ ★ ★

Acknowledgments

★ ★ ★ ★ ★ ★ ★ ★ ★ ★ ★

Many people contributed to this great project. From administrative help, to photography, to memorabilia acquisition and everything in between, it was a monumental effort on the part of some great colleagues.

Special thanks to our talented friend, John Molori, for his bat history and player-narrative contributions. John's folksy, whimsical writing style and his insightful baseball analysis combine to make this book both informative and fun to read.

Jackie Curiel deserves special recognition for her diligent work behind the scenes. From administrative assistance to acquiring images and to editing contributions, Jackie did whatever was asked with great efficiency and attention to detail. She is simply a pleasure to work with.

John Taube and Vince Malta deserve special thanks for providing the foreword for this book and for being leaders in the professional model bat world. Both of these gentlemen have brought structure to the hobby with their authentication efforts and knowledge of bat collecting, a hobby that is infinitely better off because of them.

The following collectors were kind enough to open their homes and display cases to us and allow our team to photograph some of their fine bats for this project. Thanks to Thomas Tull, Scott Foraker, Richard Angrist, Michael Pulice, Brian Seigel, Mike Heffner, Steve Masi, Don Nunnari and Nick Nunnari for their enthusiasm and support, and for sharing their collections with us. This group's willingness to share their endeavor with others can only strengthen the hobby.

We thank Memory Lane, Inc., Heritage Auctions and renowned photo expert Henry Yee for the wonderful images they provided. These beautiful images illustrate the player characteristics discussed in the text and serve to educate the reader, which is the primary purpose of this book.

Special thanks also to Tony Dube and his great staff at White Point Imaging, and to Chrissie Good, photographer for Collectors Universe. These talented people work with incredible precision in both the technical and artistic sides of the profession and the result is present throughout the book. The images are second to none.

Kudos to Ted Greenberg, key master and host to our team during one of our bat photoshoots. As organizer of one of the finest collections in the world, Ted made it possible to capture some of the hobby's most priceless pieces of lumber.

We greatly appreciate the award-winning work of Deidre Randall, Grace Peirce, Zak Johnson and the staff at Peter E. Randall Publisher. If it were not for their very talented designers and editors, this project would never have happened. Again, like all of our other books, they have stepped up to the plate and hit it out of the park.

Lastly, a heartfelt thanks to you, the collectors. The passion that you have makes it all worthwhile. We greatly appreciate every one of you. Happy collecting!

▲ *Carlton Fisk gamers, like many player bats, often exhibit unique characteristics such as identifiable knob markings. Fisk bats are often found with a circle placed around his uniform number.*

Foreword

★ ★ ★ ★ ★ ★ ★ ★ ★ ★

When Joe Orlando asked us to provide a foreword for this book, we were both honored and excited that professional model bats were being showcased not only by a fellow hobby expert who has helped provide valuable market information to the public and acted as an advocate for the hobby, but by a collector who shares our passion for the subject matter.

When we started collecting bats over 30 years ago, never did we imagine the extraordinary bats of baseball immortals that would come across our desk: Ruth, Gehrig, Cobb, Williams, Mays, Clemente—nor did we envision the tremendous growth in the interest in game-used bats. And yes, while still in its infancy as compared to other sports collectibles, it has a strong foundation to build upon as we look to the future.

This foundation is, in part, comprised of the excellent resources at our disposal, which help solidify the authenticity of a professional model bat. The availability of player ordering records, communication with the manufacturers, the wealth of information via the Internet, and the onset of MLB real-time authentication in the dugouts and clubhouses of professional teams gives collectors confidence and security as they contemplate an addition to an existing collection or the creation of a new one.

This book is a celebration of some of the greatest player bats in the hobby, and some of the bats used to illustrate each two-page spread are extraordinary relics of our National Pastime. At the very least, these bats provide us with a greater insight about the players that used them, including their habits, traits and idiosyncrasies. At the other end of the spectrum, they provide us with a direct connection to the player, and transport us back in time to the place, and in many cases, the very moment that some of our fondest memories of baseball exist.

Like other collectibles, there are only a limited number of professional model bats that will ever exist for each player, starting with their first shipment of bats and ending simultaneously with their playing career. After that time, there can be no more. Unlike other collectibles, each bat is unique, starting as a blank canvas and transformed by the player into a work of art by their preparation, use, and achievements. Yes, in a sense, we believe that Babe Ruth is akin to Pablo Picasso, with the added benefit that we can touch Ruth's masterpiece and take an imaginary swing as we call our shot and notch another home run.

We hope that you appreciate the artistic genius of each of the bats contained in this book, and thank Joe Orlando for compiling this resource and sharing this baseball art form. Be glad, not envious, that such wonderful artifacts exist, and dream about the undiscovered possibilities. Terrific bats are still out there, yet to surface, promising us more connections to the player and the era that tie us to the grand legacy of the game millions of people love.

▲ *Joe DiMaggio, Mickey Mantle, and Ted Williams pose with their bats before a game.*

Introduction

★ ★ ★ ★ ★ ★ ★ ★ ★ ★ ★

I love bats. Make no mistake about it, helping put this book together was a labor of love for me.

Like most collectors of a similar age and older, I started with baseball cards when I was a kid. My friends and I would buy packs from the store, open them together, trade with each other and then proceed to shatter our molars on those pink-colored bricks they called gum.

As I got older, I was introduced to other types of collectibles. From autographs to tickets to display pieces and more, I tried to learn about and experience as many different collectibles as I could. Eventually, I stumbled upon the world of game-used items—the tools of the trade. There were jerseys, gloves, caps, and cleats. To me, there was something so clearly different about them. These artifacts were not manufactured collectibles. They were tangible pieces of history.

▲ *Babe Ruth selecting his bat.*

As much as I loved all the collectibles that came before them, including the variety of other game-worn memorabilia, nothing was more appealing to me than professional model bats, and I still feel the same way today.

I completely understand the appeal that other items offer the collector. I get the appeal of cards and their nostalgic allure. These pieces of cardboard travel through time, reminding us of a different era and our youth. It is a part of our culture that is no longer as popular with children as it once was. For those of us who shared that experience in our earlier days, baseball cards help us recall fond memories and stay young as we get older.

Tickets are tiny time capsules that help recount a specific event or moment in history. In the not-too-distant future, with everything seemingly going digital, printed tickets will most likely become a thing of the past. They won't technically become extinct as long as collectors continue to preserve the existing population, but eventually no more paper tickets will be spawned. Someday, and someday sooner than we would like to admit, sports fans like us will be sitting around like the cranky old Muppets sitting in the balcony at the theater, reminiscing about the days they used to print tickets.

Original photos are wonderful and various kinds of display pieces can be visually stunning. I enjoy the personal touch that the autograph offers and the eye appeal of the vintage baseball flannel, yet still I am drawn to bats more than anything else.

A bat was to Babe Ruth what a paint brush or chisel was to Michelangelo. They are the tools these icons used to become legends. A bat is the sword wielded by an ancient gladiator, the weapon used to do battle with the pitcher and make history in the batter's box. For defensive wizardry, the glove is certainly its equivalent, but the crowd is more captivated by the swing and the crack of the bat than anything else as that unmistakable sound echoes through the ballpark. Some swings are graceful, smooth and seemingly effortless. Others are violent, powerful and vicious.

Bats themselves are the most customized piece of equipment a baseball player uses. They are ordered to spec. The weight, length, shape, balance, color, knob style, and more are all made to order. Some players are remarkably consistent in their ordering patterns, rarely veering from the basic look and feel of each gamer they use, while others change bats like a fashionista changes shoes.

Bats are also very personal in nature, not only in the way they are constructed, but also in the way they are prepared

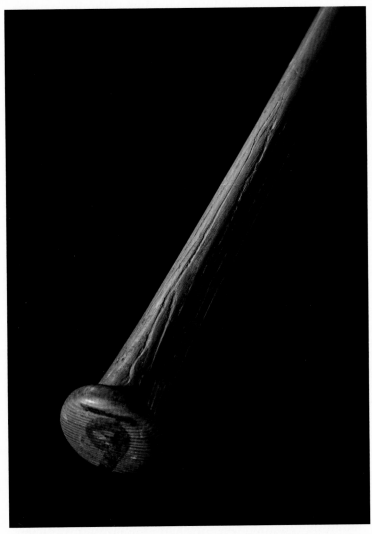

▲ *Since Stan Musial wasn't a big fan of gripping substances like pine tar, the legendary hitter would sometimes groove the handle of his bats to enhance his grip.*

▲ *Babe Ruth scores the barrel of his prized gamer.*

by the player. The handles of gamers are given all sorts of different treatments so players can enhance their grip. From tape to tar, from grooving to scoring, each hitter has their particular way of making their weapon of choice feel comfortable during the swing. This is part of the player's fingerprint, the part that can add tremendous character to each bat and help place it in their hands.

So, how cool are professional model bats compared to other collectibles?

Consider this hypothetical. Let's say that you have several Babe Ruth items placed on a table. On that table, there is a high-grade baseball card, an exquisite single-signed baseball, a ticket from the "Called Shot" game in the 1932 World Series, and even a rare flannel worn by the iconic slugger. In addition, alongside those four outstanding Ruth collectibles is a professional model bat bearing the unrivaled slugger's name.

All five Ruth items are lying on the table in front of you.

Now, one by one, you bring someone over to the table and describe what each item is. Nine times out of ten, the first item the person wants to grab is the bat. Not the card, not the autograph, not the ticket or even the jersey—the bat. All of the collectibles on the table are awe inspiring and, if you are a true collector at heart, you understand the appeal of each one. That said, whether the person standing in front of the table is a collector or not, it's the bat they are most excited to hold in their hands.

There is something about the interactive quality of a bat versus other types of collectibles, even other game-used or worn ones. You can certainly hold a glove or jersey or cap in your hands, they are all tangible pieces of history, but it's not quite the same. With a bat, you can actually swing it if you choose to or emulate the stance of the player who once ordered the specific piece of lumber. It allows the collector to connect with a bat in a way that you simply can't with most other types of collectibles.

▲ *Sometimes the barrel of the bat was planed prior to placing the side writing on a returned gamer, as was the case on this Al Simmons example.*

Sure, if you wanted to, you could try on a jersey and wear it around the house. Even former MLB pitcher David Wells once wore an authentic Babe Ruth cap while pitching for the New York Yankees. Whatever the case may be, it's just not the same thing. On a side note, do not try the "Wells approach" at home kids—even during your weekend softball tournament. A little magic happens when a person puts a bat in their hands that was once used by Babe Ruth, Willie Mays, or Derek Jeter. I don't know why it's different, it just is and it's real.

There is something about hitting a baseball, a simple joy that is almost impossible to describe in words. It doesn't matter if you played in the Major Leagues, Little League, or just messed around at the park with your friends while playing Over the Line. You know the feeling.

I had the privilege of playing baseball in college and for a very short time afterwards in an independent minor league system. During practices, my favorite time was BP—batting practice. After all the stretching, base running, defensive drills and more, it was time to cut loose at the dish on that bucket of pearls sitting on the mound. Well, truth be told, most of the time the balls looked more like rotten apples than pearls, but you get the picture.

I'm sure it's similar to the feeling a golfer gets when they strike a ball off the tee just right. Everything comes together at the right time. The timing, the stride, the weight transfer, the pivot, the hips, the hands and then—WHACK! There goes the ball. A frozen rope, a seed, a missile, a pea, a gapper, a screamer, a towering drive, a majestic blast, and even a duck fart can feel so good as long as it drops in for a hit. Hitting is fun. It's that simple. Collecting professional model bats can be a lot of fun too.

These are the weapons used by some of the best hitters and most recognizable figures who ever lived.

As collectors, we can own them, display them, or even swing them if we like. You can let your imagination run wild with these relics in your hands. They are as fun to collect as they

▲ *A closeup of Hank Greenberg and his scored handle in 1938.*

are historical in nature. All of this and more is what makes collecting bats great.

So sit back and enjoy the ride through our *Top 100* list. It's all about *Legendary Lumber* and I wouldn't have it any other way.

A Look Inside the Top 100

★ ★ ★ ★ ★ ★ ★ ★ ★ ★ ★ ★ ★ ★

The process of selecting the 100 professional model bats for this book was difficult. We considered a number of factors, including but not limited to: historical importance, rarity, popularity of the player and bat, visual appeal, and market value. The reality is that there is no right or wrong answer to the question, "What are the top 100 bats in the hobby?" The purpose of this book is to share the wonderful appeal of bats with existing collectors and potential ones. Part of the fun is stimulating friendly debates about who should make the list and who should be left off. Our top 100 is a diverse group and one bound to spark arguments.

Many of the names, and bats, on this list would fall under the category of no-brainers. Whether it's Hank Aaron, Roberto Clemente, Derek Jeter, or Babe Ruth, there were plenty of surefire picks for this amassment of legendary lumber. Once you start getting past the first 25, 50, or 75 bats, the process becomes increasingly tough. On a comprehensive list of this nature, there is room for the undisputed icons like Mickey Mantle and the ultra-popular stars of the post-1980 period such as Kirby Puckett.

There were some extreme rarities left off the list that would arguably act as the centerpieces of any fine collection, like those used by Cap Anson and Walter Johnson. We also considered bats used by Negro League stars such as Josh Gibson and Oscar Charleston. Due to the inherent difficultly in authenticating most of these Negro League relics and the virtually non-existent population of gamers that do exist, we limited the book to bats used at the Major League level.

There are many bats that did not make the cut, but that does not mean those bats do not possess serious historical importance or great value.

For every player that made the list, we include a narrative highlighting a significant moment or the accomplishments he had at the plate using the weapons that many collectors find so intriguing. Those highlights are followed by a narrative about the bat itself. This is where we break down the interesting characteristics of each gamer and provide insight about their appeal. From player ordering habits to distinct bat preparation to relative scarcity, these narratives provide important commentary for the collector.

Each two-page player spread also features the image of a stellar gamer actually used by the player. In most cases, the examples chosen for the book help illustrate some of the important features noted in the text.

To be clear, any professional model bat of the 100 players listed would qualify. With the help of some advanced collectors who made their prized gamers available to us, the bat stories come to life with the visuals provided.

▶ *A young Hank Aaron holding a handful of bats.*

The Crack of the Bat

★ ★ ★ ★ ★ ★ ★ ★ ★ ★ ★ ★ ★ ★ ★ ★ ★

If you are a bat collector, or thinking about delving into the world of bat collecting, here are some great tips from Joe Orlando, one of the foremost experts in the hobby. These invaluable tips will help you make the right decisions and choices on what to look for in your bat-world journey. If you want to learn the ropes, this chapter is a must read. Enjoy!

▶ *Ken Griffey Jr. applies his signature taping pattern.*

Five Tips for Building a Professional Model Bat Collection

★ ★

For those interested in pursuing "legendary lumber," here are a few tips that can hopefully enhance your hobby experience.

1 Buy Authenticated/ Graded Bats

The same principle that applies to virtually all other collectibles, such as coins, comic books, and baseball cards, applies here. As the hobby has matured, the importance of third-party authentication and grading services has increased. In fact, the emergence of these services has played a huge role in the hobby's evolution during the past few decades. They help provide structure in the marketplace and a better understanding of how one collectible measures up against another. The key is to ask questions and distinguish the services that have industry credibility from those that do not. Remember that a Letter of Authenticity (LOA) is only as credible as the name behind it.

Authentication is the first step in the process. This is where the experts determine whether or not the bat in question is a professional model bat, ordered by the player during their career. Here, the expert examines the ordering/ shipping records, the labeling of the bat, the length and weight and the quality of the wood, among other things. It is important that potential collectors understand there is very little gray area when it comes to separating professional model bats from other bats, such as store model, replica, or commemorative ones. This is where a large part of the bat's value comes from.

Grading is the second step in the process. Once the expert has determined the bat to be an authentic, professional

model bat, the bat is now eligible for grading on a scale of 1–10 with 10 being best. Unlike the type of grading that is used to judge most other collectibles, such as trading cards where the scale is based entirely on the sheer condition of the item, the core of the bat scale is very different. Here, the experts evaluate the general use attributes and the specific player characteristics. In essence, the experts are looking for evidence that helps place the bat in question into a player's hands. This is the closest thing to a fingerprint in the professional model bat world.

On each two-page player spread within this book, a section entitled "Tales from Joe's Bat Rack" is devoted to covering these types of characteristics. Not only can the presence of these characteristics enhance the visual appeal of some bats, but they are at the heart of the grading process. The stronger the characteristics are, the higher the grade often is. Other factors can come into play, such as provenance, degree of use, and, to a lesser extent, condition. Condition issues can lower the grade if they detract from the overall eye appeal of the bat. The affect is usually minimal, but the presence of things like water or fire damage, or missing pieces of wood from game action or other causes can be factors. This is not to be confused with the expected wear-and-tear associated with player use, such as cleat marks on the barrel or ball/stitch marks on the hitting surface.

The key to remember is that bats are not baseball cards. They were intended to be used and, often times, that use is what helps give the bat great character. The bats that usually garner the most attention from collectors are the ones that exhibit a blend of excellent characteristics, which often results in a high grade, along with an attractive look.

▼ *This 1920-21 Babe Ruth gamer exhibits the kind of barrel scoring the legendary slugger was known to employ at times during his career.*

bat preparation or use characteristics pertain to each player. Within *Legendary Lumber*, we included some fantastic examples of supporting images that help illustrate those distinct traits. If you are from the world of trading card collecting, I am sure you have heard the saying, "Buy the card, not the holder." A similar approach should be used in bat collecting. The grade of a bat is important and certainly helpful in providing a greater comprehension of its quality, but the numerical grade only tells part of the story.

Your personal growth as a collector can help put each bat in proper context, which will enable you to make wise decisions as a buyer or seller.

▲ *Babe Ruth tosses an extra bat aside before stepping to the plate.*

2 Educate Yourself

We live in the information age. Take advantage of it. There are a number of terrific resources both online and in print that can help arm you with essential information and make you a more informed collector. PSA ProBatFacts, a free online bat encyclopedia, and the book *Louisville Slugger Professional Player Bats - A Complete Reference Guide* by Vince Malta are two great examples. There are a number of great online articles and guides that are available at your fingertips. Since every professional model bat is truly unique, it is important that collectors grasp the differences between bats. Sometimes, the differences are subtle, but every aspect of a bat can impact its appeal and ultimately its value.

Part of the effort should include the study of photos or video footage, particularly of game action. This can help provide a better understanding of what specific types of

3 Find and Buy from Reputable Sellers and Network with Fellow Collectors

Buyers spend their hard-earned money on the collectibles they love, and sometimes it is a lot of money, so it is crucial that they develop relationships with sellers who possess excellent reputations. As values for collectibles increase over time, this becomes even more important. Whether the seller is a retailer or a nationally-known auction house, the standard to which collectors hold them should be the same. Often times, a seller can not only assist you with acquiring or liquidating items, they can also help provide expert advice that can help improve your overall experience.

Furthermore, if there were ever an issue with an item that you purchased, a seller of this nature would be incentivized to address it in the manner you would expect. Sellers with

▲ *Circa 1927—Lou Gehrig takes a close look at the weapon that made Babe Ruth famous.*

all learn new things every day. Cultivating friendships with other hobbyists is not only rewarding on a personal level, but sharing essential information with each other can only help elevate your experience.

Ask questions, talk to fellow collectors, evaluate references, and try to measure the reputation of the seller you are considering working with. Believe me, you will be glad you did and for a number of reasons.

4 Select a Collecting Theme and Stick to It

Prior to starting any collection, a collector should first develop a theme. Anyone who has ever participated in this hobby will tell you that if you don't take the time to do this, collecting chaos will ensue. A theme can help you stay focused and disciplined as a buyer. It can also help you stay sane. Each auction season we are inundated with terrific items offered for sale. It is easy to fall into the trap of simply buying random, unrelated collectibles you like. There's certainly nothing inherently wrong with doing so, but if you continue to go down this path, you end up with a collection that has no rhyme or reason to it.

Even if you have a virtually infinite amount of disposable income, you simply can't own everything. It is extremely advisable to start with reasonable collecting goals. Once your collection is built on a solid foundation, you can expand or complement your collection from there. It's all about developing the core as a priority. Collectors can always broaden their horizons as they move forward and gain more experience. Over time, your taste or collecting interests may change. That is all part of the endeavor of collecting. It is a natural progression most collectors go through.

Since we are talking about professional model bats, this specific genre has many potential themes to choose from. There are very traditional themes, like collecting bats used by members of the 500 Home Run and 3,000 Hit Clubs. Some collectors focus on team sets like the Brooklyn Dodgers of the 1950s, the "Big Red Machine" of the 1970s or the great New York Yankees clubs of the late-1990s/early-2000s. You can create your own Dream Team lineup, collect stars by decade, or even start a collection based on elements of this book.

The beauty of this topic is that you can create any theme you want. The most important thing is that you come up with one and actually stick to the plan.

excellent reputations are interested in preserving those reputations. It takes time to earn a certain level of respect in the marketplace, but that credibility can be lost almost instantaneously. As a result, fine sellers are often willing to provide a safety net for their clients that mere opportunists are not willing to supply.

The good news is that there are sellers who are willing to provide the kind of service you are looking for because they are equally interested in developing a longstanding relationship. If you want repeat business, then you learn to treat the customer right. They may also possess useful knowledge, and if they are willing to share that experience with you, it can prove to be invaluable. You just need to find them and distinguish those kinds of sellers from those who present a riskier proposition. Like anything else, research is the key.

Connecting with other collectors who share the same passion as you do can also prove to be vital. No matter how much you know or think you know about this hobby, you are bound to meet someone who knows more. Be a sponge and learn as much as you can from other collectors. In the hobby, we

5 Explore Different Display Options

A fair number of collectors will tell you this is one they had to learn the hard way. No matter what you collect, these things that we pursue take up space. In some cases, they can take up a lot of space. That is why it is imperative that you consider all of your options before building the collection. The first question you should ask yourself is whether or not you plan on displaying the bats in some fashion. If not, you still have to plan how you will store the bats, even if they are not presented for public viewing.

The great news is that professional model bats can be displayed in a number of ways, including those that do not take up a tremendous amount of space. So, if you desire to display your bats in your man cave or home office, there are some very attractive and creative ways to showcase your legendary lumber. Some collectors are fond of using either vintage bat racks or modern replicas to house their gamers. Although not common, vintage racks will usually appear on the auction circuit each year, while the replicas can usually be found online with relative ease.

Some collectors have customized bat racks or bat carousels (circular bat racks that can be turned on their axis) made for their collections. A collector can store a number of bats in a relatively small space if they choose the bat rack route. Without dominating an entire room, you can display dozens of bats in this manner. Other collectors, however, prefer the look of displays that are mounted on the wall. From a visual standpoint, these wall cases are terrific since you can view the bats in their entirety from across the room. There are individual bat cases and ones that hold numerous bats.

Even if you live in a mansion, wall space is limited. For that reason, keep this in mind as you build your collection. There are collectors who do not wish to display their bats, but instead prefer to store them away. Some collectors simply place their bats inside traditional bat tubes and bank them inside their

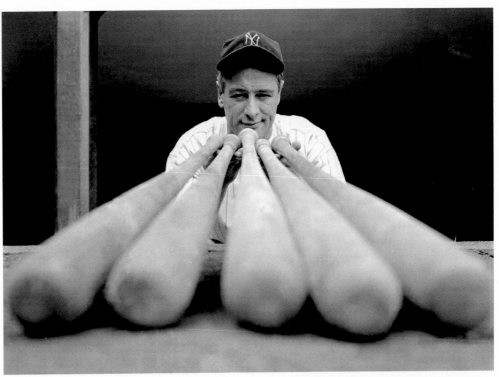

▲ *Lou Gehrig tries to pick a winner.*

▲ *Joe DiMaggio and Ted Williams pose with a bat in 1941.*

▲ *Some Ted Williams gamers from the late-1940s and 1950s feature his number painted on the knob.*

▲ *Ted Williams prepares his bat for battle.*

home safe. I know several collectors who use gun-style safes for their bats because of the accommodating dimensions. In other cases, collectors may simply place the bats in a closet or another secluded area so their collectibles are not out in the open.

Whatever you choose to do, it is important that you think ahead and plan before making acquisitions. Owning any collectible can be fun, but thinking about space can help a hobbyist enjoy those collectibles to the fullest.

A Final Thought

Beyond the sport and the hobby we love, the baseball bat possesses a symbolic power in our culture. All you have to do is think about the range of television shows and movies where unforgettable scenes featured baseball bats. Of course, there are iconic moments in baseball movies like *The Natural* (1984) that come to mind right away. Who can forget when Roy Hobbs (played by Robert Redford) splits his favorite bat—"Wonderboy"—in half on a foul ball and asks the batboy to pick out a winner for him? The batboy,

Bobby Savoy, goes back to the dugout and brings Hobbs his own homemade bat—the "Savoy Special." We all know what happens next as Hobbs clobbers a fastball into the light tower in right field.

Aside from baseball movies, there have been comedic moments like the one seen in *Office Space* (1999) when a bunch of coworkers decide to take a constantly malfunctioning printer out to a field for a beating as hardcore rap music plays in the background. There have been shocking moments like those seen in the movie *The Untouchables* (1987), where Al Capone (played by Robert De Niro) makes an example out of one of his men by proceeding to tee off on his head during a sit-down meeting, and the hit show *The Walking Dead*, where the evil Negan (played by Jeffrey Dean Morgan) introduces us to his favorite bat—"Lucille"—in the Season Six finale.

Bats have been used as a weapon against evil too. Who can forget the creepy scene in *The Shining* (1980) where Wendy Torrance (played by Shelley Duvall) tries to defend herself when Jack Torrance (played by Jack Nicholson) follows her up a flight of stairs in a crazed state? In *Inglourious Basterds* (2009), Donny Donowitz (played by Eli Roth) uses his favorite piece of lumber to punish Nazi soldiers during WWII. And how about the climax to the 2002 movie, *Signs*? As Graham Hess (played by Mel Gibson) emerges from his state of shock after seeing his unconscious son in the hands of an alien, he instructs his brother Merrill (played by Joaquin Phoenix) to "swing away." Merrill, a former minor league baseball player and home run record holder, grabs his bat from the wall mount above and proceeds to rescue his nephew by laying the wood to the intruder.

One could argue that the baseball bat is the most recognizable piece of sports equipment in our culture. It transcends baseball and sports, but the bats used by the men who made history on the field are the ones that collectors hold dear. It's time to sift through the pages of this book and visit the legendary lumber that captivates collectors around the world.

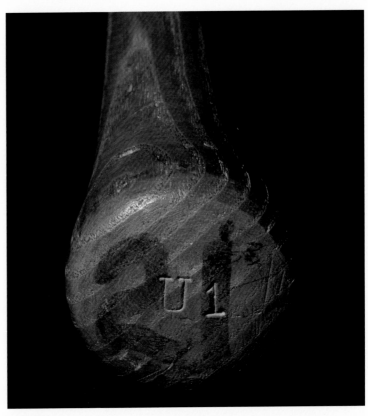

▲ *While other player bats feature the same type of handle, Roberto Clemente made the U1 model famous.*

◄ *Paul Waner removes his gamer from the bat rack.*

Crushed, Cracked and Corked

★ ★ ★ ★ ★ ★ ★ ★ ★ ★ ★ ★ ★ ★ ★ ★ ★ ★ ★

Before we begin our journey into the world of bats, we thought that it would be appropriate to first look at the evolution of these hardwood gems. From trees come bats, from bats come ballplayers, from ballplayers come home runs, but there is a little more to the story. Sit back and enjoy our short primer on the history of the baseball bat. Our colleague John Molori, along with some great insight from Chris Meiman Curator of Louisville Slugger Museum & Factory, enlightens us on bat history and how some of these bats used by the greats truly became legendary lumber.

◄ *A trio of bat knobs from the gamers of three baseball legends – Ted Williams, Roberto Clemente, and George Brett.*

The History and Lore of the Baseball Bat

★ ★

Bat Beginnings

To those who revere the game, a baseball bat is no inanimate object. It is a living, breathing part of the game, one that has transformed, grown, and matured, just as the players themselves. Whether it is a thin-handled weapon built for bat speed or a hefty war club crafted for durability, the bat is the baseball player's most customized piece of equipment. An individual player's preferred bat size, shape, and contents can often be a mystery, but what of the baseball bat's history?

As far back as the 1840s, players fashioned their own baseball bats with no set standards or guidelines for weight, length, type of wood, or size. In many cases, bats had previous lives as tools or other wooden items. In fact, most players used bats with a flat, rather than rounded, surface. Bat selection was a matter of personal taste, from long, slender sticks to stout, heavier models. Many of these self-made bats shattered easily and were mended with tape or string near the handle. This served the dual purpose of making the bat easier to handle.

The Professional National Association of Baseball Players Governing Committee finally passed an edict limiting the size of bats in 1859. The ruling stated that bats must be rounded and no more than 2.5 inches in diameter at the thickest point, but it did not set limitations regarding bat length. A decade later, in 1869, the committee set a maximum length of 42 inches, which is still the Major League Baseball standard today. By 1879, most players were using a long, slender bat with a knob at the bottom for better control. Despite the rule on rounded bats, some players still used flat bats for bunting. In 1893, flat bats were banned completely but the barrel limit was increased to 2.75 inches.

The knob plays a key part in bat history, specifically in the case of Hall of Famer Napoleon "Nap" Lajoie. In the early 1900s, Wright and Ditson created the "Nap Bat" in their Boston shop. Produced with a double-ringed knob, it was designed to improve bat control for players who hit with their hands apart or who tended to choke up on the bat. A bat with options, it came in a variety of weights and lengths, with Lajoie's name branded on each model.

▲ *Ty Cobb inspects his bat before the game.*

Regardless of the era or bat style, batting is pure frustration. Imagine trying to hit a Satchel Paige fastball, Sandy Koufax curveball, Gaylord Perry spitter, or Mariano Rivera cutter. It is fitting that the modern-day baseball bat truly began with frustration.

In 1884, 17-year-old John "Bud" Hillerich, the son of Louisville, Kentucky, woodworker J. F. Hillerich, ditched work to take in a ballgame featuring the local nine, the Louisville Eclipse. During the game, Pete Browning, a talented but slumping player for the Eclipse, broke his bat. "After the game, Bud Hillerich offered to make Browning a new bat," explains Chris Meiman, curator of Louisville Slugger Museum & Factory in Louisville, Kentucky. "The next game, Browning got three hits with the bat and the legend was born. At first, J. F. Hillerich was not interested in making baseball bats. He believed the nineteenth-century game was tainted by gambling and alcohol. Eventually, he relented and 'Hillerich Bats' were soon followed by 'Falls City Sluggers' and, in 1894, Hillerich trademarked the 'Louisville Slugger.'"

In 1905, Honus Wagner signed a deal that emblazoned his name on the "Slugger." Players like Babe Ruth, Ty Cobb, Nap Lajoie, Joe Jackson, and Lou Gehrig followed suit and popularized the Louisville Slugger name beyond all others. Says Meiman, "The agreement with Wagner was the first endorsement deal between a player and product manufacturer. It allowed Hillerich to brand Wagner's signature on bats sold to the public and use his name and likeness in advertising. Soon after, other big stars of the day signed on to have their signature on their bats."

Although Hillerich is recognized as the first family of bats, mention should be made of A. G. Spalding. In a seven-year big league pitching career, Albert Goodwell Spalding was 252–65 with an ERA of 2.13, but he quit baseball in 1878 at the age of 27 to run A. G. Spalding and Brothers, the Chicago-based sporting goods company he formed in 1876. By 1900, Spalding was the largest manufacturer of baseball bats in the United States, producing one million bats annually with factories across the country, but, eventually, Hillerich & Bradsby, Co. would dominate the bat marketplace.

Meiman points to three significant turning points for Hillerich early in the twentieth century: the 1901 move to the Finzer Street facility that only made baseball bats and served as the company's home for more than seven decades; the hiring of St. Louis sporting goods salesman Frank Bradsby and his 1916 promotion to business partner; and the fortunate signing of George Herman "Babe" Ruth to a bat contract in 1918, his first season as a primary hitter. The soon famous Ruth became an unabashed cheerleader for Hillerich & Bradsby and the Louisville Slugger brand.

Good Wood

According to Meiman, the earliest bats were often handmade with whatever wood was available. About a half-dozen species of wood were used for bats, but two species started the twentieth century as the favorites: northern white ash and true hickory. Though most players preferred ash bats, several early baseball stars used hickory, including Babe Ruth. Hickory is much stronger than ash and is less prone to

▲ *Babe Ruth boning his bat.*

breaking. Many bats of the era were 35 to 36 inches in length and sometimes weighed more than 40 ounces. The theory of the time was that the batter would have more power with heavier, stronger wood.

A. G. Spalding's Gold Medal bat was fashioned from traditional white ash wood. Each bat was registered and inspected, and included a guarantee against any failings. In addition, many Spalding bats were made from durable wagon tongue wood that came from the sturdy spokes of wagons used throughout the 1800s. Around the turn of the century, Spalding also popularized the "Mushroom Bat," which had a round knob for better balance and weight distribution.

As players and times changed, so did the bats, says Meiman. "Led by Ted Williams and Stan Musial in the 1940s, players began to look for lighter, more flexible bats. The sizes of the bats also began to shrink to between 34 and 36 inches and 33 to 36 ounces. Looking for an edge, some smaller companies began experimenting with other types of wood, including maple."

Many Major Leaguers now prefer maple due to its unique hardness, sound, and feel. "Maple offers added strength at impact," notes Meiman. "Closed grains eliminate flaking, commonly seen with ash, allowing superior durability against delamination. Barry Bonds was an early adopter of maple, and players sought out what the man who hit 73 home runs was using. Now, more than half of MLB players use maple bats. The physical structure of the bat continues to shrink as players continue to get larger and stronger. Most bats are now between 33 inches and 34.5 inches, and weigh between 30 to 32 ounces."

Bonds followed a long tradition of player involvement in bat creation and selection. "Ted Williams made several trips to the bat factory and often hand-picked the billets he wanted made into his bats," explains Meiman. "When a new bat type is created, it becomes its own unique model. In the earliest days, these models were named after the player and the date it was created. Babe Ruth's first model was called 'Babe Ruth 3/23/1923.' In the 1930s, this was changed to an alphanumeric system organized by the player who created the model. For example, when Hank Aaron created a bat model in 1961, he was the 99th player with the last name beginning with A to make a new model and it was called an 'A99.'"

In addition to standard white ash and popular maple, birch has become the fastest growing wood used for baseball bats. Says Meiman, "It features the ideal combination of surface hardness and flexibility for increased durability, decreasing the chance of fractured breakage. Birch also affords lighter swing weights for comparable turning models. It isn't quite as light as ash, but does provide another option in the growing marketplace."

Hitting High Jinks

Memorable offensive statistics in MLB history were all accomplished by great baseball bats, but that is not the entire history of the instrument. On the contrary, some unforgettable bat moments have nothing to do with immense talent. Some of the juiciest bat banter is downright nefarious!

Who could forget the 2000 Subway World Series between the Mets and Yankees? In Game Two, Mike Piazza shattered his bat against a Roger Clemens' first inning pitch. Clemens picked up the dangerously pointed scrap of lumber and seemed to toss it at Piazza as the Mets catcher made his way to first base. Similarly, was there ever a more violent maneuver than when fiery A's shortstop Bert Campaneris

hurled his bat at Tigers pitcher Lerrin LaGrow in Game Two of the 1972 American League playoffs?

How about that August day in 1965 when the Dodgers-Giants rivalry exploded as San Francisco pitcher Juan Marichal angrily took a bat to Johnny Roseboro's head? Some bat-related wounds were even self-inflicted. A case in point is Bo Jackson, who regularly shattered bats on his own thighs, knees, shins, and head!

Bat history is not all home runs and high fives. Here are two of the most notorious baseball bat moments told by those who were there:

Tarred and Measured

New York. July 24, 1983. In the top of the ninth inning, with the Royals trailing the Yankees 4–3, future Hall of Famer George Brett swatted a two-run homer giving Kansas City a 5–4 lead. Yankees manager Billy Martin wanted Brett's bat checked to see if it had more than the permitted 18 inches of pine tar.

Merritt Riley, a 17-year-old Yankees batboy assigned to the Royals' bench, was a Yankees fan but also a Brett fan. In 2013, Riley told Daniel Barbarisi of the *Wall Street Journal* about that day. "George Brett was a very outgoing, easygoing, friendly guy. He called me Spaulding. I thought that was so cool. The Yankees had a rule, you had to go to home plate, get the bat, and run back to the dugout. You couldn't stand there and wait for the player to round the bases, to high-five him. Something kept me there, with the bat in my hand. I gave [Brett] a high-five, and then started to go back to the dugout. And that is when Billy Martin started yelling from the Yankees dugout to check the bat. If I would have just picked it up, and run back, they wouldn't have been able to get to it in time." After Brett's bat was found to have too much pine tar and he was called out, he emerged from the dugout in a fit of rage.

Riley saw Brett after the game. He told Barbarisi, "We made eye contact. He looked at me and said, 'Why the [expletive] didn't you pick up the bat?' And then he started laughing. He said, 'Spaulding, I'm only kidding you. But you do owe me.'" The American League eventually overruled the decision, allowing Brett's home run. The game was resumed a month later and the Royals prevailed 5–4.

Bat Man and Robbing

Chicago. July 15, 1994. Early in a game vs. Cleveland, White Sox manager Gene Lamont asked umpire Dave Phillips to check Albert Belle's bat for cork. Phillips took the bat, secured it in his locker and said it would be checked after the game. Jason Grimsley was a pitcher for Cleveland that day and, in 2014, told Fox Sports what happened next.

"I looked at [coach] Buddy Bell and said, 'I bet I can make my way back to the umpires' room, crawl down, and get that bat.' I looked over at Mike Hargrove, who gave me a thumbs up and we were off. I went inside, took my jersey off, put some tennis shoes on, and put some batting gloves on. I needed a flashlight, and a sanitary [mask] wrapped around my face. Albert didn't have one bat, BP or game, that was not corked, so we found a bat that was similar, put some pine tar on it, put a little resin on it, and put it in a sanitary [plastic wrap].

"I went into Hargrove's office, lifted up the [ceiling] tile, got on the cinder block walls and started making my way to the umpires' room. It was close to 95 or 100 degrees. I couldn't really breathe. I found the room, picked up the ceiling tile, and dropped down. I found the bat in one of the umpire's lockers and replaced it. That was pretty intense."

After the game, White Sox general manager Ron Schueler told Phillips that there was a break-in. The White Sox employed an ex-FBI agent to check out the crime scene. Cleveland GM John Hart finally surrendered the bat with the stipulation that the robber not be identified or punished.

The Walk-Off

The Louisville Slugger remains the "Official Bat of Major League Baseball," but there is more competition in the wood bat industry than ever. According to Meiman, players who used to swing two or three bat companies in their career will now use that many in a series. Although Hillerich & Bradsby, Co., sold the rights to the Louisville Slugger brand to Wilson Sporting Goods in 2015, it maintains ownership of the factory and the attached museum that opened in Louisville in 1996.

Bat making is big business, but the baseball bat is less about cents and more about the senses. In Ken Burns' celebrated PBS film *Baseball*, Negro League legend Buck O'Neil recalled hearing a certain sound only on three occasions—when Babe Ruth, Josh Gibson, and Bo Jackson smacked the baseball.

Size, shape, barrel diameter, and knob style are tangible assets, but there is a metaphysical magic to a baseball bat.

▲ *George Brett would occasionally place his childhood nickname (Lou) on the knobs of his bats. Lou is short for Looney Tunes. Brett's oldest brother gave him the nickname because of George's love of cartoons.*

How does the bat feel in the hands of a hitter? How does it turn and connect with an oncoming pitch? How does it bounce back from an inside fastball on the handle or after being tossed aside in disgust after an untimely strikeout?

At the 1999 All-Star Game at Fenway Park in Boston, Ted Williams famously asked home run king Mark McGwire if he smelled burnt wood when one of his mighty swings met the ball. Williams also said he could see the stitches on a baseball as it neared his bat. The Splendid Splinter could probably even taste the combination of white ash and cowhide as the ball and bat met!

Hitting a baseball is one of the most difficult tasks in sports and the baseball bat is the instrument to accomplish this tough task. Regardless of the way it is boned, bludgeoned, blessed, or bashed, the baseball bat remains a steadfast symbol of the game. Its history creates baseball's timeline, its stories bring color to baseball's present, and its continued technological development brings progress to baseball's future.

The Top 25

★ ★ ★ ★ ★ ★ ★ ★ ★ ★ ★ ★ ★ ★ ★ ★ ★

This chapter highlights the top 25 pieces of lumber in the hobby along with player profiles about the greats that held them in their hands. This list does not necessarily mean that these are the top 25 players that ever played the game—although most are, in fact, at the top of the mountain—but rather that these players used the bats that are now the most sought after in the hobby. From tree trunks to light lumber, it is all here. From Ruth to Foxx to Jeter, this list is based on the research done by the leading bat experts in the country. Enjoy *The Top 25*.

▲ *A young Willie Mays poses for the camera with his bat.*

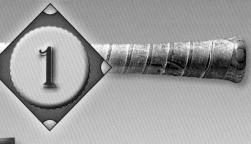

★ ★ ★ ★ ★ ★ ★ ★ ★ ★ ★ ★

slapping the ball to all fields, and stretching a double to a triple. Ruth's mound magnificence ended voluntarily when, in 1920, he became a full-time outfielder for the Yankees. Over 15 seasons in New York, he would pound the baseball at an incredible rate, and the Yankees would win four World Series.

Ruth batted .342 for his career, and is the all-time leader in slugging percentage (.690) and OPS (1.164). He smashed a record 60 home runs in 1927, a mark that stood for 34 years, and he finished his career as baseball's all-time home run king with 714 blasts. Part of baseball's inaugural Hall of Fame class in 1936, Ruth passed away in 1948, but his immortality exists in the

The most famous baseball player who ever lived, George Herman Ruth's colossal exploits on the baseball field were surpassed only by his legendary drinking, eating, and partying. Ruth's playing career spanned from 1914 to 1935, a Golden Age of sports legends who were canonized, not demonized, by the press. Reporters of the day constructed Ruth's iconic status as they destructed bottles of beer and whiskey alongside him.

As a baseball player, Ruth is still considered by most to be the greatest of all time. With the Red Sox, Ruth won three World Series and posted 23 wins with a league-leading ERA of 1.75 in 1916. Three years later, in 1919, he hit a record 29 home runs, forever altering the National Pastime of speed, bunting,

enormity of his feats, none more memorable or controversial than his still-debated called home run shot in the 1932 World Series. In Game Three, with the score tied 4–4 in the fifth inning, Ruth came to bat having already hit a homer in the ballgame. He reportedly extended two fingers toward Cubs pitcher Charlie Root, and some say he also pointed his bat toward centerfield to let Root know where his next pitch was going. The fact is, Ruth did send Root's 2–2 pitch deep to center for another home run. With the help of the icon-building press, Ruth's "called shot" lore was created. Whether or not he actually called the shot doesn't matter, it all adds to the enduring legend that is Babe Ruth.

★ ★ ★ ★ ★ ★ ★ ★ ★ ★ ★ ★

> " *I swing as hard as I can, and I try to swing right through the ball...The harder you grip the bat, the more you can swing it through the ball, and the farther the ball will go. I swing big, with everything I've got. I hit big or I miss big. I like to live as big as I can.*" – Babe Ruth

The Ultimate Season:				Career:			
Year/Team: 1927 NYY				Years: 22			
G:	151	HR:	60	G:	2503	HR:	714
AB:	540	RBI:	165	AB:	8399	RBI:	2214
R:	158	SB:	7	R:	2174	SB:	123
H:	192	BB:	137	H:	2873	BB:	2062
2B:	29	OPS:	1.258	2B:	506	OPS:	1.164
3B:	8	BA:	.356	3B:	136	BA:	.342

Tales from Joe's Bat Rack

At the very top of any professional model bat list is the weapon made for the "Sultan of Swat." Early in Ruth's career, this larger-than-life star was known for using a monstrous piece of wood, often exceeding 40 ounces in weight. Ruth bats from this period look more like small trees than baseball bats. He signed an endorsement contract with H&B in the summer of 1918, so bats featuring Ruth's name in block letters can and do exist. As Ruth gained more experience and knowledge about the science of hitting, the slugger started ordering lighter bats, but even these sticks would still be considered heavy by today's standards. Ruth realized that greater bat speed and enhanced bat control were more important than trying to get a massive log through the strike zone. In fact, Ruth's thoughts about this subject have been documented in interviews with the Yankees icon.

For much of his career, Ruth hit with the center brand facing down, resulting in most of the contact appearing on the left barrel. You can see this hitting approach in a large number of images from his playing days. In fact, the handful of scored examples that exist for Ruth, a practice of bat preparation that Ruth employed at times during his career, exhibit the modification on the left barrel. This further supports the label-down hitting approach since the barrel scoring is done where the hitter intends to strike the ball. Some documented Ruth gamers not only feature scored barrels, but they also exhibit scoring along the handle as well for enhanced grip.

During a very brief period of his career, Ruth carved notches into his bats around the center brand to keep track of every home run he hit. Yes, it sounds like the stuff of legend, but it's true. At the time of this writing, there were a total of five such bats known, with one on permanent display in the Baseball Hall of Fame (28 notches) and one in the Louisville Slugger Museum (21 notches). The remaining three are privately owned. Finally, the very first bat to ever eclipse the $1,000,000 mark was a bat used by Ruth to hit the first home run in Yankee Stadium history on Opening Day in 1923. It sold for $1,265,000 in 2004.

▲ Babe Ruth's 1932 scored H&B bat.

Ty Cobb

★ ★ ★ ★ ★ ★ ★ ★ ★ ★ ★ ★

.945, and only 681 Ks in 11,434 at-bats. In reality, the famous and infamous Georgia Peach was both meticulous and methodical in his approach to hitting.

In 1938, the left-handed batting Cobb answered a letter from Athletics rookie and future All-Star Sam Chapman, giving the lad some hitting advice. Among Cobb's words of wisdom: position yourself near the back of the batter's box, stand away from the plate to hit the ball to right-center or center, use a slightly closed stance with more weight on your front foot, keep your left elbow cocked and either level or slightly higher than your hands, keep your back leg straight, and move up in the box against a hard-throwing lefty. As for hard-throwing righties, Cobb was at his best against the very best. Choosing the greatest moments of Cobb's career is akin to choosing the greatest Shakespeare sonnet, but his .366 career batting average against legendary righty Walter Johnson is worth mentioning. Cobb crowded the plate vs. Johnson and worked the count until The Big Train served up a hittable pitch.

Ironically, Cobb's career average was also .366, which is tops all-time, and his consistency is the reason why. In his final two seasons, 1927 and 1928 at the ages of 40 and 41, Cobb hit a combined .343 with 289 hits, 59 doubles, and an OBP of .419. Many great hitters have marred their career averages with sub-par seasons late in their careers. Wade Boggs stood with a career average of .352 in 1989 at the age of 31, but several sub-.300 seasons lowered his career mark to .328. Cobb maintained his excellence and most likely put the all-time batting mark well out of reach.

A quintessential Deadball Era hitter, Tyrus Raymond Cobb eschewed power for persistence. He was a perennial leader in hits, doubles, and triples, and his intellectual mastery of hitting confounded pitchers. When he was not using his

A glance at Ty Cobb's statistics implies that he could have hit over .300 holding a piece of straw: 4,189 hits, .366 lifetime batting average, 12 batting titles, a .400-plus average three times, 897 steals, nine seasons of 200-plus hits, a career OPS of

★ ★ ★ ★ ★ ★ ★ ★ ★ ★ ★

flair, Cobb was using his fists. Mercilessly hazed as a young player in 1905 and 1906, Cobb carved a rather large chip on the shoulders of his 6-foot, 1-inch, and 175-pound frame. Throughout his career, he engaged in violent fights with teammates, opponents, and fans. Never the most tolerant sort, Cobb also had numerous altercations with African-Americans, burgeoning his life-long reputation as a racist. As a ballplayer, Cobb was both virtuoso and venomous, equally adept at using his knowledge and knuckles.

The Ultimate Season:			Career:		
Year/Team: 1911 DET			Years: 24		
G:	146	HR:	8		
AB:	591	RBI:	127		
R:	147	SB:	83		
H:	248	BB:	44		
2B:	47	OPS:	1.088		
3B:	24	BA:	.420		

Career:			
Years: 24			
G:	3034	HR:	117
AB:	11434	RBI:	1933
R:	2244	SB:	897
H:	4189	BB:	1249
2B:	724	OPS:	.945
3B:	295	BA:	.366

Tales From Joe's Bat Rack

Ty Cobb professional model bats have a tremendous amount of appeal due to Cobb's historical importance and the character his well-used gamers often present. With a career batting average that is hard to imagine ever being approached, Cobb's place in history as a hitter is clearly established and his bats remain high on the list of desirability. In the fall of 1908, Cobb signed an endorsement contract with H&B. Most of the known Cobb bats were made by the company, but some Spalding gamers exist as well. Heavily-used Cobb gamers commonly possess a few different traits.

Many baseball fans are familiar with the ferocity and aggression of Cobb's running approach on the bases. Never shy about coming in spikes high when sliding, Cobb was also never shy about banging the barrels of his bats against those spikes, which often left distinct marks near the end of his bats. Beyond the presence of spike marks, there are Cobb bats that actually exhibit discoloration along the barrel from tobacco juice. Some of the best examples in the hobby

feature this staining, which can be evident to the naked eye. Furthermore, since professional model bats from Cobb's era were not cracked at near the frequency we see in the game today, a small number of Cobb gamers have a virtually flattened hitting surface from repeated contact.

Perhaps the most interesting Cobb bat characteristic is one involving his use of tape. There are two different styles that collectors might encounter. One pattern features tape ringlets, which are spread apart on the handle. While this taping method is the less common of the two styles, it might be a product of Cobb's hitting approach, which often started with his hands spread apart before the pitch was delivered. The more common application of tape was spiral in nature, a consistent and overlapping wrap that started at the base of the handle. This style is documented in a number of vintage images.

" *A ball bat is a wondrous weapon.*"
– *Ty Cobb*

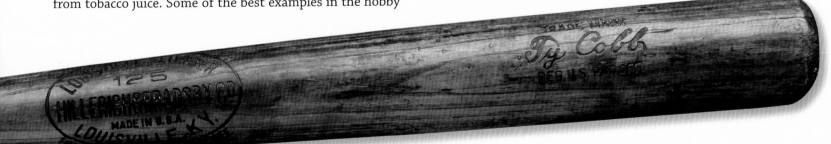

▲ *Ty Cobb's 1923–1925 H&B bat from the family of Luke Sewell.*

★ ★ ★ ★ ★ ★ ★ ★ ★ ★ ★ ★ ★

Hulton Archive/Archive Photos/Getty Images

an amazing .482 OBP. He played 19 years over a 21-year span from 1939 to 1960, all with the Red Sox, but baseball itself experienced generations of change during that time frame.

When Williams broke in, Mel Ott, Bill Dickey, and Lefty Grove were still making All-Star teams. There were no teams west of St. Louis, and the game was lily-white in terms of race. When he retired, there were two teams in California and the National League All-Star team included Ernie Banks, Hank Aaron, and Willie Mays. Always a proponent of positive change, at his Hall of Fame induction speech in 1966, Williams stated, "I hope that one day Satchel Paige and Josh Gibson will be voted into the Hall of Fame as symbols of the great Negro players who are not here only because they weren't given the chance." Perhaps Williams' humanistic perspective was forged while serving as a U.S. Navy and Marine Corps pilot in World War II and in the Korean War. The 34-year-old decorated war hero returned from Korea in time for the 1953 All-Star game, and continued as the Sox star player for seven more seasons.

The Red Sox were behind 4–2 at the end of the eighth inning with one out and no one on base when Williams stepped to the plate at Fenway Park for what would be his final at-bat on September 28, 1960, against Baltimore. Williams had walked in the first, and lifted a fly ball in both the third and the fifth innings. After a lengthy standing ovation, the crowd quieted to take in this historic moment. With a 1–1 count, Williams used his signature and singularly sweet swing to deposit Jack Fisher's pitch deep into the right field seats, and ran the bases for the final time to the roar of the crowd. For most men, this would be legendary, but Ted Williams was an icon long before that final swing. As John Updike eloquently

Charitable. Churlish. Charming. Hero. Theodore Samuel Williams was all of these things and then some. The San Diego native won six batting crowns and two Triple Crowns. He led the American League in home runs four times, was a 19-time All-Star and was named league MVP in 1946 and 1949. The last man to reach the .400-mark pinnacle, Williams batted .406 in 1941. For his career, he hit .344, clouted 521 home runs, and had

★ ★ ★ ★ ★ ★ ★ ★ ★ ★ ★ ★ ★

> "*Ted [Williams] was the greatest hitter of our era...He loved talking about hitting and was a great student of hitting and pitchers.*"
> – Stan Musial

The Ultimate Season:				Career:			
Year/Team: 1941 BOS				Years: 19			
G:	143	HR:	37	G:	2292	HR:	521
AB:	456	RBI:	120	AB:	7706	RBI:	1839
R:	135	SB:	2	R:	1798	SB:	24
H:	185	BB:	147	H:	2654	BB:	2021
2B:	33	OPS:	1.287	2B:	525	OPS:	1.116
3B:	3	BA:	.406	3B:	71	BA:	.344

stated in his essay *Hub Fans Bid Kid Adieu,* "William's last word had been so exquisitely chosen, such a perfect fusion of expectation, intention, and execution, that already it felt a little unreal in my head." Teddy Ballgame. Splendid Splinter. The Kid. Let's just make it easy and call him what he was—one of the greatest hitters who ever lived.

Tales from Joe's Bat Rack

Along with Babe Ruth, Ted Williams is often referred to as one of the best all-around hitters in baseball history, so you can imagine how prized his professional model bats are. Williams, who was not blessed with incredible physical strength like Jimmie Foxx or Mickey Mantle, understood the science of the swing as well as anyone of the era—and maybe ever. Williams realized that a lighter bat meant increased bat speed, which helped generate power at the plate.

When it came to bat preparation, Williams was known to use pine tar or a combination of olive oil and rosin to enhance the grip on his bats at different times in his career. Williams would often clean the handles of his bats with alcohol to prevent heavy buildup since he didn't want to alter the weight of his weapons.

Collectors may also encounter Williams gamers that exhibit some degree of scoring along the handle to further improve his grip, but this was not a consistent practice. Starting around the very late-1940s and early-1950s, the bat boy for the Boston Red Sox used to hand paint Williams' uniform number "9" on the knobs of many of Ted's gamers. Most of the time the number "9" was underlined and other times it was not, but the painted number is very distinct. Towards the end of Williams' career, the uniform number would be noted in black marker. It is important to mention that not all of his professional model bats from this period feature his uniform number, but the number notation is supported by numerous vintage images of the iconic hitter.

According to Williams himself in the book *Crack of the Bat: The Louisville Slugger Story* (2000), he used H&B bats exclusively after signing an endorsement contract with the company in 1937, even though some professional model Adirondack bats have been found bearing his name.

▲ *Ted Williams' 1956 H&B bat used to hit career home run #400.*

Lou Gehrig

★ ★ ★ ★ ★ ★ ★ ★ ★ ★ ★

one of the greatest and most beloved players in the history of the game. Famously depicted in the film *Pride of the Yankees*, Henry Louis Gehrig was born in New York of German immigrant parents and attended Columbia University. He eventually joined the Yankees as a rookie in 1923, and the story of how he got into the lineup has become part of legend. As the story goes, Yankees first baseman Wally Pipp asked for a day off due to a headache in 1925 and Gehrig was inserted into the lineup at first base as a substitute. Number "4" would never look back, playing in 2,130 consecutive games and earning the nickname "The Iron Horse." His consecutive games record would remain unchallenged until 1995 when it was broken by Cal Ripken, Jr., of the Orioles.

That, however, is not the only number of which Gehrig can be proud. He led the American League in RBI five times, highlighted by 173 in 1927 and 1930, and 185 in 1931. He was a two-time MVP (1927, 1936) and smacked over 40 homers five times. His run totals were outstanding including 163 in 1931 and 167 in 1936, both league-highs. An incredibly patient batter for a power hitter, Gehrig regularly drew over 100 walks a season, but never reached the century mark in strikeouts. In 17 seasons (1923–1939), he hit 493 home runs, drove in 1,995 runs, batted .340, slammed 534 doubles, and slugged .632.

Known for both the tragic end to his career as well as his glorious career itself, Lou Gehrig left an impression on the game that remains indelible. Amyotrophic lateral sclerosis (ALS), the disease that eventually took Gehrig's name, robbed baseball fans of

The consecutive games streak will always be Gehrig's greatest feat, but his best moments at the plate came in postseason play. He played in seven World Series for the Yanks, winning six of them and batting .361 with 10 home runs and 35 RBI.

★ ★ ★ ★ ★ ★ ★ ★ ★ ★ ★

In both the 1928 and 1932 Series, he hit over .500. That 1928 Fall Classic was his best with 4 homers, 9 RBI, a .545 average, .706 OBP, and 1.727 slugging. The Yanks swept St. Louis in four games. A seven-time All-Star, one can only imagine the numbers Gehrig would have put up if his career had not been cut short in 1939. He was elected to the Hall of Fame by special election that year and died in 1941 at the age of 37. Gehrig's grace in the face of suffering made him an icon. He famously called himself "the luckiest man on the face of the earth," but those who had a chance to see Lou Gehrig play were truly the lucky ones.

The Ultimate Season:			Career:		
Year/Team: 1927 NYY			Years: 17		
G:	155	HR: 47	G:	2164	HR: 493
AB:	584	RBI: 173	AB:	8001	RBI: 1995
R:	149	SB: 10	R:	1888	SB: 102
H:	218	BB: 109	H:	2721	BB: 1508
2B:	52	OPS: 1.240	2B:	534	OPS: 1.080
3B:	18	BA: .373	3B:	163	BA: .340

Tales from Joe's Bat Rack

Lou Gehrig professional model bats are some of the true rarities in the hobby. Less than 20 examples are known to exist at the time of this writing, which makes Gehrig bats clearly tougher to find than some of his contemporaries, including those of his slugging teammate Babe Ruth. Some Gehrig gamers have been found with a unique taping method along the handle: with spacing

> *"Lou Gehrig was a guy who could really hit the ball, was dependable and seemed so durable that many of us thought he could have played forever." – George Selkirk*

in between ringlets of tape. This kind of handle preparation can be viewed in images from the "Iron Horse's" playing days. It is important to note that Gehrig did not employ this taping method, or any taping method at all, on all of his bats. In fact, most Gehrig bats do not possess this characteristic. In addition, due to his declining strength later in his career, Gehrig's bats were gradually reduced in weight by the manufacturer so he could handle them at the plate.

For most of his career, Gehrig preferred H&B bats, and he signed an endorsement contract with the company late in the fall of 1923. From the spring of 1933 until the end of his career, Gehrig did order bats with the weight marked or stamped into the knob or barrel end according to his shipping records. That said, Gehrig did experiment with other brands such as Kren and Hanna Batrite. In fact, one photo-matched Hanna Batrite gamer was brought to the market in 2015, and it proceeded to set an auction record at the time. Absent extraordinary documentation such as ironclad provenance, side writing or photo-matching, the less popular bat brands usually sell for a fraction of the bats made by H&B. With such a small number of authentic examples in existence, combined with his legendary status, Gehrig bats remain extremely desirable.

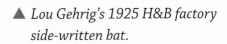

▲ *Lou Gehrig's 1925 H&B factory side-written bat.*

Jackie Robinson

★ ★ ★ ★ ★ ★ ★ ★ ★ ★ ★ ★ ★

extra base and made the nearly-impossible act of stealing home into a commonplace occurrence. In fact, he stole 197 bases in his career, leading the National League in both 1947 and 1949. He was named the 1947 Rookie of the Year and in an epic 1949 season, Robinson won the batting title with his .342 average, while stroking 203 hits with 124 RBI and 16 home runs to win league MVP honors. Robinson's Brooklyn Dodgers were a National League dynasty, playing in six World Series and winning the title in 1955.

Born in Cairo, Georgia, Robinson was the Major League's first documented African-American player, selected by general manager Branch Rickey to join the Brooklyn Dodgers in 1947. Prior to that year, men of color were banned from the Major Leagues. Among the owners, it was called a "Gentlemen's Agreement," but it was anything but gentlemanly. A Negro League star with the Kansas City Monarchs, it was Robinson's ability and respectability that made him the perfect choice to break down walls and break up the old boys' network. Robinson had to bite his tongue, turn his cheek, and control his temper as he endured ceaseless and merciless racist jabs from teammates, opponents, fans, and the media. If he cracked, the so-called "Great Experiment" would fail and the game, perhaps, would have remained in the "whites only" realm.

The versatile and multi-talented Jackie Robinson made the All-Star team six times in his ten-year MLB career, posted a .311 career batting average and finished with a .409 career OBP. With an expert eye and pitch judgment, he drew 740 walks compared to just 291 strikeouts in 4,877 career at-bats. He had over 30 doubles six times and smacked 19 home runs in both 1951 and 1952. Robinson used his UCLA track speed to take that

Robinson did not fail. His career was outstanding and he was inducted into the Hall of Fame in 1962. Just 10 years later, suffering from diabetes and, no doubt, years of stress from what he had endured as a trailblazer, Robinson succumbed to a heart attack at age 53. Jackie Robinson's eye was not only on the ball, but the globe. His courage and talent paved the

★ ★ ★ ★ ★ ★ ★ ★ ★ ★ ★

> "*I don't know any other ball player who could have done what he did. To be able to hit with everybody yelling at him. He had to block...everything but this ball that is coming in at a hundred miles an hour.*"
> – *Pee Wee Reese*

The Ultimate Season:				Career:			
Year/Team: 1949 BRO				Years: 10			
G:	156	HR:	16	G:	1382	HR:	137
AB:	593	RBI:	124	AB:	4877	RBI:	734
R:	122	SB:	37	R:	947	SB:	197
H:	203	BB:	86	H:	1518	BB:	740
2B:	38	OPS:	.960	2B:	273	OPS:	.883
3B:	12	BA:	.342	3B:	54	BA:	.311

way for generations to follow. Robinson's greatest moment came in that game-changing year of 1947. On April 15, Robinson took the field and stepped to the plate for Brooklyn for the first time. With all due respect to astronaut Neil Armstrong who walked on the moon in 1969, the "one small step for man, one giant leap for mankind" occurred 22 years earlier at a ballpark in Brooklyn with one movement, one motion, one man—Jackie Roosevelt Robinson.

Tales from Joe's Bat Rack

Pound for pound, Jackie Robinson professional model bats are the most valuable pieces of wood from the era in which he played (1947–1956). There are some exceptions, like special bats used by the likes of Mickey Mantle or Ted Williams, but Robinson bats, on average, sell for the most. In fact, extremely high-end Robinson examples, ones that exhibit excellent characteristics and/or have ironclad provenance, have fetched well in excess of $100,000 on a consistent basis—a price

point reserved for an elite group of lumber. In 2013 and 2014, four different Robinson bats sold for more than $150,000 each at auction.

Robinson signed an endorsement contract with H&B in 1946, prior to making his unforgettable debut, so all of the bats made for him at the Major League level featured his facsimile signature. According to factory records, Robinson used a fairly hefty piece of lumber. Many of his bats are in the 34–36-ounce range, and the majority of his gamers were made with a thick handle and smaller knob. You will occasionally see Robinson bats with his uniform number "42" marked on the knob, but most known gamers do not possess this trait. The bats that do feature his number are almost always found with a smaller, painted "42" in black.

This use of paint was a somewhat common practice in the Dodger organization during that period. Most Brooklyn Dodger game bats, like those made for Roy Campanella and Pee Wee Reese, do not possess numbers on the knob, but when they do, the numbers are often found in black paint. This kind of knob marking is evident in numerous vintage images capturing Dodger players holding their bats with the knob directly facing the camera. Finally, Robinson was not known for using heavy amounts of pine tar or modifying his bats with tape or scoring/grooving.

▲ *Jackie Robinson's 1952 H&B bat.*

Mickey Mantle

★ ★ ★ ★ ★ ★ ★ ★ ★ ★ ★ ★

Neil Leifer/Neil Leifer Collection/Getty Images

Mickey Mantle's speed, power, boyish charm, and good looks made him a matinee idol among fans of all ages. He debuted in the majors in 1951, just as the game was entering a golden age of popularity and progress, quite heady stuff for a country boy from Commerce, Oklahoma. In the Bronx, Mantle was seen as the successor to Joe DiMaggio, not only in center field, but also as the symbol of the Yankees. He wanted no part of that and asked that his number be changed from "6" to "7" so he would not be part of the Yankees numeric lineage: Ruth "3," Gehrig "4," DiMaggio "5."

After a rookie season in which he hit .267, Mantle embarked on a 17-season assault on big league pitching. He made the All-Star team 16 times, won three MVP Awards, led the league in runs five times, home runs four times, and walks and Ks five times each. In his Hall of Fame career, Mantle had 536 homers, 1,509 RBI, batted .298, and scored an amazing 1,676 runs, all the while missing numerous games to knee injuries and other ailments. His determination to play through pain further endeared him to the Yankees faithful. In 1956, he won the Triple Crown with 52 home runs, 130 RBI, and a .353 batting average. In 1961, Mantle and teammate Roger Maris waged an epic assault on Babe Ruth's single-season home run record of 60. Maris would blast 61, while Mantle, beset by injuries, would "settle" for 54.

Mantle won seven World Series rings with New York including 1952 when, at age 20, he batted .345 and experienced perhaps his greatest moment. In Game Seven vs. Brooklyn, Mantle crushed a massive home run in the sixth inning to break a 2–2 tie and give the Yanks the lead. He knocked in another run the following inning with a base hit, helping his team to a 4–2 win and the title. Mantle's tape measure home runs were legendary, as was his penchant for excessive partying and carousing. This

★ ★ ★ ★ ★ ★ ★ ★ ★ ★ ★ ★

contributed to several health problems later in life and an untimely death in 1995 at age 63. Mickey Charles Mantle sits on that rare perch of players whose skills were only half of the story. His charisma made him a household name and one of the greatest stars the game has ever known.

The Ultimate Season:					Career:				
Year/Team: 1956 NYY					Years: 18				
G:	150	HR:	52		G:	2401	HR:	536	
AB:	533	RBI:	130		AB:	8102	RBI:	1509	
R:	132	SB:	10		R:	1676	SB:	153	
H:	188	BB:	112		H:	2415	BB:	1733	
2B:	22	OPS:	1.169		2B:	344	OPS:	.977	
3B:	5	BA:	.353		3B:	72	BA:	.298	

Tales from Joe's Bat Rack

The witness accounts of Mantle's raw power make the Yankees Hall of Famer sound more like a fairy tale character than a real person. That said, if you saw the way the barrels of his well-used bats look up close, you might start to believe Mantle was more than human. Gamers used by the iconic slugger often possess some of the most deeply embedded ball and stitch marks you will ever see, evidence of his strength and vicious cut. Since Mantle was a switch-hitter and the majority of pitchers in the league were right handed, a great deal of the use tends to be located on the right barrel, the location where nearly all hitters would strike the ball if they were batting with the label facing up.

During his career, Mantle alternated between H&B (endorsement contract) and Adirondack (block letter) bats, but collectors usually prefer the former. Based on photo studies and more, it seems as if Mantle may have used a fair number of Adirondack bats during the late 1950s and early 1960s, but he preferred H&B during most of his playing days. He signed an endorsement contract with the company prior to his rookie season in 1951, which means all the H&B bats made for MLB use feature his facsimile signature.

One of Mantle's signature characteristics didn't really develop until several years after his first plate appearance. Mantle bats that date to the pre-1960 period rarely show a significant application of pine tar, but that changed in the following decade. You can find numerous photos of Mantle at the plate during the 1960s with a bat covered in pine tar, starting about 8–12 inches up the handle. While Mantle did not cake all of his bats in this manner, its presence helps place the bat in his hands.

One very interesting aspect to Mantle professional model bats is that the bulk of the known examples do not feature his primary uniform number "7" or rookie season number "6" on the knob or barrel end, as he was not nearly as consistent as other players of the era about marking his bats. While there are some authentic "7"s that appear to be vintage from the late-1950s and 1960s, in certain cases, the uniform number is believed to have been added at a later time.

" *That kid can hit balls over buildings." – Casey Stengel*

▲ *Mickey Mantle's 1964 H&B bat.*

Joe DiMaggio

★ ★ ★ ★ ★ ★ ★ ★ ★ ★ ★

Clipper" hit safely in 56 consecutive games. During that stretch, he batted at a torrid pace—a .408 average with 15 homers and 55 RBI. On July 17, 1941, nearly 70,000 fans packed Municipal Stadium in Cleveland. They certainly were not there to see the mediocre Tribe, a team that would eventually fade to fourth place with a 75–79 record. No, the Cleveland faithful were there to see DiMaggio. However, the star of the game would be Ken Keltner, a 24-year-old third baseman who made two outstanding defensive plays, swiping would-be hits from DiMaggio. After Keltner's heroics ended the streak, DiMaggio hit safely in another 16 consecutive

Joe DiMaggio was an American icon of the highest status. He transcended the fame of a mere ballplayer and stood as the epitome of a golden era of baseball. His celebrated marriage to film star Marilyn Monroe took DiMaggio to another level of pop culture status. Despite his fame and social status, Joseph Paul DiMaggio always carried himself with an air of dignity and serenity.

In 1941, DiMaggio captivated the baseball world and accomplished a feat that remains as iconic as the man himself. That season, he batted .357 with 30 home runs and 125 RBI, but that was merely a side dish. The main course was served from May 15 until July 17 when the "Yankee

games. Indians pitchers held DiMaggio to 0-for-3 with a walk the day the streak ended, but he was still something to watch.

At bat, DiMaggio dissected the opposing pitcher and calmly waited for a pitch to hit. His strong and silent stance exploded with a vicious roundhouse swing fraught with power. The word "class" is always associated with DiMaggio. Can't you see the 6-foot, 2-inch, and 193-pound DiMaggio smashing a ball to centerfield and effortlessly galloping to first base, the sleeves of his jersey blowing in the summer breeze? When he retired in 1951, Joe DiMaggio had 361 home runs, over 1,500 RBI and a .325 batting average.

★ ★ ★ ★ ★ ★ ★ ★ ★ ★ ★ ★

> "*He had great wrists and hit balls like rockets, with top-spin, that exploded past third basemen.*"
> – Bobby Doerr

The Ultimate Season:				Career:			
Year/Team: 1937 NYY				Years: 13			
G:	151	HR:	46	G:	1736	HR:	361
AB:	621	RBI:	167	AB:	6821	RBI:	1537
R:	151	SB:	3	R:	1390	SB:	30
H:	215	BB:	64	H:	2214	BB:	790
2B:	35	OPS:	1.085	2B:	389	OPS:	.977
3B:	15	BA:	.346	3B:	131	BA:	.325

Moreover, he had the respect and love of millions. He was inducted into the Hall of Fame in 1955, and, though he passed away in 1999, Joe DiMaggio remains a vivid beacon of baseball's glorious past.

Tales from Joe's Bat Rack

The "Yankee Clipper" is considered by many to be one of the greatest all-around players in baseball history, but it was his work with the bat that made him famous. Joe DiMaggio professional model bats are highly desired by collectors, with early examples fetching a premium. The one aspect of DiMaggio bats that may confuse some collectors is the great disparity that can exist between the values of his bats. There is no question that the special nature of any player bat can dramatically impact the value, but there are some players, like DiMaggio and his teammate Mickey Mantle, where the price gaps seem more dramatic. A bat used during DiMaggio's 1941, 56-game hitting streak sold for $345,596 in 2004, one of the highest prices ever paid for a bat at that time. There are DiMaggio bats that sell for as much as $75,000–$100,000 or more, while others sell for under $40,000.

Most DiMaggio bats exhibit ball marks on the left barrel, as he was known to hit, predominantly, with the center brand facing upward. It is important to note that his bats do not usually exhibit the types of unique characteristics often tied to other major stars, such as a particular style of handle preparation. That said, there was a period of time during the 1940s when DiMaggio did use a relatively healthy amount of pine tar. In fact, this pattern can be verified in some vintage images of the Yankees icon. Furthermore, collectors may encounter DiMaggio gamers with evidence of sanding along the barrel, which is something the Yankees great did for a period to modify his bats.

While game-used items from his days with the San Francisco Seals are rare and desirable, most collectors prefer bats from his New York Yankees days. That is where DiMaggio did his damage as a Major Leaguer and became a legend. DiMaggio signed an endorsement contract with H&B in 1933, long before making his debut, so all of his bats feature his facsimile signature on the barrel. At one time, DiMaggio bats were considered to be among the scarcest in the hobby. While a few more have been found over the years, they remain one of the tougher Hall of Famer bats to find from the period.

▲ *Joe DiMaggio's 1939 H&B factory side-written/vault-marked bat.*

Joe Jackson

★ ★ ★ ★ ★ ★ ★ ★ ★ ★ ★ ★

Joseph Jefferson Jackson was the oldest of eight siblings and was sent to work at the local textile mill when he should have been attending first grade. Although he never learned to read or write, young Jackson learned to excel at baseball while playing for the mill-sponsored team as a young teen. Fans came to see the young phenom hit massive home runs they called "Saturday Specials."

The country boy did not take to the big city, only hitting .130 and .176 respectively in his first two seasons with the Philadelphia Athletics (1908–1909), but he would never hit under .300 again. In one of Connie Mack's rare blunders, the A's sent Jackson to the Cleveland Naps in 1910. There Jackson thrived, batting .387, .408, and .395 in 1910, 1911, and 1912, and slugging over .500 every year from 1910 to 1913. In that 1913 season, he batted .373 and led the American League in hits, doubles, slugging, and OPS with an amazing 1.011 clip. After six years in Cleveland in which he batted .375, Jackson was traded to the White Sox in August of 1915. It would be the best and worst thing that ever happened to him. He batted .340 in his six seasons in the Windy City, and led the league in triples in both 1916 and 1920. Joining a powerful White Sox team gave Jackson the chance to play in his first World Series in 1917, and he did not disappoint, batting .304 in the six-game victory over the Giants.

O>ne of the greatest hitters of all-time, Shoeless Joe Jackson is best known for his dubious role in the 1919 Chicago White Sox World Series fixing scandal. While no one is really sure how black Jackson's Sox were, he was banished from the game he adored in 1920, putting him forever in the realm of baseball limbo. Born to poverty in Pickens County, South Carolina,

Jackson was also an excellent outfielder whose anticipation was rare. Because of his illiteracy some thought he was intellectually challenged, but Jackson was truly a baseball genius who played the sport with a pure joy and fervor. Did he help throw the 1919 Series? Although banned with his teammates, it is interesting to note that Jackson's .375 BA

★ ★ ★ ★ ★ ★ ★ ★ ★ ★ ★ ★ ★

for the Series was the highest of any player from either team that played all eight games, and he hit the only homer in the contest. Jackson's final season, 1920, was outstanding with 218 hits, 42 doubles, 20 triples, .444 OBP, .589 SLG, 1.033 OPS and career-highs in home runs (12) and RBI (121). Most incredibly, in 570 at-bats, he struck out just 14 times. Banned from baseball at age 32 by Commissioner Judge Kenesaw Mountain Landis, Jackson continued to play the game anywhere he could. His legend as a phenomenal hitter lives on to this day.

The Ultimate Season:			Career:		
Year/Team: 1911 CLE			Years: 13		
G:	147	HR: 7	G:	1332	HR: 54
AB:	571	RBI: 83	AB:	4981	RBI: 785
R:	126	SB: 41	R:	873	SB: 202
H:	233	BB: 56	H:	1772	BB: 519
2B:	45	OPS: 1.058	2B:	307	OPS: .940
3B:	19	BA: .408	3B:	168	BA: .356

Tales from Joe's Bat Rack

There are many great rarities in the bat collecting world, but professional model bats that can be linked to this legendary figure rank near the very top in terms of difficulty. For collectors, owning a piece of lumber from "Shoeless Joe" is often wishful thinking. Only a handful of documented examples are known from his playing days, and one of those examples is a vault-marked, signature model H&B gamer from his rookie season in 1911. Four examples have sold for more than $500,000, including $577,610 (2001), $956,000 (2014), $605,077 (2015) and $583,500 (2016) respectively, proving the intense demand for his bats. Joe Jackson, who was known for using very heavy, thick-handled bats, was a player who often hit with the center brand facing down. This approach was copied by Babe Ruth, an avid fan of Jackson's, and some of the best hitters in the modern era have used the same approach.

Jackson was also known for naming his bats, and the most famous bat of all was his Black Betsy—a name that would

"Everything he hit was really blessed. He could break bones with his shots. Blindfold me and I could tell you when Joe hit the ball. It had a special crack." – Ernie Shore

eventually be used to create a particular model years later. After his 1920 ban from baseball, Jackson was relegated to barnstorming tours, and you will see bats from this time period offered on occasion. These bats, while valuable in their own right, do not command near the price that an example from his MLB career would, but they have still fetched well into five figures at auction. Keep in mind that after Jackson's banishment, professional model bats featuring his full name were not produced for the iconic hitter any longer. Bats manufactured after 1920 only feature his last name, "Jackson," near the barrel end in script or block letters.

▲ *Shoeless Joe Jackson's 1905–1910 J. F. Hillerich & Son bat factory side-written/vault-marked to 1911.*

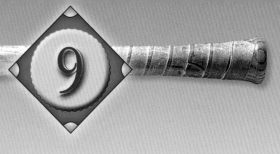

Honus Wagner

★ ★ ★ ★ ★ ★ ★ ★ ★ ★ ★ ★

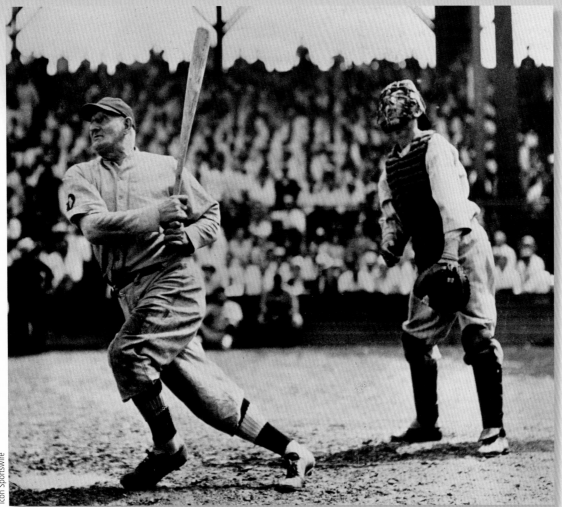

Icon Sportswire

Wagner hit higher than .320 for 14 straight seasons, eclipsing .350 in six of those years.

A Louisville Colonel as a rookie in 1897, Wagner was dealt to Pittsburgh in 1899. While Hall of Famer Jack Chesbro moved to Louisville in the deal, it still ranks as one of the worst trades in history. Wagner was known as "The Flying Dutchman," but it was the Pirates whom he took to new heights. Pittsburgh won the pennant in both 1903 and 1909. The World Series of 1909 was really the Honus Wagner Show. He hit at a .333 clip and drove in six runs in the championship series victory vs. Detroit. A member of baseball's inaugural Hall of Fame class of 1936, Honus Wagner's name is synonymous with an era of baseball that was more about guts than glory, more about determination than dollars, and more about fight than fame.

From 1897 to 1917, Honus Wagner set a standard of excellence attained by a scant few. His versatility was second to none as he pitched, played the outfield, and suited up at every infield position except catcher during his career. Deemed by many as the best shortstop ever to play the game, Wagner was a tough-as-nails, old-fashioned, pain-in-the-neck ballplayer. He could field, hit, run, and generally drive opponents crazy, spraying the ball to all fields and stretching singles to extra bases. He won eight batting titles and led the Senior Circuit in hits on two occasions. In one of those mind-boggling baseball stats,

A sublime player who, upon his retirement in 1917, held a bevy of NL and MLB records, Wagner led the league in doubles seven times, triples three times, and OPS eight times. He was not a home run man, but eclipsed the 100 RBI plateau nine times. As with any ballplayer, time marches on, and by 1914, Wagner was no longer a lock for a .300 average and 100 RBI. On June 9 of that year, however, he

★ ★ ★ ★ ★ ★ ★ ★ ★ ★ ☆ ★

experienced perhaps his most telling moment at the plate. With his ninth-inning double off Phillies Erskine Mayer, Wagner made history as the first player in the twentieth century to reach the 3,000-hit mark. Johannes Peter Wagner passed away at the age of 81 in 1955. Over the years, many players would join that 3,000 Hit Club, but none of them can lay claim to the overall talent of Honus Wagner.

The Ultimate Season:			Career:		
Year/Team: 1900 PIT			Years: 21		
G:	135	HR: 4	G:	2794	HR: 101
AB:	527	RBI: 100	AB:	10439	RBI: 1732
R:	107	SB: 38	R:	1739	SB: 723
H:	201	BB: 41	H:	3420	BB: 963
2B:	45	OPS: 1.007	2B:	643	OPS: .858
3B:	22	BA: .381	3B:	252	BA: .328

Tales from Joe's Bat Rack

On September 1, 1905, Honus Wagner signed an endorsement contract with J. F. Hillerich & Son, giving the company permission to use a facsimile of his signature on their bats. Wagner became the first baseball player ever to sign a contract of this nature and one of the first athletes in any sport to endorse a specific sporting goods product. As much as Wagner is known for his T206 baseball card, perhaps he should be as well known for his role in launching the practice of player bat endorsements. Of course, years later (1916) the company Wagner signed with became known as Hillerich & Bradsby or H&B, which is the name more bat collectors are familiar with.

During his career, Honus Wagner ordered a number of bats that came with a "Kork" grip affixed to the handle, added by the bat manufacturer. This grip is evident in some vintage images of Wagner posing with his bat. On other occasions, Wagner added tape along the handles of his gamers, with some applications covering a substantial portion of the bat. One of the rare but documented Wagner examples exhibits this style of taping. The tape can extend from the grip area all the way to the center brand. It is not uncommon for the

tape, which resembles black electrician's tape at first sight, to cover a portion of the handle already encased with "Kork" grip from the factory.

Wagner was also known for spreading his hands apart when gripping the bat, so it makes sense that he would order bats with such expansive coverage of customized "Kork" grip or tape his handles so severely. Either form of handle preparation would help compensate for the movement of his hands since they covered such a large surface area. It is important to note that not all of his bats possess the "Kork" grip from the factory or exhibit the aforementioned taping method. Whether the bats possess these characteristics or not, however, all Wagner professional model bats are in high demand due to their incredible scarcity.

"The way to get a ball past Honus is to hit it eight feet over his head."
– John McGraw

▲ *Honus Wagner's 1900–1905 J. F. Hillerich & Son bat.*

★ ★ ★ ★ ★ ★ ★ ★ ★ ★ ★ ★ ★

lifetime batting average, followed by 534 home runs, a Triple Crown, nine All-Star Games, three Most Valuable Player Awards, and two World Series Championships? Oh yeah, and let's not forget that Foxx was a three-time RBI leader and two-time American League Batting Champ.

Simply put, James Emory Foxx was one of the greatest ballplayers ever. Also known as "The Beast," for his prodigious tape measure blasts, Foxx's most productive years were with Connie Mack's Philadelphia Athletics. The teenaged farm boy from Maryland joined the A's in 1925 and became a superstar during his 11 years in Philly. The pinnacle of his career was in 1933 when he batted .356, drove in 163 runs, and hit 48 homers to win the Triple Crown. However, Foxx said his most memorable career moment was his performance in Game Five of the 1930 World Series against the St. Louis Cardinals. The Series was tied 2–2 going into the game on October 6, 1930, at Sportsman's Park in St. Louis. With a scoreless tie going into the ninth, and Mickey Cochrane on first base following a walk and one out, Foxx came up to the plate. While in the dugout, he told his teammates to relax because he "was gonna bust one out." Facing the Cards excellent pitcher Burleigh Grimes, Foxx launched a two-run shot into the stands to win the game. That Foxx blast ended up being the catalyst for the championship as the A's went on to win Game Six and the World Series.

I f you were to flip a coin to determine the greatest first baseman of all time, you would likely see an image of Lou Gherig on one side and Jimmie Foxx on the other. Some give the edge to "Larrupin' Lou," but others swear by "Double X." Of course, there are also Greenberg, Pujols, Thomas, and Murray fans, but Foxx and Gehrig are usually at the top of the list. Right now, the discussion will revolve around Mr. Foxx. How about a .325

After Mack's famous team dismantling, Foxx went to the Red Sox in 1936, where he continued his success. His 175 RBI in 1938 still stands as the Red Sox record, and his 50 home runs that year stood as the Sox record until David Ortiz beat it in 2006. Known for his good nature and generosity, Foxx befriended and mentored a young batting

★ ★ ★ ★ ★ ★ ★ ★ ★ ★ ★ ★

> "He [Foxx] had great powerful arms, and he used to wear his sleeves cut off way up, and when he dug in and raised that bat, his muscles would bulge and ripple." – Ted Lyons

The Ultimate Season:			Career:		
Year/Team: 1933 PHA			Years: 20		
G:	149	HR: 48	G:	2317	HR: 534
AB:	573	RBI: 163	AB:	8134	RBI: 1922
R:	125	SB: 2	R:	1751	SB: 87
H:	204	BB: 96	H:	2646	BB: 1452
2B:	37	OPS: 1.153	2B:	458	OPS: 1.038
3B:	9	BA: .356	3B:	125	BA: .325

prodigy named Ted Williams. After his 20-year career, Jimmie Foxx struggled. Some bad investments eroded his baseball earnings and although he was well-liked, a drinking problem kept him from steady employment in baseball. He was elected to the Hall of Fame in 1951. Double X choked on his food in a restaurant in 1967 and died from asphyxia. The greatest first baseman? Maybe, maybe not. It makes for a great debate though.

Tales from Joe's Bat Rack

Professional model bats made for "The Beast" find themselves in elite company, and for good reason. The combination of Jimmie Foxx's offensive numbers, intimidating presence, and the relative scarcity of his gamers make his inclusion an easy choice for most collectors of elite lumber. During his prime, the only two hitters that could stack up against Foxx were a dynamic duo in New York—Babe Ruth and Lou Gehrig. Far tougher to find than Babe Ruth professional model bats, Foxx gamers

are considered the second toughest of the popular 500 Home Run Club. While Mel Ott bats are technically harder to find, Foxx is slightly more popular with collectors.

Foxx often used ash bats, but he also used hickory bats from time to time. The hickory bats have a darker appearance and offer excellent eye appeal. While he did occasionally use less popular brands such as Spalding-model bats, his preference was clearly H&B during his career. Foxx signed an endorsement contract with the company in the summer of 1926. Although Foxx did make his debut in 1925, it was very brief, netting nine total plate appearances that season.

In addition, like Ruth gamers, some Foxx bats have been found with heavy scoring along the barrel. Keep in mind, however, that this was not the usual practice employed by Foxx. Furthermore, as was the case with most of his contemporaries, Foxx was not known for using any distinct taping method or gripping substance like pine tar during his playing days. Early examples from Foxx's time with the legendary Philadelphia Athletics teams of the 1920s and early 1930s sell for a premium. Finally, a handful of Foxx bats have been discovered with factory side writing and vault marks.

▲ Jimmie Foxx's 1933 Triple Crown season H&B vault-marked bat.

Willie Mays

★ ★ ★ ★ ★ ★ ★ ★ ★ ★ ★

MLB Photos/Major League Baseball Collection/Getty Images

base running, Mays had it all and put it on display with a joy and enthusiasm that remains singular and unforgettable. His statistics are enough to make anyone yell, "Say Hey!" 660 home runs, 1,903 RBI, a batting average of .302, 338 steals, and 2,062 runs scored in a 22-year career.

It was not just the numbers, however, it was the method in which those numbers were recorded. Mays played all-out, all the time. He ran the bases with ardent verve—his cap or helmet invariably blowing off his head as he took that extra base. No one will forget the magnificent manner in which he patrolled the outfield. His over the shoulder catch off the bat of Cleveland's Vic Wertz in the 1954 World Series is still looked upon as one of the eternally terrific plays in all of sports. That catch was a product of Mays' athletic skill, intelligence, judgment, fearlessness, and the child-like, carefree style he brought to the field every day.

While the Wertz catch is Mays' signature moment, his most significant may have been the first of his 3,283 hits. Just 20 years old, Mays debuted with the Giants in May of 1951 but the Rookie of the Year started slow at the plate. Hitless in his first three games, Mays finally did it in his fourth game, at home vs. the Boston Braves. He blasted a first inning home run off future Hall of Famer Warren Spahn, who was just the first in a long line of Mays' pitching victims. From 1951 to 1973, Mays was the star attraction, first in New York with the Giants, then on the West Coast when the team moved to San Francisco, and back in the Big Apple with the Mets. After missing the 1953 season in military service, Mays went on a decade-plus rampage through the National League, leading the senior circuit, at one time or another, in

The mere mention of the name Willie Mays conjures up images that tantalize and touch any true baseball fan. He is regarded by many to be the greatest player who ever lived—the closest thing to the total package. Power, speed, defense, hitting skills,

> "*He [Mays] could hit, hit with power, run, throw and field. And he had the other magic ingredient that turns a superstar into a super Superstar. Charisma.*" – Leo Durocher

The Ultimate Season:				Career:			
Year/Team: 1955 NYG				Years: 22			
G:	152	HR:	51	G:	2992	HR:	660
AB:	580	RBI:	127	AB:	10881	RBI:	1903
R:	123	SB:	24	R:	2062	SB:	338
H:	185	BB:	79	H:	3283	BB:	1464
2B:	18	OPS:	1.059	2B:	523	OPS:	.941
3B:	13	BA:	.319	3B:	140	BA:	.302

home runs, hits, steals, triples, runs, walks, slugging, and batting average. He won a batting title in 1954 and crushed 52 home runs in 1965. The two-time MVP had 20 All-Star appearances and 12 straight Gold Gloves. Hall of Famer Willie Howard Mays, Jr. was much more than a player. His passion and attitude made him an iconic ambassador of the game, a legend in every sense of the word.

Tales from Joe's Bat Rack

Much like fellow power hitter Mickey Mantle, Willie Mays alternated between H&B and Adirondack professional model bats throughout his career. While his Adirondack bats do feature his signature on the barrel, Mays' H&B bats are of the block letter variety only since he did not have a signature contract with the company. A small number of the known examples do possess either "W. Mays" on some of his early bats or his full name from the latter portion of his career, but most Mays H&B gamers only feature his last name. Another interesting similarity to Mantle was Mays' use of pine tar,

which evolved over the course of his career. Early on, Mays was inconsistent about his use of the gripping substance. By the mid-1960s, that all changed.

Mays was known to apply a coat of pine tar that would sometimes extend from the base of the handle up past the center brand, a pattern documented in many photos. As a result, well-used bats from this period until the end of his career are as distinct looking as any gamer of the era. In addition, many of the known Mays gamers do feature his primary uniform number "24" marked on the knob. Mays did wear number "14" for a short time during his rookie season, but many of his early bats do not possess a vintage uniform number notation.

Keep in mind that Mays was a player who often hit with the label facing downward, which caused ball marks to cluster on the left barrel in such cases. You will, however, find that heavily-used Mays bats often have contact marks on both sides, which is consistent with his free-swinging approach. Finally, Mays gamers from his time with the New York Giants are far tougher to locate than bats manufactured during his time in San Francisco and with the New York Mets.

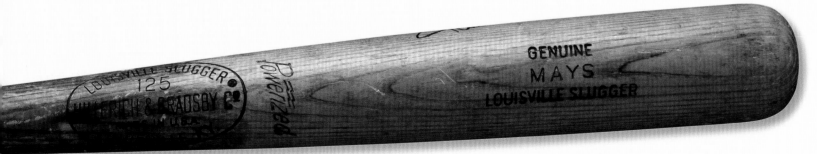

▲ *Willie Mays' 1965–68 H&B bat.*

Rogers Hornsby

★ ★ ★ ★ ★ ★ ★ ★ ★ ★ ★

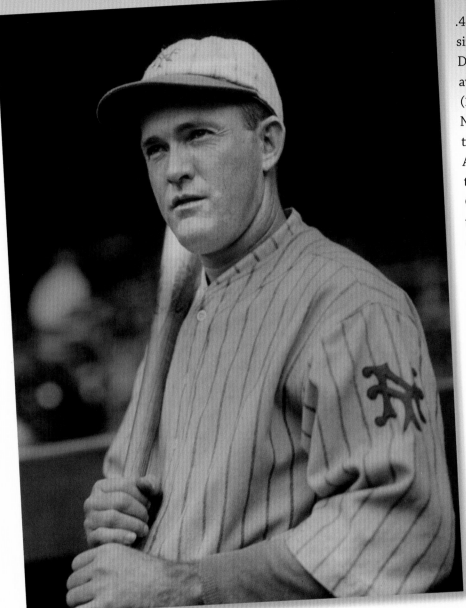

.424 batting average in 1924, the second highest single-season mark in the twentieth century. Did you know he batted .400 three seasons and averaged a composite of .402 over five seasons (1921–1925), or that he was a seven-time National League Batting Champ? Throw in the two National League Most Valuable Player Awards in 1925 and 1929, the two home run titles in 1922 and 1925, the 1926 World Series Championship as player-manager of the of the St. Louis Cardinals, and the fact that most consider him the greatest second baseman of all time. Now you have the total offensive package. As a matter of fact, Ted Williams once said that unequivocally, Rogers Hornsby was "the greatest hitter for average and power in baseball history."

Known as "The Rajah," the 19-year-old Winters, Texas, native started off in 1915 as a scrawny 5-foot, 11-inch, and 135-pound infielder who was just a bit too weak to hit with any consistency. When manager Miller Huggins suggested that Hornsby get on a weight gaining and strength program, the young man listened, and worked on a farm in the offseason to build strength and muscle mass. The next season he reported 30 pounds of muscle heavier and quickly became a prolific hitter. Fanatical about his conditioning, Hornsby abstained from drinking alcohol, smoking, and even refrained from reading or going to the movies fearing that it would affect his vision.

It is impossible to choose one defining moment in the career of Rogers Hornsby. There were just too many. How about the fact that he won not one, but two Triple Crowns? On the other hand, we could mention that his .358 career batting average is the second highest in Major League history, and the highest for a right-hander. If that doesn't impress you, we can talk about his

Not the easiest guy to get along with, Hornsby was tough, condescending and aloof to fellow teammates and opponents alike, which is probably why he played for five different teams during his 23-year career. He had run-ins with managers, teammates and front office personnel over salary,

★ ★ ★ ★ ★ ★ ★ ★ ★ ★

baseball philosophy or just plain old personalities. Hornsby also had a penchant for gambling at the racetrack, and was usually behind the eight ball financially. He was player-manager from 1925 to 1937 for the Cards, Giants, Braves, Cubs and Browns, and came back to manage the Browns in 1952 and the Reds in 1952–1953. As a manager he was 701–812. His greatest success as manager was his 1926 world championship team but his contentious style always seemed to get in the way.

From an offensive standpoint, in his own way, Rogers Hornsby is right up there with the gods of twentieth century baseball. He was elected to the Hall of Fame in 1942, incredibly on the fifth ballot.

Tales from Joe's Bat Rack

Rogers Hornsby professional model bats often find their way into the upper echelon of collector want lists based on a combination of historical importance and scarcity. Hornsby was widely considered one of the great complete hitters of the era and, today, he remains a player whose name is mentioned as one of the best all-around batsmen ever. His ability to hit for average and power, at a time when few players hit with real power, helps make his bats a hot commodity. This is despite his surly reputation on the field. Hornsby signed an endorsement contract with H&B in the spring of 1926, several years after making his debut, so a number of bats were manufactured with his name in block letters.

When it comes to Hornsby bats, the most notable aspect is the style of his knobs. Hornsby-style knobs, as they are

The Ultimate Season:			Career:		
Year/Team: 1922 STL			**Years: 23**		
G:	154	HR: 42	G:	2259	HR: 301
AB:	623	RBI: 152	AB:	8173	RBI: 1584
R:	141	SB: 17	R:	1579	SB: 135
H:	250	BB: 65	H:	2930	BB: 1038
2B:	46	OPS: 1.181	2B:	541	OPS: 1.010
3B:	14	BA: .401	3B:	169	BA: .358

referred to today, appear to be a compromise between the traditional protruding knobs seen on most bats and the flared knob (which is really no knob at all) seen on some gamers. The most notable name to use bats with a flared knob would be Roberto Clemente, who played many years later. The Hornsby knob or flare knob would allow for a hitter to comfortably place his bottom hand around the base of the bat. In addition, Hornsby would occasionally employ a spiral taping pattern along the handle. Some examples found today show evidence of the tape residue left by Hornsby's application. This handle preparation can be seen in various images from Hornsby's playing days.

Finally, at the time of this writing, there is only one autographed Hornsby gamer known to exist.

" *To be a good hitter you've got to do one thing—Get a good ball to hit.*"
– *Rogers Hornsby*

▲ *Rogers Hornsby's 1924–28 H&B factory side-written bat.*

Mel Ott

★ ★ ★ ★ ★ ★ ★ ★ ★ ★ ★

13

unusual batting stance of kicking his right leg before making contact with the ball added to his power. Master Melvin smacked 25 or more dingers 13 times and led the National League in homers six times, including 1932 when he clouted 38 along with 123 RBI and a batting average of .318.

Selected as an All-Star each season from 1934 to 1944, Ott was as patient as he was powerful, regularly walking twice as often as he struck out. In fact, Ott led the league in free passes six times and eclipsed the 100-walk milestone on ten occasions. For his career, Ott walked 1,708 times and struck out just 896 times in 9,456 at-bats. Ott had an amazing .414 career OBP, and once he did get on base, he usually scored. He led the NL in runs twice, topping out at 138 in 1929. His first All-Star season of 1934 was one of his best with 35 homers, 135 RBI and a batting average of .326. Ott roamed the Giants outfield with superb skill, saving his most clutch performances for the most crucial games.

With 2,876 career hits, Ott had numerous great moments at the plate, but none more important than his performance in the 1933 World Series vs. Washington. The Giants beat the Senators in five games and Ott was spectacular with 7 hits, 2 homers, 4 RBI, a .389 batting average, and .500 OBP while slugging .722. It was in Game Five on October 7, 1933, however, that Ott came through with his famous clutch home run. With the Giants up 3–1 in the Series and the score tied at 3–3 with 2 outs at the top of the 10th inning, Ott came up to bat and blasted Jack Russell's offering into Griffith Stadium's center-field bleachers to win the Series.

Born to working class Dutch parents in Gretna, Louisiana, Melvin Thomas Ott was signed by the Giants while a

One of the game's early home run specialists, during his 22-season career spent entirely with the New York Giants, Mel Ott hit 511 homers with 1,860 RBI, a .304 average, and 488 doubles. The 5-foot, 9-inch, and 170-pound lefty-hitting mighty mite's

★ ★ ★ ★ ★ ★ ★ ★ ★ ★ ★

16-year-old high school student in January 1926 and was personally trained and mentored by John McGraw. Ott would climb from poverty to immense popularity with his natural talent, hardscrabble work ethic, and likable attitude. Player-manager of the Giants from 1942 to 1947, Ott continued as manager until 1948, when he was replaced by Leo Durocher. A successful broadcaster after his retirement, Mel Ott was inducted into the Hall of Fame in 1951 but, just seven years later, he passed away at age 49 due to injuries suffered in an automobile accident in Louisiana.

The Ultimate Season:			Career:		
Year/Team: 1934 NYG			Years: 22		
G:	153	HR: 35	G:	2730	HR: 511
AB:	582	RBI: 135	AB:	9456	RBI: 1860
R:	119	SB: 0	R:	1859	SB: 89
H:	190	BB: 85	H:	2876	BB: 1708
2B:	29	OPS: 1.006	2B:	488	OPS: .947
3B:	10	BA: .326	3B:	72	BA: .304

Tales from Joe's Bat Rack

Of all the fashionable bat-collecting themes, perhaps no other is as popular as collecting legendary lumber from members of the 500 Home Run Club. Many of the most recognizable names in baseball history are part of this exclusive club—from Babe Ruth to Mickey Mantle to Barry Bonds. This club is comprised of the hitters who captivated fans and left crowds in awe as their majestic drives often traveled great distances. There are some very difficult professional model bats needed to complete this intriguing set, but of all the bats on the list, none is more arduous to find than those wielded by this man—a man who used an exaggerated leg kick to help power pitches over the right-field wall.

Unlike many of the bats on this list, Mel Ott gamers do not possess obvious, identifiable characteristics such as a unique taping method, scoring, grooving, a specific pine tar application or handwritten notations. This is due, in part, to the era in which Ott played. Players did not place their numbers on the knobs of their bats and rarely used gripping substances like pine tar or applied handle tape. Ott signed an endorsement contract with H&B in the summer of 1927, one season after making his debut, leaving the possibility of finding one with Ott's name in block letters.

Furthermore, the left-handed slugger did order a fair number of hickory bats from the manufacturer during his career, in addition to the more traditional ash bats. Ott is a fixture on any elite bat checklist since his bats usually represent the final hole to fill for a collector of super sluggers.

> "That kid [Ott] is remarkable. He's like a golfer; his body moves but he keeps his head still with his eyes fixed on the ball. He's got the most natural swing I've seen in years."
> – John McGraw

▲ *Mel Ott's 1927 H&B factory side-written bat.*

Roberto Clemente

★ ★ ★ ★ ★ ★ ★ ★ ★ ★ ★

Louis Requena/Major League Baseball Collection/Getty Images

Brooklyn minor league system by Pittsburgh. In 1956, Clemente blossomed, batting .311 with 60 RBI and 169 hits. His average dipped below .300 for the next three seasons, but in 1960, he fashioned the first of 12 All-Star campaigns, batting .314 with 16 homers, 94 RBI, and 179 hits. That season, he led Pittsburgh to a memorable World Series win vs. the Yankees, batting .310 with 9 hits and 3 RBI is the Series. In 1961, Clemente won the National League batting crown with a .351 average and his outfield play netted him the first of 12 consecutive Gold Gloves. In 1966, he garnered the NL MVP award with 29 homers and 119 RBI. The next season, he led the league with 209 hits and a .357 average. Clemente eclipsed the 200-hit mark four times and finished his wondrous career with a .317 average, 240 home runs, 1,305 RBI, and exactly 3,000 hits.

With a fiery approach to the game and a sensational fervor for excellence, Roberto Clemente embodied the true essence of what it means to be a ballplayer. A lifelong Pittsburgh Pirate, the strong, fast, wiry and tough Clemente is truly the godfather of today's Latino stars. At a time when Latino players were the exception, not the norm, Clemente won over a fickle fan base with his passion and soul. He was a mentor to his teammates, a role model to youngsters, and a humanitarian to the world.

Born in Puerto Rico in 1934, Clemente was signed by the Brooklyn Dodgers in 1954, but was soon plucked from the

That final round number is tinged with great sadness. On September 30, 1972, in the final series of the season at home against the Mets, Clemente stepped to the plate against Jon Matlack sitting at 2,999 hits. He launched a patented bomb to left-center field for a double and number 3,000. It was his last at-bat of the regular season. In December of 1972, the city of Managua, Nicaragua, was victimized by a horrific earthquake. Ever the activist, Clemente organized a relief effort and boarded a supply plane to the troubled region on New Year's Eve. It would be his final act of heroism. Clemente's plane crashed that night, tragically ending an extraordinary life. He was

★ ★ ★ ★ ★ ★ ★ ★ ★ ★ ★

inducted into the Hall of Fame by Special Election in 1973, but in the end, this is a man who will be remembered more for heart and commitment than hits and catches.

The Ultimate Season:				Career:			
Year/Team: 1967 PIT				Years: 18			
G:	147	HR:	23	G:	2433	HR:	240
AB:	585	RBI:	110	AB:	9454	RBI:	1305
R:	103	SB:	9	R:	1416	SB:	83
H:	209	BB:	41	H:	3000	BB:	621
2B:	26	OPS:	.954	2B:	440	OPS:	.834
3B:	10	BA:	.357	3B:	166	BA:	.317

Tales from Joe's Bat Rack

Like the man himself, Roberto Clemente professional model bats tend to have a flair all their own. While Clemente was of modest size at around 175 pounds during his playing career, he wielded one of the biggest bats in the game. Many of his bats weigh in the 36–38-ounce range, with a small number actually exceeding that weight. Compared to contemporary stars like Hank Aaron and Willie Mays, Clemente gamers look like caveman clubs. The majority of the known Clemente bats feature his primary uniform number "21" on the knob or barrel in black marker, but there are two distinct styles: One "21" contains a loop at the bottom of the "2" while the other does not. The iconic Pirate did wear number "13" during his rookie year, but it was for a brief period of time.

A distinct characteristic that you will occasionally see on a Clemente gamer is grooving along the hitting surface of the barrel. Clemente would carve light grooves into the barrel, usually several of them, in order to create spin on the ball after contact. It is important to note that the vast majority of his bats do not possess this type of modification. Early in Clemente's career, his nickname "Momen" was burned into the barrel instead of "Roberto." The "Momen" bats were shipped to Clemente until about 1960. Bats featuring his nickname are certainly more difficult to find than the latter and often sell for a premium. Speaking of premiums,

due to Clemente's early death in 1972, finding autographed professional model bats can be challenging. There are some authentic examples that exist, but they are tough to locate.

For the bulk of his career, Clemente preferred H&B bats (endorsement contract) and signed with the company in 1954, but he did use some Adirondack (block letter) bats during the final few years of his career. The knob style of his bats tended to vary as well, from the more traditional-looking knobs to the distinct flared knobs. Finally, Clemente had a propensity to change bats more often than the average player, which resulted in the majority of his gamers exhibiting only moderate use.

"The big thing about Clemente is that he can hit any pitch. I don't mean only strikes. He can hit a ball off his ankles or off his ear."
– Juan Marichal

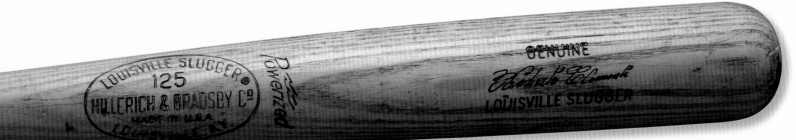

▲ *Roberto Clemente's 1966 MVP season H&B bat.*

Hank Aaron

★ ★ ★ ★ ★ ★ ★ ★ ★ ★ ★

"Guessing what the pitcher is going to throw is 80 percent of being a successful hitter. The other 20 percent is just execution." – Hank Aaron

The Mobile, Alabama, native is on that extremely short list of players who can be argued as the greatest of all time. Still, many seem to dwell on what Hank Aaron did not do. They say he never hit 50 home runs. No, but he hit over 40 homers eight times. They say he did not win multiple MVP Awards. No, but in an era that featured some of baseball's true legends, he finished in the top five in voting eight times. They say he was not as great a fielder as Willie Mays. No, but who was? And Aaron did win three Gold Gloves in his career.

What is not debatable is the greatest moment in Hank Aaron's career. April 8, 1974. Atlanta, Georgia. Dodgers vs. Braves. Al Downing on the mound. Hank Aaron at the plate. Fourth inning. History and the very foundations of baseball at stake. Aaron had tied Babe Ruth on the all-time home run list four days earlier with a shot against Jack Billingham of the Reds. Now, he was poised to pass him. To say that Aaron was a reluctant legend would be an understatement. A quiet man of grace and dignity, his outward demeanor masked the burning competitor within.

For a player who is the all-time leader in RBI and total bases, it might seem difficult to choose a greatest moment. To be sure, Hall of Famer, Henry Louis Aaron slugged and swatted his way into history, thrilling fans with season after season of prolific power.

★ ★ ★ ★ ★ ★ ★ ★ ★ ★ ★ ★

Aaron idolized the great Jackie Robinson who bravely broke baseball's color barrier in 1947. Both men endured the slings, arrows, aches, and scars of racism along the way. Robinson died nearly two years prior to Aaron digging in against Downing on that night in 1974, but he was with him in all ways but earthly.

Aaron's batting stance, like his personality, was quiet, basic, and workmanlike. There was no shoulder pumping, ritualistic motions, or endless batting glove machinations. Aaron just waited, and on that night, Downing delivered. There was no doubt that it was a home run. Onlookers had seen that swing 714 previous times. A scrappy Dodgers left fielder named Bill Buckner scaled the fence trying to catch the ball, but it nestled into the glove of Braves reliever Tom House in the bullpen. This moment belonged to Aaron. As he rounded the bases, two fans emerged from the stands and joined Aaron in his trot. Think about that. An African-American man from Alabama, playing in the cradle of slavery, breaking the game's most hallowed record held by its most beloved player, gleefully escorted by two white men. That is not mere baseball history. It is American history.

The Ultimate Season:				Career:			
Year/Team: 1959 MLN				Years: 23			
G:	154	HR:	39	G:	3298	HR:	755
AB:	629	RBI:	123	AB:	12364	RBI:	2297
R:	116	SB:	8	R:	2174	SB:	240
H:	223	BB:	51	H:	3771	BB:	1402
2B:	46	OPS:	1.037	2B:	624	OPS:	.928
3B:	7	BA:	.355	3B:	98	BA:	.305

in his career, Aaron was not known for using heavy pine tar, but that changed in the late-1960s/early-1970s. Some of his 1970s examples are found with very heavy tar. Most Aaron gamers do feature his primary uniform number "44" on the knob and sometimes on the barrel end as well. During his rookie year, Aaron did wear number "5" for a very brief period of time.

Due to his assault on Ruth's home run record in the early 1970s, many Aaron bats were either taken from the locker room or given away during the time period. This is the main reason why you see many early 1970s examples with little-to-no use. People knew Aaron was ultimately going to break the record, so his bats became a hot commodity.

Some of the most challenging Aaron bats to find would be gamers from the 1950s, which are much harder to find than those manufactured during the second half of his career. In addition, and much like the bats used by fellow superstar Willie Mays, gamers from this period usually lack the evident character that later bats often do. Keep in mind that there are some documented Aaron home run bats in the hobby. Only a few regular season examples and one All-Star Aaron home run bat (1972) have been made available for sale. These are great pieces to own, but make sure you have rock-solid documentation to accompany the bat.

Tales from Joe's Bat Rack

During his career, Hank Aaron was known for using both H&B (endorsement contract) and Adirondack (block letter) professional model bats. Aaron signed his contract with H&B prior to his rookie season, so all of the bats used at the Major League level feature his facsimile signature on the barrel. His final year came in 1976 when he used the popular Bicentennial H&B bats, which contained the special Liberty Bell brand. Early

▲ *Hank Aaron's 1969 Adirondack bat used to hit career home run #521.*

★ ★ ★ ★ ★ ★ ★ ★ ★ ★ ★

just 414 times in over 7,500 at-bats. Berra was a 15-time All-Star and three-time MVP. The rock-solid catcher played in 75 postseason games and 14 World Series, winning ten rings. In both the 1953 and 1955 World Series, Berra batted over .400. Yes, one of the greatest winners in baseball history was a short and scruffy 5-foot, 7-inch, and 185-pound keg-shaped catcher, but he had a smoldering will to lead and win.

Similar to longtime teammate Billy Martin, Berra was more about fire than fame. He willed New York to become the greatest dynasty the game has ever known, calling masterful games including Don Larsen's perfect game in the 1956 World Series, and chewing out umpires with that incendiary temper. Berra was an enigma. On the field, he was committed. Off the field, he was rather comical. Indeed, Yogi Berra became as well-known for his mouth as his mitt. "You wouldn't have won if we'd beaten you." "I usually take a two-hour nap from one to four." "Never answer an anonymous letter." And of course, "It ain't over till it's over." These are just some of the quotes that made Berra one of the most beloved ballplayers and raconteurs in history.

Ironically, perhaps Berra's most memorable moment at the plate was one of failure. In Game Seven of the 1955 World Series vs. Brooklyn, the Yankees trailed 2–0 heading into the bottom of the sixth inning. With Billy Martin on second, Gil McDougald on first and nobody out, Berra stepped to the plate. With that wide stance and powerful stroke, Berra slapped a Johnny Podres pitch the opposite way to left field, something he rarely did. It looked like a sure extra-base hit, perhaps even a home run. Dodgers left fielder Sandy Amoros, shaded far toward

If ever there was an athlete whose appearance and statistics did not match, it is Lawrence Peter "Yogi" Berra. A New York Yankee for 18 seasons (1946–1963), Berra hit 358 home runs and drove in 1,430 runs. He had a career batting average of .285 and struck out

★ ★ ★ ★ ★ ★ ★ ★ ★ ★ ★

> "He [Berra] stopped everything behind the plate and hit everything in front of it." – Mel Ott

The Ultimate Season:			Career:		
Year/Team: 1950 NYY			Years: 19		
G:	151	HR: 28	G:	2120	HR: 358
AB:	597	RBI: 124	AB:	7555	RBI: 1430
R:	116	SB: 4	R:	1175	SB: 30
H:	192	BB: 55	H:	2150	BB: 704
2B:	30	OPS: .915	2B:	321	OPS: .830
3B:	6	BA: .322	3B:	49	BA: .285

center, sped toward the ball, reached out his glove, made a game-saving catch, and then fired to the infield to double off McDougald. The Yanks lost that World Series, but for Berra it was just a small glitch in his storied career. Berra was inducted into the Hall of Fame in 1972 and passed away in 2015 at the age of 90. With his play and his words, we shall certainly not see the likes of Yogi Berra again, or as he once said, "The future ain't what it used to be."

Tales from Joe's Bat Rack

Owning a professional model bat of the man who won more World Series championships than any other player in history certainly ranks high on the collector's list. When it comes to Yogi Berra gamers, there are a few key things to look for. First, while the majority of Berra bats do not feature his primary uniform number "8" on the knob, the ones that do have a particular style. Some hobbyists refer to it as a "snowman 8" because it has the look of two circles placed on top of each other. Keep in mind that Berra did wear numbers "38" and "35" during his first couple of seasons, but players did not often mark their knobs during that time. Second,

there are examples of this style in both paint and marker form at different stages of his career. The painted style, as with most other players, is seen on bats from a slightly earlier period before markers became the preferred method.

An interesting feature, one that is evident on some Berra bats, is the positioning of the grain in relation to the labeling. Berra, who signed an endorsement contract with H&B in the summer of 1947, had a strange request for the company. Near the beginning of the 1958 season, Berra started ordering bats branded across the grain, versus branded in the open grain. As a result, the sweet spot of the hitting area appeared near the back of the barrel versus the immediate left or right of the stamped barrel end. Berra did this in order to compensate for the rolling of his hands during the swing.

As a final note, keep in mind that early Berra gamers have "Larry" instead of "Yogi" stamped into the barrel. The change from "Larry" to "Yogi" took place in 1953. Like a large number of his contemporaries, bats that date to earlier in his career often sell for a premium and are tougher to locate than those manufactured later.

▲ Yogi Berra's 1960 H&B All-Star Game bat.

Stan Musial

★ ★ ★ ★ ★ ★ ★ ★ ★ ★ ★ ★

Superb hitters, like Stan Musial, have many memorable moments over the course of their great careers. Game winning hits and superb offensive plays seem to come naturally to the truly special hitters. As a 24-time All-Star, three-time National League

Most Valuable Player, and a seven-time NL Batting Champion with three World Series crowns, "Stan the Man" enjoyed many special moments. Taking a look at his overall career, Stanley Frank Musial can certainly be mentioned in the same breath as Williams, DiMaggio, Aaron, Mays, Cobb, and even Ruth. He also played the game with class, dignity, and compassion.

One of Musial's great career moments took place at Busch Stadium on May 2, 1954. That day, under clear skies, the St. Louis Cardinals played an early season doubleheader vs. the New York Giants. It would be a good indicator of how the season would progress, as both teams expected to be in the hunt for the National League pennant. In front of a crowd of 26,662 rabid fans, Musial put on an offensive display for the ages. In the first inning of Game One, with Giants lefty Johnny Antonelli on the mound, Musial drew a walk. Then, in his second at-bat in the third, Musial hit a rocket onto the roof for his first home run of the day. In the fifth inning, with a man on base, Musial launched another shot off Antonelli for his second homer of the day. With reliever Jim Hearn in for Antonelli in the sixth inning, Musial ripped a single. This was followed by his third home run—a tie-breaking shot launched onto the roof off a Hearn slider which put the Cards in the lead. The Redbirds went on to win the first game of the contest 10–6, with Musial knocking in six runs.

Musial continued to spin his magic in the nightcap.

Facing Don Liddle, Musial drew a walk in his first at-bat in the first, followed by a deep fly to right in the third inning tracked by Willie Mays. With the great knuckleballer Hoyt Wilhelm relieving Liddle in the fifth, Musial mashed one onto the right field roof for home run number four. In the seventh inning, with St. Louis fans in frenzy, Musial stepped up to the plate to face Wilhelm and went yard for the fifth time. Although he popped up in his final at-bat that day, "Stan the Man" finished with a record-setting 5 home runs and 9 RBI. Interestingly, an eight-year-old boy and his dad were in the stands watching Musial smack home run, after home run. He said to his father, "I'm going to do that someday." Eighteen years later that little boy, Nate Colbert, tied Musial's record when he hit 5 home runs while playing for the San Diego Padres. Who was one of the first to congratulate him? Stan the Man.

The Ultimate Season:				Career:			
Year/Team: 1948 STL				Years: 22			
G:	155	HR:	39	G:	3026	HR:	475
AB:	611	RBI:	131	AB:	10972	RBI:	1951
R:	135	SB:	7	R:	1949	SB:	78
H:	230	BB:	79	H:	3630	BB:	1599
2B:	46	OPS:	1.152	2B:	725	OPS:	.976
3B:	18	BA:	.376	3B:	177	BA:	.331

Tales from Joe's Bat Rack

As a result of his all-around offensive capabilities and popularity, Stan Musial professional model bats remain a hot commodity. During his career, Musial was an avid user of H&B bats, but the iconic Cardinal did order some Adirondacks as well. In his early playing days, Musial did have a signature model produced, but the vast majority of the known examples are from the 1950s and beyond, which instead have "Musial Model" in block letters on the barrel end. You will often find well-used gamers from this period with his uniform number "6" underlined on the knob in black marker, but not all of his bats exhibit his number.

The most unique Musial bat characteristic of note is the occasional presence of grooving or scoring along the handle, which has been documented in various books. Musial used a jackknife to carve up the handle of his bats for extra grip since he wasn't a fan of substances like pine tar. A direct quote from Musial detailing this practice can be found in *Crack of the Bat: The Louisville Slugger Story* (2000). "I had the thinnest bat in the Major Leagues. I made my bat with a Babe Ruth handle and a Jimmie Foxx barrel and I would scrape down the handle to make it even thinner. I never used tar and I didn't like wax. I'd scrape up the handle a little bit so I could hold it better."

While this feature is certainly coveted by collectors, it is important to note that most known Musial gamers do not possess handle preparation of this nature. This includes a photo-matched bat used to hit the game-winning home run during the 1955 All-Star Game.

> "*When a pitcher's throwing a spitball, don't worry and don't complain, just hit the dry side like I do.*" – Stan Musial

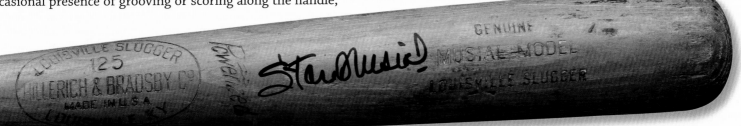

▲ *Stan Musial's 1952 H&B bat.*

Pete Rose

★ ★ ★ ★ ★ ★ ★ ★ ★ ★ ★

Bettmann/Bettmann Collection/Getty Images

(1975, 1976, 1980) and was named 1975 Series MVP. Rose led the league in hits seven times, runs four times, doubles five times, and garnered three batting crowns. Named NL MVP in 1973, he has a Silver Slugger Award and two Gold Gloves. Playing left field, right field, first base, second base, and the hot corner, Rose led the league at various times in putouts, assists, and fielding percentage.

Rose was the leadoff hitter for Cincinnati's "Big Red Machine" in the 1970s before joining the Phillies in 1979. At 39 years old, he led the Phillies to their first-ever Series win in 1980. He played briefly for the Montreal Expos, logging hit number 4,000 in 1984 before returning to Cincinnati as player-manager of the Reds. Probably his greatest achievement took place on September 11, 1985. Rose made baseball history that day, breaking Ty Cobb's record of 4,191 career hits. He retired in 1986 with 4,256 career hits and continued as Cincinnati's manager until he was banned from baseball for life in 1989. Unfortunately, Rose had a gambling problem, and apparently bet on games while a manager. He applied for reinstatement several times but, at this point, Rose is still on the outside looking in. However, MLB has allowed him on the field for ceremonies marking career achievements and, in June 2016, the Reds retired his uniform number "14" and inducted Rose into the Reds Hall of Fame. He has provided analysis for Fox Sports since 2015.

Whether or not Pete Rose ever gets into the Hall of Fame, there is no denying he was one heck of a ballplayer. Thirty years after his last game, Rose still holds the MLB career record for games played, at-bats, plate appearances, hits, and singles. A controversial figure throughout his 24-year career, Peter Edward Rose played aggressively, some say with reckless abandon. He did whatever it took to win, inspiring teammates and intimidating opponents along the way.

The Cincinnati, Ohio, native was signed by his hometown Reds right out of high school, in 1960. He took Rookie of the Year honors in 1963 and, in 1965, his first of 17 All-Star seasons, Rose led the National League with 209 hits and batted .312—the first of fifteen .300-plus seasons. His achievements are astounding. The switch-hitter played on six pennant winners and three World Series championship teams

★ ★ ★ ★ ★ ★ ★ ★ ★ ★ ★ ★ ★

> "*Hitting. That's what I enjoy most. Realistically, it's probably the hardest thing to do in all of sport. Think about it. You've got a round ball, a round bat, and the object is to hit it square." – Pete Rose*

The Ultimate Season:				Career:			
Year/Team: 1969 CIN				Years: 24			
G:	156	HR:	16	G:	3562	HR:	160
AB:	627	RBI:	82	AB:	14053	RBI:	1314
R:	120	SB:	7	R:	2165	SB:	198
H:	218	BB:	88	H:	4256	BB:	1566
2B:	33	OPS:	.940	2B:	746	OPS:	.784
3B:	11	BA:	.348	3B:	135	BA:	.303

Tales from Joe's Bat Rack

Compared to other players of the period, Pete Rose used a fairly diverse selection of bats during his career. During the first couple of decades, Rose switched from using H&B (endorsement contract) bats to Adirondack (block letter) bats on a regular basis. Later in his career, Rose started using Mizuno bats of various styles as he marched towards the all-time career hits record held by Ty Cobb. In fact, perhaps to provide extra motivation, Mizuno had the number "4192" added to the barrel of Rose's bats. That was the number needed to break Cobb's record, although his official career total has been reduced to 4,189 since. After Rose surpassed Cobb in the record books, Mizuno replaced the "4192" with the acronym "ATHL" (All Time Hit Leader). Most of these Mizuno bats were made with a black finish, but some had a more natural blonde-looking appearance.

Rose also changed his bat preparation method like he mixed up the use of certain bat models and brands during his career. From the 1960s and 1970s, you will encounter Rose bats with varying degrees of pine tar applications. Later on and during his transition to Mizuno bats, Rose utilized one of the more unique taping methods a collector will ever see. Rose would often affix several small ringlets of tape along the handle, while adding a large wrap of tape just north of the ringlets at the top of the handle. This taping pattern is evident in many Rose photos from the era. In some cases, you will find Rose gamers from this stage of his career with the tape wrap only, absent any ringlets. Rose's uniform number "14" is often found marked on the knob, from the 1960s until the end of his career, but not all of his gamers possess this notation.

Finally, gamers that date to Rose's early playing days are much tougher to locate than those from the mid-1970s and later. When Hank Aaron was chasing the all-time home run record, his bats became hot commodities, and the same is true for Rose gamers as he approached the career hits record. The price range for Rose gamers can be as wide ranging as any professional model bat in the hobby, and it depends on a number of variables.

▲ *Pete Rose's 1985 Mizuno bat used to register career hit #4,192.*

George Brett

★ ★ ★ ★ ★ ★ ★ ★ ★ ★ ★ ★

Ron Vesely/Getty Images Sport Classic Collection/Getty Images

third basemen in history. In his 21-season career, Brett batted .305 with 317 home runs and 1,596 RBI. A doubles machine, he attained 40 or more five times, registering 665 in his career. Brett dominated his position for more than a decade, earning All-Star status each season from 1976 to 1988. A solid third sacker, he won a Gold Glove in 1985 at age 32.

It was Brett who spearheaded Kansas City's rise from a 1969 expansion team to an American League powerhouse. Known for his 1983 meltdown at Yankee Stadium after the well-documented pine tar incident, Brett's greatest moment also involved the Yankees, Kansas City's chief rival in the American League. New York had beaten Kansas City in the ALCS in 1976, 1977, and 1978. In 1980, the two teams met again for American League supremacy. Brett made a serious run at hitting .400 that season, finishing at .390, but once again, the Yankees stood between him and a trip to the World Series. The Royals won the first two games of the best-of-five series and, on October 10, 1980, headed to Yankee Stadium with a chance for the pennant. The veteran Yanks had a 2–1 lead as the Royals came to bat in the seventh inning. With Rich Gossage on the hill, two men on base and two outs, Brett came to the plate, launched a three-run homer into the right field seats and the Royals went on to win the game 4–2, clinching the pennant. Brett's clutch clout finally vanquished the Yankees. Kansas City lost the World Series to the Phillies, but Brett batted .375 in that Fall Classic.

George Brett batted .337 in seven postseasons and eventually led the Royals to their first World Series title in 1985. He won three batting crowns in his career, two of them a decade apart. His .390 average in 1980 was, at the time, the highest average since Ted Williams hit .406 in 1941. The 1980 MVP Award winner twice had over

O**ne of the most dogged** competitors of his generation, George Brett was a rare batter who could hit for average and power. A lifelong Kansas City Royal, Brett ranks among the best

★ ★ ★ ★ ★ ★ ★ ★ ★ ★ ★

200 hits. George Howard Brett was inducted into the Hall of Fame in 1999. He is Kansas City Royals royalty and one of the most tireless competitors and productive third basemen of all time.

The Ultimate Season:			Career:		
Year/Team: 1980 KCR			Years: 21		
G:	117	HR: 24	G:	2707	HR: 317
AB:	449	RBI: 118	AB:	10349	RBI: 1596
R:	87	SB: 15	R:	1583	SB: 201
H:	175	BB: 58	H:	3154	BB: 1096
2B:	33	OPS: 1.118	2B:	665	OPS: .857
3B:	9	BA: .390	3B:	137	BA: .305

Tales from Joe's Bat Rack

George Brett was a terrific hitter and a popular player, but that is only part of why his professional model bats find their way into many of the very best collections in the world. Visual appeal plays a key role in all collectibles. It is no different in the world of professional model bats, and when it comes to well-used Brett gamers, not many bats can compete with the eye-catching nature of his lumber. Classic, heavily-used Brett bats look more like props from the hit movie *Braveheart* than baseball game equipment.

Of course, the Brett bat characteristic that sticks out above all others is the heavy use of pine tar. Some of his gamers look like they were repeatedly dipped in the substance like a vanilla ice cream bar dipped in chocolate. The pattern is usually consistent, with concentrated areas visible near the center brand (where the initial application was made) and on the lower-to-mid handle (where the tar was transferred by hand). The one exception to this rule would be bats that date to the early portion of Brett's career. The degree of pine tar use seemed to increase over time, so some early gamers don't possess the same look. The contact area for Brett is usually concentrated on the right barrel as a result of the career Royal batting with the label facing up.

Brett signed an endorsement contract with H&B (which later became Louisville Slugger) in 1971, prior to making his debut, and he clearly preferred their bats throughout his career. In addition, the knobs of Brett gamers were occasionally marked in a unique fashion. While many of his gamers feature his primary uniform number "5" in black marker, some are marked "GB" along with the "5" directly underneath. At times, you will see Brett bats with "LOU" (one of Brett's nicknames) written on the knob, often in large letters. Brett's oldest brother nicknamed George "Looney Toons" growing up because of his younger sibling's fascination with cartoons. "Looney Toons" was eventually shortened to "Lou" over time. Keep in mind that Brett did wear number "25" during his first couple of season with the Royals.

Near the end of his career, it is important to note that Brett did document some "hit" bats by adding special inscriptions to the barrel.

> **"***George Brett could get good wood on an aspirin.***"** – Jim Frey

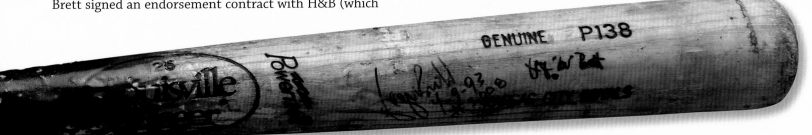

▲ *George Brett's 1993 Louisville Slugger bat used to register career hit #3,008.*

Derek Jeter

There have been a slew of Jeter moments over the years, but there are two real highlights that define what Derek Jeter was all about. It was October 31, 2001. The Yankees were behind 2–1 going into Game Four of the World Series vs. the Arizona Diamondbacks. The score was 3–3 in the bottom of the 10th inning when Jeter stepped up to the plate. He patiently worked a nine-pitch at-bat and finally, at four minutes past midnight, Jeter blasted one over the right field fence to win the game. For this feat, he earned the nickname "Mr. November."

Is it time to ask Honus Wagner to move over a bit? Derek Jeter could very well be moving into the top spot as the greatest shortstop of all time. Blasphemy? Well, if anything, it's worth discussing. The offensive numbers are darn close. Wagner hit for a higher average, Jeter hit more home runs. Wagner had a higher OPS, Jeter had slightly more hits. In any event, Jeter is certainly in the argument. Derek Sanderson Jeter accumulated 3,465 hits and a .310 batting average over his 20-year career. Along with those impressive numbers, you can add his 14 All-Star appearances, the Roberto Clemente award in 2009, the five World Series championship rings, five Silver Slugger Awards, five Gold Gloves, the Rookie of the Year Award in 1996 and World Series Most Valuable Player Award in 2000.

The other defining moment took place at Fenway Park in front of Red Sox fans. On July 1, 2004, with the game on the line in the 12th inning, Sox outfielder Trot Nixon hit a fly down the left field line. With total reckless abandon, Jeter sprinted from his shortstop position and threw himself over the third-base rail to make a head-first diving catch two rows into the crowd, smashing his face on a seat. Jeter came up with a cut chin and bruised face but had the ball in his glove. Even the Boston fans cheered the Yankees captain for his amazing effort.

Held in high esteem by fans and foes alike, Jeter presented

★ ★ ★ ★ ★ ★ ★ ★ ★ ★ ★

> "He really knows how to work the pitcher and work the count... that's 'professional' hitting."
> – Dave Campbell, ESPN analyst

The Ultimate Season:				Career:			
Year/Team: 1999 NYY				Years: 20			
G:	158	HR:	24	G:	2747	HR:	260
AB:	627	RBI:	102	AB:	11195	RBI:	1311
R:	134	SB:	19	R:	1923	SB:	358
H:	219	BB:	91	H:	3465	BB:	1082
2B:	37	OPS:	.989	2B:	544	OPS:	.817
3B:	9	BA:	.349	3B:	66	BA:	.310

himself with dignity and class throughout his career. Even with the legendary Yankees-Red Sox rivalry, Jeter was the player that Sox fans hated to hate. In his final game at Fenway Park, Jeter received a prolonged standing ovation when he was honored for his great contributions to the game. Jeter later joked that Sox fans had "gone soft." Off the field, Jeter was great fodder for the New York gossip columns. With his movie star looks and an almost mysterious, private personality, he was considered the most eligible bachelor in New York. It's not often that one gets to say "he was the greatest of all time," but in Derek Jeter's case, he very well may have been.

Tales from Joe's Bat Rack

Let's get this straight...Derek Jeter professional model bats are not scarce. Nevertheless, his lumber may be the most popular of all the names in any comprehensive collection. Jeter had a long, prosperous career and he worked with Steiner—a hobby staple—for a great deal of it. Jeter not only signed autographs for the entity, but they also helped bring Jeter game-used equipment to the marketplace direct from the New York Yankees. While this wasn't the only way Jeter bats made their way to the hobby, this long relationship provided a great opportunity for collectors to obtain an authentic gamer.

Many heavily-used Jeter bats have one thing in common: a generous helping of Mota stick or pine tar along the handle. In some cases, the application of gripping substance extends from the base of the handle through the center brand. In these instances, the eye appeal of his gamers is terrific since the application adds so much character. The majority of the time Jeter used a solid, black-colored Louisville Slugger bat, but he also used some natural-colored gamers earlier in his career. These early gamers feature Jeter's name in block letters, but the bulk of his bats are of the endorsement contract variety and contain his facsimile signature.

Interestingly enough, most of Jeter's gamers are not found with his uniform number "2" noted on the knob. This is also true of some of his Yankees teammates like Jorge Posada and Paul O'Neill. Finally, like bats used by fellow shortstop Cal Ripken, Jr., Jeter bats often exhibit cleat marks on the top portion of the bat along the barrel.

▲ *Derek Jeter's Louisville Slugger bat used in the 2001 World Series.*

★ ★ ★ ★ ★ ★ ★ ★ ★ ★ ★

on the streets of Philadelphia, Campanella was a boulder of a man at 5-foot, 9-inches, and 190 pounds—strong and smart, all wrapped in an All-Star package. Make that an eight-time All-Star package. Arguably the best catcher in the National League, in his ten seasons with Brooklyn, he won three NL MVP awards and slammed 242 career home runs with 856 RBI. His toughness was unquestionable and his leadership was key in carrying "Dem Bums" to five pennants and one glorious world championship in 1955. Campanella had over 100 RBI three times in his career. In 1953, he registered 41 homers, scored 103 runs and posted a colossal 142 RBI while batting .312. Much like his crosstown rival, the Yankees' Yogi Berra, Campanella was no matinee idol, but the broad-shouldered backstop was a steadying influence behind the plate. He built pitching staffs, which included Sandy Koufax, Carl Erskine, Clem Labine, Don Newcombe, and 1955 World Series hero Johnny Podres.

Campanella joined the Dodgers one year after Jackie Robinson broke baseball's color barrier. He followed Robinson as the second African-American MVP in 1951, and the second African-American Hall of Famer in 1969. As strong as Campanella was, he was beset by injuries throughout

The Brooklyn Dodgers of the 1950s were more a human body than a baseball team. Pee Wee Reese was the heart. Duke Snider was the nerve. Gil Hodges was the mind, and Jackie Robinson was the soul. All of these great superstars, however, depended on the guts of that club—Roy Campanella. Raised

his career and constantly played with pain. In the midst of a great 1955 season, Campanella seriously injured his knee on a foul tip setting the backdrop for his finest moments as a hitter. After rehabbing for weeks, he pushed himself to return to the Dodgers lineup. Despite bad wheels and aching hands from the rigors of catching, he had an MVP-winning

★ ★ ★ ★ ★ ★ ★ ★ ★ ★

season with 32 homers, 107 RBI, and a .318 batting average. Moreover, he had two home runs in the 1955 Series as the Dodgers finally prevailed over the hated Yanks. Campanella's career came to a sudden and sad end in January of 1958 when he was permanently paralyzed in an automobile accident on Long Island. He would never leave the confines of his wheelchair again, but in the hearts and minds of Dodgers fans, he remained a shining hero until his death in 1993.

The Ultimate Season:				Career:			
Year/Team: 1953 BRO				Years: 10			
G:	144	HR:	41	G:	1215	HR:	242
AB:	519	RBI:	142	AB:	4205	RBI:	856
R:	103	SB:	4	R:	627	SB:	25
H:	162	BB:	67	H:	1161	BB:	533
2B:	26	OPS:	1.006	2B:	178	OPS:	.860
3B:	3	BA:	.312	3B:	18	BA:	.276

Tales from Joe's Bat Rack

Roy Campanella professional model bats are amongst the scarcest of the 1948–1957 era. Part of that scarcity is a product of his short time in the majors, and part of it is strictly about the survival rate. During his impactful run, Campanella's bat of choice was H&B, although he did not have an endorsement contract with the bat manufacturer. As a result, his bats were branded with his last name, "Campanella," in block letters on the barrel. Furthermore, his tragic career-ending accident in 1958 also limited the opportunity to obtain a signed Campanella gamer.

Most players, including the likes of Mickey Mantle and Ted Williams, signed more gamers after their careers were over than during. These were vintage bats often presented to them for signing during the 1980s and 1990s. So, with Campanella, you would be hard-pressed to find a pre-accident signature on one of his gamers. Post-accident signatures on vintage Campanella gamers are slightly more likely after he regained some use of his arms after rehabilitation, but they are still very rare.

The key characteristic that is clearly visible in numerous photos from Campanella's playing days is the presence of pine tar near the lower handle of his bats. It can be a fairly heavy application, but it usually doesn't extend too far up the handle. In addition, Campanella was inconsistent about noting his primary uniform number "39" on the knobs of his bats. You will find some gamers today that feature a painted "39" or one added in black marker, but they are very rare. Most of his bats, even well-used examples, do not possess his number. Keep in mind that Campanella did wear number "33" for a brief time during his rookie season in 1948. With Campanella's free-swinging, aggressive hitting style, you will find that his bats often exhibit evidence of use all over the barrel, and some of them showcase cleat marks towards the end of the bat.

> " *A flawlessly graceful catcher and an astute handler of pitchers, Campanella was also a feared slugger.*" – New York Times, *1993*

▲ *Roy Campanella's 1957 H&B bat with original factory-ordered cork grip.*

Cal Ripken, Jr.

22

★ ★ ★ ★ ★ ★ ★ ★ ★ ★ ★

Icon Sportswire

he worked through illness and injury to play every game. Calvin Edwin Ripken, Jr., played his 2,131st game on September 6, 1995, to much fanfare and continued for three more years, ending the streak on September 19, 1998, having set a new record of 2,632 consecutive games played.

At 6-foot, 4-inches, and 200 pounds, Ripken was not the typical shortstop of his era. With his offensive power, defensive skills, dedication, work ethic, and focus on fundamentals, Ripken essentially redefined the shortstop position. The two-time Gold Glove winner led the American League in assists seven times, double plays turned eight times, putouts six times, and fielding percentage four times. No slouch offensively, he batted over .300 five times, owns eight Silver Slugger Awards, and slammed 20-plus home runs for ten consecutive seasons with a career-high 34 dingers in 1991.

Signed out of high school in 1978, the Maryland native played his entire 21-year career for the Baltimore Orioles. Ripken won the Rookie of the Year Award in 1982 and followed that in 1983 with his first AL MVP Award, his first Silver Slugger, and his first of 19 consecutive All-Star appearances. Also named 1983 Major League Player of the Year, the 22-year-old Ripken batted .318, hit 27 homers, led the league in doubles, hits, runs, at-bats, and games played, and helped to lead the Orioles to a 4–1 World Series win over the Phillies.

A baseball superhero for sure, the "Iron Man" brought disenchanted fans back to the game after the 1994 players strike with his quest to break Lou Gehrig's 2,130 consecutive games-played streak. Ripken's epic streak began on May 30, 1982, and for 17 years

Besides his games-played streak, Ripken, Jr., put together an amazing 8,264 consecutive innings-played streak from June 4, 1982, to September 14, 1987. A consistent force at the plate and in the field, he had another MVP season in 1991, batting .323 with 34 homers and a league-leading 368 total bases. He won the Home Run

★ ★ ★ ★ ★ ★ ★ ★ ★ ★ ★

> " *He was a great player, a great ambassador of the game, and shattered one of the most hallowed records in sports.*" – Brady Anderson

The Ultimate Season:				Career:			
Year/Team: 1991 BAL				Years: 21			
G:	162	HR:	34	G:	3001	HR:	431
AB:	650	RBI:	114	AB:	11551	RBI:	1695
R:	99	SB:	6	R:	1647	SB:	36
H:	210	BB:	53	H:	3184	BB:	1129
2B:	46	OPS:	.940	2B:	603	OPS:	.788
3B:	5	BA:	.323	3B:	44	BA:	.276

Derby and was named 1991 Major League Player of the Year. Ripken, Jr., retired at the end of the 2001 season, at age 41, with a career 3,184 hits, 431 home runs, and a .276 batting average. He is owner of the Aberdeen Ironbirds, a minor-league affiliate of the Orioles, and is involved in youth baseball. Ripken was appointed Special Sports Envoy for the State Department in 2007 and was inducted into the Hall of Fame that year with 98.5% of the vote.

Tales from Joe's Bat Rack

Rumor has it that Cal Ripken, Jr., was very protective of his equipment during his career. So, by post-1980 standards, Ripken gamers are tougher to find than bats used by many of his contemporaries. By different means, professional model bats have their way of making it out of the clubhouse or the bat rack. Sometimes, the players can be generous with their equipment. Other times, the equipment is poached and finds its way into the hobby without the player's knowledge or permission.

Ripken was not only guarded about his bats, but he was also one of the small percentage of players that actually kept a decent amount of his game-used equipment from his playing days. Once in a while, collectors may encounter bats that are signed by "Iron Man" and inscribed as "Gamer" on the barrel. These are bats that originated from Ripken's personal collection. As expected, bats featuring this special inscription often sell for premiums. Ripken did use both Louisville Slugger and Rawlings/Adirondack bats during his career, but he clearly preferred the former. Ripken had a very early signature model (1978), dating to the minor leagues, with Louisville Slugger (H&B). In addition, Ripken ordered many bats with either a two-toned or solid, dark-colored appearance, but some—especially earlier examples—were of the more traditional blonde tone.

Two key Ripken characteristics to look for are cleat marks on the upper barrel and the style of his uniform number "8" on the knobs of his gamers. Ripken was known for banging his cleats with his bats while at the plate, so some heavily-used bats have a plethora of cleat marks along the barrel. Furthermore, the style of the "8" often seen on the knobs of his bats is of the snowman variety, like those seen on Yogi Berra bats. It is usually large and appears like two circles placed on top of each other. On occasion, the "8" is circled in marker as well. Keep in mind that a good portion of his bats do not feature the uniform number, as Ripken was inconsistent about adding his "8" to the knobs.

▲ Cal Ripken, Jr.'s, 1987–88 Louisville Slugger bat.

Mike Schmidt

★ ★ ★ ★ ★ ★ ★ ★ ★ ★ ★

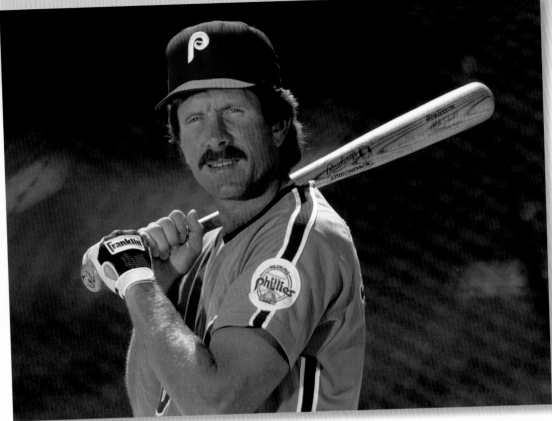

In 1980, Schmidt powered the Phillies to their first-ever world championship with 48 home runs and 121 RBI, winning World Series MVP honors and the first of his three NL MVP Awards. A model of consistency, Schmidt had over 30 home runs in 13 of 14 seasons from 1974 to 1987, and won six Silver Sluggers in a seven-year period. The third baseman won Gold Gloves in nine straight seasons (1976–1984), and another in 1986. A 12-time All-Star, Schmidt played his entire 18-year career in Philadelphia. The 1983 Phillies, known as the "Wheeze Kids" for their veteran roster, won the National League pennant with a lineup that included Pete Rose, Joe Morgan, and Tony Perez.

The history of baseball is filled with amazingly talented players, but only a scant few can be counted among the best at their respective positions. Michael Jack Schmidt is one of those players. Although his stoic demeanor and expressionless face did not endear him to fans or the press, Schmidt set the standard for pure power in the 1970s and 1980s, before both stats and sluggers became bloated through performance enhancing drugs. Born in Dayton, Ohio, Schmidt brought a Midwestern humility to superstardom. In his career spanning from 1972 to 1989, he had 548 home runs while driving in 1,595 runs. Not a patient hitter, Schmidt led the National League in strikeouts on four occasions, but also led the league in OBP three times. In 1974, 1975, and 1976, Schmidt led the National League in home runs, a feat he accomplished eight times in his career.

The most memorable at-bat of Mike Schmidt's career completely belied his stony exterior. On April 18, 1987, in Pittsburgh against the rival Pirates, the Phillies had blown a 5–2 lead and the score was 6–5 Pirates going into the ninth inning. With two men on base and two outs, Schmidt launched a home run off Don Robinson over the left-field wall giving the Phillies an 8–6 lead. It would prove to be the game-winner and, more importantly, the 500th home run of his career. Showing more emotion than he had his entire career, Schmidt pumped his fists, clapped his hands, and practically danced around the bases. Two years later, emotion would once again rule as the man known as "Captain Cool" was anything but in a tearful farewell to the Phillies and

★ ★ ★ ★ ★ ★ ★ ★ ★ ★ ★ ★

Major League Baseball. Mike Schmidt was inducted into the Hall of Fame in 1995 and, taking into account offense and defense, is arguably the greatest third baseman in the history of baseball.

The Ultimate Season:				Career:			
Year/Team: 1980 PHI				Years: 18			
G:	150	HR:	48	G:	2404	HR:	548
AB:	548	RBI:	121	AB:	8352	RBI:	1595
R:	104	SB:	12	R:	1506	SB:	174
H:	157	BB:	89	H:	2234	BB:	1507
2B:	25	OPS:	1.004	2B:	408	OPS:	.908
3B:	8	BA:	.286	3B:	59	BA:	.267

Tales from Joe's Bat Rack

For most of his career, Mike Schmidt preferred using Adirondack bats (endorsement contract), but the perennial home run champion did use a fair number of H&B/Louisville Slugger (block letter) bats as well. This is particularly true during the first several years of Schmidt's career. In some cases, you may encounter a Schmidt H&B professional model bat with a red tape ring added around the midsection of the bat. This was likely done as a result of being under contract with the rival bat manufacturer. The purpose of the tape was to make the bat appear like an Adirondack on television, as Adirondack bats are made with a colored ring often consistent with the team colors. While this practice was certainly not commonplace, collectors may encounter gamers that feature this tape addition.

Many of the existing Schmidt gamers do possess his primary uniform number "20" marked on the knob in marker. Most of the time, the "20" is large and it covers a substantial portion of the knob. Schmidt did wear number "22" during his debut season, but it only lasted for 13 games. Though not a player known for any extreme handle preparation, the slugger did use pine tar throughout his career. You will often see Schmidt gamers with pine tar along the handle and, in some cases, a moderate coating of the gripping substance on the upper portion of the handle, which is where some players like to grab extra tar before stepping in the box.

Keep in mind that during the last several years of his career, Schmidt was known for marking some of his home run bats as he marched towards 500 career dingers. These bats are marked in different ways. A percentage of his gamers were marked with dots representing the home runs near the center brand and either the actual home run number or the number needed (a countdown) to reach 500. Other bats are signed and/or inscribed with the specific home run number. These bats sell for premiums in the marketplace.

> "*Natural ability like the raw power Schmidt had is a rare gift you see maybe once in a lifetime*"
> – Bob Wren, Schmidt's Ohio University baseball coach

▲ *Mike Schmidt's 1984 Rawlings/ Adirondack bat used to hit career home run #400.*

Johnny Bench

★ ★ ★ ★ ★ ★ ★ ★ ★ ★ ★ ★

24

the team into the 1972 NL playoffs, while earning him the National League Most Valuable Player Award. With the addition of players like Joe Morgan from Houston, along with key players like Cesar Geronimo, Denis Menke, and pitcher Jack Billingham, the Reds won 95 games and faced the Pittsburgh Pirates, with their 96 wins, for the National League crown.

The first four games of the best of five series were split, with the two very evenly matched teams going head to head. Game Five would decide which team would play in the World Series. The Pirates took an early 2–0 lead, but the Reds came back on a Pete Rose double to cut the score to 2–1. In the fourth inning, the Pirates padded their lead on a run-scoring hit by Dave Cash. In the bottom of the fifth inning, Cincinnati's Cesar Geronimo smashed a home run to bring the Reds to within one.

For the next four innings, into the bottom of the ninth, the Reds could not close the gap.

With Pirates steady reliever Dave Giusti on the mound to face the 4, 5, and 6 hitters, and with the Reds down to their last three outs, Johnny Bench stepped up to the plate. The Pirates reliever quickly got ahead of Bench 1–2. On the next pitch, Giusti threw a big sweeping changeup. Not being fooled, the Little General stepped into the pitch and drove the ball into the right field stands with a dramatic home run to tie the game. With arms raised and Cinci fans going berserk, Johnny Bench circled the bases into the arms of his teammates at the top of the dugout steps.

Twenty-four-year-old Johnny Bench went into the 1972 season with very high expectations. After all, the Reds were coming off a dismal 1971 season, finishing fourth in the tough National League West. "Redemption for the Reds" became the battle cry for 1972. The Little General and his teammates were ready to make amends. The pieces were coming together to form one of the greatest teams in baseball history—the "Big Red Machine."

Bench's 40 home runs, 125 RBI, and dynamic defense led

★ ★ ★ ★ ★ ★ ★ ★ ★ ★ ★ ★

After singles by Tony Perez and Denis Menke, Bob Moose replaced Giusti. Moose threw a wild pitch to Hal McRae, scoring George Foster who was pinch running for Perez, and there was pandemonium on the field. The Cincinnati Reds won the National League pennant, and the Bench home run started it all. The Reds would lose the World Series to the Oakland A's that year, but they went on to win the championship in 1975 and 1976. By the time his 17-year career was said and done, Johnny Lee Bench was considered by many to be the greatest catcher of all time. That special moment in 1972 personifies what Bench and the Big Red Machine were all about. He was an extraordinary talent who led his team to dominate the game for many years.

The Ultimate Season:			Career:		
Year/Team: 1970 CIN			Years: 17		
G:	158	HR:	45	G:	2158	HR:	389
AB:	605	RBI:	148	AB:	7658	RBI:	1376
R:	97	SB:	5	R:	1091	SB:	68
H:	177	BB:	54	H:	2048	BB:	891
2B:	35	OPS:	.932	2B:	381	OPS:	.817
3B:	4	BA:	.293	3B:	24	BA:	.267

Tales from Joe's Bat Rack

If you are looking for a stellar professional model bat used by the player many people consider to be the greatest catcher of all time, there are a couple of key characteristics to note. From very early on in his career to the end, Johnny Bench was an avid user of pine tar. He was also extremely consistent in how he applied the gripping substance. Well-used Bench gamers often exhibit a heavy coating of pine tar that starts near the base of the handle, extending towards the center brand. This is the most prominent Bench characteristic, and its presence adds a tremendous amount of visual appeal to his bats. From time to time, collectors will encounter a Bench gamer that exhibits scoring along the handle or barrel, but the majority of his bats do not possess this bat modification.

In addition, a large number of Bench gamers do feature his uniform number "5" written on the knob in either red or black marker. The number is usually fairly large and its shape or style varies throughout his career. Bench ordered bats with a number of different finishes, and he clearly preferred H&B (endorsement contract) bats during his career after signing with the company in 1965 prior to his Major League debut. You will occasionally see an Adirondack (block letter), but these usually date to Bench's early playing days. Bench bats that were manufactured during his time as the field general for the "Big Red Machine" in the 1970s tend to sell for a premium. Keep in mind that some of Bench's keepsakes, which include game-used items, were damaged or destroyed during a residential fire in the early 1980s.

" *They're [hitting slumps] like sleeping in a soft bed. Easy to get into and hard to get out of.*"
– Johnny Bench

▲ *Johnny Bench's 1975 H&B World Series bat.*

Albert Pujols

Icon Sportswire

batting average of .328, but Pujols became the leader of the clubhouse, a revered figure of class and dignity.

After finishing fourth in MVP voting in his rookie season, Pujols would win the award in 2005, 2008, and 2009. Amazingly, he finished in the top five in MVP voting in seven other seasons between 2001 and 2011. He made the All-Star team nine times and won two Gold Gloves at first base. Moreover, he led the Cards to two world titles and was named MVP of the 2004 NLCS. In his 11 years in St. Louis, the Redbirds qualified for the postseason seven times. Pujols thrilled his many fans with huge hits in big moments, but perhaps his most crucial came in Game One of the 2006 World Series at Detroit. In the third inning against Rookie of the Year and 17-game winner Justin Verlander, Pujols jacked a two-run homer to right field. The clout gave the Cards a lead they would not relinquish, drawing first blood in the Series and eventually winning it in five games. Pujols batted just .200 in the Series, but that home run set the tone. It also catapulted the Cardinals, perennial bridesmaids, to their first world championship since 1982.

Following the 2011 season, Pujols signed a free agent contract with the Los Angeles Angels of Anaheim. Despite changing leagues and heading into his late 30s, Pujols has remained incredibly productive. He smashed

Baseball is a tough game, one that takes even the most talented players years to master. There are talented players, and then there is Albert Pujols. The Dominican Republic native was drafted by the St. Louis Cardinals in the 13th round of the 1999 draft. A scant two years later, he exploded into the MLB scene with a dazzling Rookie of the Year performance. In 2001, Pujols delivered 194 hits, 47 doubles, 37 homers, 130 RBI, and a .329 batting average that season and captured the hearts of the rabid Cardinal faithful. He had starred at Fort Osage High School and Maple Woods Community College, both in Missouri. Over his 11 seasons with the Cards, Pujols would show the "Show Me" state what he was all about. Not only did he hit 445 home runs with more than 1,300 RBI and a

★ ★ ★ ★ ★ ★ ★ ★ ★ ★ ★ ★

> " *I've never seen anything like it. He's [Pujols] quick to the ball with his bat, he hits to all fields, he rarely goes out of the strike zone, and no situation seems to rattle him.*"
> – Lloyd McClendon, Pirates manager

The Ultimate Season:				Career To Date:			
Year/Team: 2003 STL				Years: 16			
G:	157	HR:	43	G:	2426	HR:	591
AB:	591	RBI:	124	AB:	9138	RBI:	1817
R:	137	SB:	5	R:	1670	SB:	107
H:	212	BB:	79	H:	2825	BB:	1214
2B:	51	OPS:	1.106	2B:	602	OPS:	.965
3B:	1	BA:	.359	3B:	16	BA:	.309

40 home runs with 95 RBI in 2015, making his first All-Star team since 2010. Pujols eclipsed the 500 home run plateau in 2014 and is a sure-fire Hall of Famer. Moreover, his unassuming and quiet demeanor sits in stark contrast to the "look at me" attitude of many modern-day professional athletes. Jose Alberto Pujols is an intelligent, articulate man, but since 2001, he has let his bat do the talking, and it has spoken loud and clear.

Tales from Joe's Bat Rack

Albert Pujols is one of the few players from the 2000–present era to garner the kind of respect usually reserved for the past offensive greats of the game, which keeps his bats on the minds of most advanced collectors. Pujols has used a variety of professional model bat brands throughout his career. They include, but are not limited to, Louisville Slugger, Adirondack, Carolina Clubs, Old Hickory, SAM, and his current bat of choice: Marucci.

Pujols has not only ordered a wide variety of bat brands, but he has also ordered a broad selection of bat designs. He has used natural-colored, solid-black, and two-toned bats, including two-toned bats where the handle is manufactured with a darker color and the barrel is natural-colored—a design which is the exact opposite of most traditional two-toned gamers. Pujols also prefers maple wood bats, although he used a fair amount of ash bats earlier in his career.

One thing you may notice about Pujols gamers is that you rarely find them with heavy use. This is by design as Pujols, generally speaking, does not like to use any one gamer for an extended period of time. Many of his gamers have a light coating of pine tar on the upper handle and his use of tar has seemingly increased since about 2011. Moreover, finding his uniform number "5" on the knob or barrel end, in either black marker or in pre-stamped fashion, is fairly common. You may encounter gamers from early in his career with the word "Game" noted on the knob. A number of the Pujols bats in circulation feature his name in block letters on the barrel, but some of them possess his facsimile signature instead. Finally, you will find autographed gamers in the marketplace with a specially-designed Pujols hologram as the slugger has provided memorabilia through KLF Sports Investments.

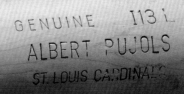

▲ *Albert Pujols' 2004 Louisville Slugger bat from the 2004 postseason.*

The Battery

★ ★ ★ ★ ★ ★ ★ ★ ★ ★ ★ ★ ★ ★ ★ ★ ★ ★

The pitchers, the catchers and the bats that they used are featured in this chapter. Well, actually there are only two pitchers and you may be asking yourself "why"? The long and the short of it is that one was an excellent hitting pitcher and the other ordered so few bats that they became extremely desirable. The catchers on the other hand were all lethal with their bats. Read along and find out why. Enjoy!

▶ *Jorge Posada applies pine tar to his gamer.*

Icon Sportswire

Gary Carter

★ ★ ★ ★ ★ ★ ★ ★ ★ ★ ★ ★

Heinz Kluetmeier/Sports Illustrated Collection/Getty Images

Montreal Expos, his most memorable moment was as a New York Met. A clutch hitter, he became part of baseball folklore when the Mets faced the Boston Red Sox on October 25, 1986, in Game Six of the World Series.

The Mets trailed the Sox three games to two going into an unbelievable World Series game. After tying the game in the bottom of the eighth on a blown save by Boston reliever Calvin Schiraldi, the Mets forced the game into extra innings. In a seesaw battle for the ages, New York gave up two runs in the top of the 10th and fell behind 5–3. In the bottom of the frame, Schiraldi got two quick outs on Wally Backman and Keith Hernandez fly-outs. Boston fans were already celebrating the end of the 68-year "Curse of the Bambino," but then it all unraveled for the Sox.

With two outs and the season on the line, Carter stepped up to the plate, determined not to make the last out of the season. With the count 2–1, he lined a single into left field. Little did Gary Edmund Carter realize that this would be the biggest hit of his career. Pinch hitter Kevin Mitchell came up next and stroked a single, advancing Carter to second. Then Ray Knight stepped up to the plate. With an 0–2 count and the Sox on the verge of clinching, Knight singled, scoring Carter and bringing the Mets within one run. Mitchell was on third and reliever Bob Stanley was pitching for the Sox when Mookie Wilson came up to bat. Wilson worked a 10 pitch at-bat and with the count 2–2, Stanley threw an inside pitch, the ball got away from catcher Rich Gedman, and Mitchell scored to tie the game. On the 10th pitch, Wilson hit a routine grounder to Red Sox first baseman, Bill Buckner. Unbelievably, the ball trickled through Buckner's legs, scoring Knight. The Mets were still alive, forcing a Game

An excellent defensive catcher and solid hitter over his 19-year career with the Expos, Mets, Dodgers, and Giants, Gary Carter was an 11-time All-Star and was voted the All-Star MVP in 1981 and 1984. Although Carter's glory days were with the

Seven, and it all started with the Gary Carter single. New York went on to win Game Seven to take the championship.

Known as the "Kid" for his youthful enthusiasm, Carter won five Silver Sluggers, three Gold Gloves, and finished at age 38, in 1992, with a career .262 batting average. He was inducted into the Hall of Fame in 2003. Diagnosed with a brain tumor in 2011, Carter left us way too early at the age of 57, but not before he left his mark as one of baseball's great catchers.

The Ultimate Season:			Career:		
Year/Team: 1984 MON			Years: 19		
G:	159	HR:	27	G:	2296	HR:	324
AB:	596	RBI:	106	AB:	7971	RBI:	1225
R:	75	SB:	2	R:	1025	SB:	39
H:	175	BB:	64	H:	2092	BB:	848
2B:	32	OPS:	.853	2B:	371	OPS:	.773
3B:	1	BA:	.294	3B:	31	BA:	.262

Tales from Joe's Bat Rack

Gary Carter professional model bats are amongst the most affordable bats on the entire Hall of Fame list. While he used more than one bat brand during his career, including Rawlings/Adirondack (block letter) gamers, Carter seemed to prefer H&B/ Louisville Slugger bats for the majority of it after signing an endorsement contract with them in 1973. The only exception would be for a short stretch in the late 1980s, when Carter

dramatically reduced the number of bats ordered from the factory.

Most Carter gamers are found with his primary uniform number "8" on the knob, and sometimes the barrel end, in black marker. Keep in mind that Carter did wear the number "57" for a very brief period of time during his debut season in 1974. Carter played in a mere nine games that year, so finding a true gamer with a vintage "57" would be virtually impossible.

Early Carter examples will occasionally exhibit a crisscross taping pattern along the handle area, which is somewhat similar to the taping pattern seen on Duke Snider bats. Carter was also known for applying modest amounts of pine tar to the handles of his bats during his career. In some cases, the pine tar is clustered near the lower handle area of his bats. Playing in three different decades, Carter gamers from the 1970s are much tougher to find than ones used during his post-1980 playing days. Nevertheless, some collectors prefer bats from his time with the New York Mets (1985–1989) since he was a part of the fabled 1986 World Series champion team.

> " *I'll always be grateful for the dream season of 1986. In a corner of my mind I will stand forever with my bat cocked, waiting for the two-one pitch from Calvin Schiraldi."*
> *– Gary Carter*

▲ *Gary Carter's 1975 H&B rookie year bat.*

Mickey Cochrane

★ ★ ★ ★ ★ ★ ★ ★ ★ ★ ★ ★ ★ ★

George Rinhart/Corbis Historical Collection/Getty Images

by a Bump Hadley speedball. The 34-year-old Cochrane, AL MVP in 1928 and 1934, fractured his skull and, with it, the remainder of his Hall of Fame career. Before joining Detroit in 1934, Cochrane was the glue that held Connie Mack's Philadelphia A's together. He backboned the club to World Series titles in 1929 and 1930, batting .400 in the 1929 Fall Classic. With the Athletics, Cochrane batted .321 in nine seasons with an OBP of .412 and OPS of .902. He was a sturdy leader behind the dish, a man among men, taking charge on the field—a veritable extension of the great Mack himself. In 1930, he batted .357, a career high.

Beyond the stats, Cochrane was an unselfish player who stressed team success more than personal stardom. In his career, he won five pennants and three World Series. After a typical Connie Mack fire sale, Cochrane found himself in Detroit in 1934 as player-manager. He immediately won two pennants and the 1935 World Series made him a Motown icon. The Massachusetts native and Boston University product would eventually become the first catcher in history elected to the Hall of Fame by the Baseball Writers Association of America. Interestingly enough, baseball was not "Black Mike's" best sport. As a youth, he excelled more prominently in both football and basketball. He put this athleticism to good use on the diamond, however, as a gritty and fearless catcher—a true gem in the game's most physically grueling position.

Ox May 25, 1937, one of the great catching careers in baseball history came to a violent denouement. On that day, legendary Detroit Tiger backstop Mickey Cochrane was struck in the head

Still, Cochrane's physical toughness masked the demons that lived within him. One year before being beaned by Hadley, he suffered an emotional breakdown in his triple role as a

★ ★ ★ ★ ★ ★ ★ ★ ★ ★ ★ ★

player, manager, and general manager in Detroit. Beset by physical and mental woes, Cochrane's big league managerial career ended for good in 1938. In his five years at the helm in Detroit, Cochrane put together an exceptional 348–250 won-loss record. When the best catchers in history are mentioned, names such as Berra, Campanella, Bench, Carter, and Fisk are bandied about but true baseball experts begin and end such a conversation with Mickey Cochrane. He batted over .300 in nine of his 13 seasons, drew 857 career walks, consistently got on base, and sacrificed his body and soul for his teammates. He was a doubles and triples machine and darn near gave his life for the grand old game. Gordon Stanley Cochrane died of lymphatic cancer in 1962 at the young age of 59. He remains the ultimate example of what it means to be a catcher.

The Ultimate Season:			Career:		
Year/Team: 1930 PHA			Years: 13		
G:	130	HR: 10	G:	1482	HR: 119
AB:	487	RBI: 85	AB:	5169	RBI: 830
R:	110	SB: 5	R:	1041	SB: 64
H:	174	BB: 55	H:	1652	BB: 857
2B:	42	OPS: .954	2B:	333	OPS: .834
3B:	5	BA: .357	3B:	64	BA: .320

When it comes to specific player characteristics, Cochrane was not known for things such as unique handle preparation or knob markings. Cochrane, however, was known for using both ash and hickory bats during his career. This can be confirmed in his ordering records and in various period images. In addition, it appears that Cochrane often hit with the label facing down, which causes most of the ball contact marks to appear on the left barrel. While both teams Cochrane played for are popular franchises, the aforementioned Athletics and the Detroit Tigers, the bats that date to his time with A's are considered more desirable. Cochrane was a part of a core that featured the likes of fellow greats Jimmie Foxx, Al Simmons, and Lefty Grove.

Tales from Joe's Bat Rack

Mickey Cochrane professional model bats are some of the toughest bats to find in the entire hobby. In fact, there are only a handful of Cochrane bats known at the time of this writing. Of the few of Cochrane bats that do exist, two are documented (either side-written or vault-marked) from the factory. So, while this two-time American League MVP could certainly swing the bat, the rarity of his gamers is what takes his bats to another level with collectors. Cochrane signed an endorsement contract with H&B in the spring of 1925 during his rookie season with the Philadelphia Athletics, so almost all of his gamers feature his facsimile signature on the barrel.

" *He can hit. He has a great arm. He is fast. Best of all he likes the game and his spirit is an inspiration to the rest of the boys."*
– Connie Mack, 1925

▲ *Mickey Cochrane's early-1930s H&B bat - factory side-written to 1933.*

Bill Dickey

★ ★ ★ ★ ★ ★ ★ ★ ★ ★ ★ ★

"He [Dickey] was a great catcher, great hitter and a great man to have on the ball club." – Joe McCarthy

A career-long New York Yankee, Bill Dickey became a standard-bearer for Major League Baseball catchers. His career spanned from 1928 to 1946, and he was a key cog in the Yankees dynasty that dominated the game and headlines. Dickey was born in Louisiana and raised in Arkansas, but this country boy had big city talent, swatting 202 career dingers with 1,209 RBI and a .313 batting average. Dickey was an All-Star every year he played from 1936 to 1946, and was voted to 11 Midsummer Classics overall. He batted over .300 11 times, highlighted by a .362 clip in 1936, adding 22 homers and 107 RBI that season. In 1937, his average "dropped" to .332, but he had career highs in homers with 29 and RBI with 133.

You would seldom find Dickey's name among the league leaders in any particular category, unless of course, they had a category for consistency. In his prime, you could pretty much pencil him in for 15 to 20 homers, 100 RBI, a .300-plus average, and 20 to 30 doubles. Dickey's toughness was unquestionable. He played catcher in each of his 17 big league seasons—never moving to first base or the outfield to save his knees. He was a backstop, pure and simple, one of the true rocks on which Yankees glory was built, and what glory it was! Dickey's Yankees played in eight World Series and won seven of them. His greatest postseason, and perhaps career, offensive moments came in the 1932 and 1938 Series. In 1932, while Babe Ruth was calling his fabled home run shot, all Dickey did was hit .438 with 7 hits in 16 at-bats in a four-game sweep of the Cubs. Six years later, New York again swept Chicago, and Dickey batted .400 with 6 hits and a home run.

★ ★ ★ ★ ★ ★ ★ ★ ★ ★ ★

The left-handed batting Dickey was a sturdy 6-foot, 1-inch, and 185 pounds. He was a menacing figure at the plate and had a catapult of an arm behind the plate. Over the years, Dickey became a source of guidance and leadership for the Yankees pitching staff. He truly bridged two eras of Bronx greatness, playing alongside Ruth and Gehrig, and tutoring the likes of Yogi Berra, who would succeed him and wear his number "8," behind the dish for New York. Dickey managed the Yanks for a brief stint in 1946, served as coach and scout for the team, and eventually joined Casey Stengel's coaching staff with the Mets. He became a Hall of Famer in 1954. Dickey's uniform number "8" was retired in 1972, and in 1988 he was immortalized in Yankee Stadium's Monument Park. William Malcolm Dickey died five years later at the age of 86, leaving a legacy of catching, clutch hitting, and character.

The Ultimate Season: Year/Team: 1936 NYY				Career: Years: 17			
G:	112	HR:	22	G:	1789	HR:	202
AB:	423	RBI:	107	AB:	6300	RBI:	1209
R:	99	SB:	0	R:	930	SB:	36
H:	153	BB:	46	H:	1969	BB:	678
2B:	26	OPS:	1.045	2B:	343	OPS:	.868
3B:	8	BA:	.362	3B:	72	BA:	.313

Tales from Joe's Bat Rack

Much like professional model bats of fellow standout catcher Mickey Cochrane, Bill Dickey gamers are amongst the toughest bats in the entire hobby. They are also considered very desirable since Dickey, a fantastic offensive player, was a key figure on the great New York Yankees teams of the late-1920s through the early-1940s. Interestingly, Dickey's bats are far tougher to find than those used by several of his legendary teammates, such as Joe DiMaggio, Lou Gehrig, and Babe Ruth.

Dickey had signature-model H&B bats produced throughout his career, signing an endorsement contract with the company in the spring of 1928. Like some players of the period, Dickey served in the military in the mid-1940s but came back for a brief time in 1946. That playing career gap and the fact that Dickey coached for the Yankees after 1946 is important to note for collectors. There are Dickey coaching-era bats that may be mistaken by some for playing career gamers in the marketplace.

During Dickey's playing days, the Hall of Fame catcher was one of the few players whose bats had a very distinct appearance based on the way they were prepped for game action. There are two key characteristics to look for on Dickey gamers. First, he applied a very unique taping method to the handle of his bats. Dickey would often place two small, but fairly thick, ringlets of tape near the base of the handle with slight gaps between the two ringlets. This taping method can be seen in many vintage photographs and is a key bat preparation characteristic for Dickey. On rare occasions, Dickey can be seen holding a bat with three ringlets, but two was clearly the norm. Secondly, Dickey often hit with the label facing downward, causing most ball contact marks to appear on the left barrel.

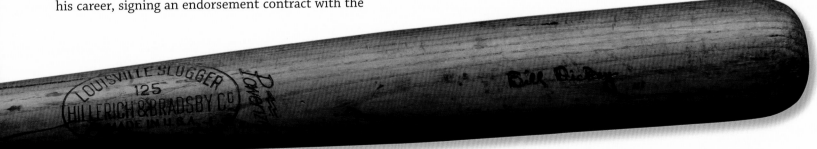

▲ *Bill Dickey's 1940 H&B bat.*

Don Drysdale

★ ★ ★ ★ ★ ★ ★ ★ ★ ★ ★ ★

Icon Sportswire

Drysdale was 17–9 with an ERA of 2.69. He staked his claim as a frightening mound presence the next season, leading the National League in hit batsmen with 14. A massive innings-eater, Drysdale racked up over 300 innings-pitched four straight seasons from 1962 to 1965. Those years marked a fantastic run of dominance. In that span, Drysdale won 85 games, struck out 930 batters and started 165 games, logging over 1,250 innings.

Drysdale came to the mound with bad intentions and great stuff—a lethal combination. He had no patience for batters who crowded the plate. If you were so much as in the on deck circle, he might whistle one past your ears. In 14 seasons, Drysdale won 209 games and struck out 2,486 batters in 3,432 innings. He

The first two seasons of his big-league career were spent in Brooklyn, but Don Drysdale was the quintessential Los Angeles Dodger. At 6-foot, 5-inches, and 190 pounds, with Hollywood good looks, the Van Nuys, California, native looked the part of a 1960s movie dreamboat. Drysdale would have been at home frolicking on a sandy Southern California beach, but his sandy beach was a pitcher's mound, and with a lightning fastball and menacing attitude, there was not much room for frolicking—especially for opposing batters. His first great season was in 1957, the Dodgers' swan song in Brooklyn.

hit 154 batters, many of them just to send a message. He owned home plate. Batters were merely temporary tenants. Drysdale was a stalwart on a pitching staff that included the sublime Sandy Koufax. This pair helped lead the Dodgers to World Series titles in 1959, 1963, and 1965. An eight-time All-Star, Drysdale won the Cy Young Award in 1962 with a 25–9 record and 232 Ks, both NL highs. As if his mound mastery were not enough, Drysdale could also hit. His best moments at the plate came in 1965 when he batted .300, the only Dodger in the regular lineup to do so that year. With

★ ★ ★ ★ ★ ★ ★ ★ ★ ★ ★ ★ ★ ★

> *"I hate all hitters. I start a game mad and I stay that way until it's over."*
> – Don Drysdale

The Ultimate Season:				Career:			
Year/Team: 1965 LAD				Years: 14			
G:	58	HR:	7	G:	547	HR:	29
AB:	130	RBI:	19	AB:	1169	RBI:	113
R:	18	SB:	0	R:	96	SB:	0
H:	39	BB:	5	H:	218	BB:	60
2B:	4	OPS:	.839	2B:	26	OPS:	.523
3B:	1	BA:	.300	3B:	7	BA:	.186

39 hits in 130 at-bats, he slugged 7 home runs and knocked in 19 runs with an OBP of .331 and slugging percentage of .508. He retired in 1969 to start a successful career in sports broadcasting and was inducted into the Hall of Fame in 1984. Tragically, he died of a heart attack on July 3, 1993, in Montreal at the age of 56. His nickname was "Big D" and it fit. Donald Scott Drysdale—at times dangerous, always distinguished, and totally dominant.

Tales from Joe's Bat Rack

On this entire list of elite lumber, we only included two slots for pitchers: Sandy Koufax, because he is *Sandy Koufax*, and his hulking teammate Don Drysdale. This one-two punch was a lethal combination for the Los Angeles Dodgers during the 1960s. The dynamic duo helped bring home three World Series titles in 1959, 1963 and 1965. Beyond his pitching exploits, Drysdale was no slouch with the bat. In fact, Drysdale hit 29 career home runs and twice hit seven in a season. He was so good with the bat that he was actually called on to pinch hit from time to time, and who could blame the Dodgers? Drysdale hit an even .300 in 1965! For those not old enough to have seen him play or hit, Madison Bumgarner is a great point of reference.

Drysdale's ability to swing the bat with authority is only part of the reason his professional model bats remain popular with collectors. In addition to his hitting prowess, the visual appeal and character of Drysdale's gamers is what separates them from most other professional model pitcher bats. Drysdale was a big man. At 6-foot, 5-inches and 190-plus pounds, "Big D" was as menacing-looking at the plate as he was on the mound. Add to that the fact that his gamers often look more like small trees or a giant's club than a baseball bat and you have your explanation. Most of the bats Drysdale ordered from H&B measure 35–37 inches in length, and a number of them were manufactured with large handles.

Drysdale received his first signature model from H&B in the spring of 1964, several years after making his MLB debut. Prior to that time, Drysdale's bats were made with his last name in block letters only. Collectors may encounter Adirondack examples as well, as Drysdale used both bat brands throughout his career. The Adirondack bats were only made with his name in block letters. Finally, a number of Drysdale's gamers can be found with his uniform number "53" marked on the knob in black marker.

▲ *Don Drysdale's 1965 H&B bat.*

Carlton Fisk

★ ★ ★ ★ ★ ★ ★ ★ ★ ★ ★ ★

Photo File/Getty Images Sport Classic Collection/Getty Images

and a Gold Glove. Over his 24-year career, Fisk hit 376 home runs, compiled a .269 batting average, and worked an incredible 2,226 games behind the dish. Beyond the stats, the well-documented rivalry between Fisk and Yankees catcher Thurman Munson made for very entertaining baseball with occasional brawling and frequent jawing between the two top American League catchers.

One of the iconic moments in baseball history took place on October 21, 1975, when Carlton Fisk hit a dramatic home run to beat the Cincinnati Reds in Game Six of the World Series. With the Sox down 3–2 going into the Game Six, the atmosphere at Fenway Park was tense. Boston was hoping for its first World Series championship in 57 years. Going into the bottom of the eighth, the Sox trailed Cinci 6–3. Bernie Carbo set the stage for the dramatics that came later in the game by blasting a three-run homer off Cinci relief pitcher Rawley Eastwick to tie the game at 6–6. In an incredible nailbiter, Boston had the bases loaded in the bottom of the ninth but could not score. Then in the 11th, Sox right fielder Dwight Evans made a spectacular circus catch off Joe Morgan to save the game.

An elite catcher, Carlton "Pudge" Fisk brought his tremendous work ethic and competitive zeal to both the Boston Red Sox and Chicago White Sox. Voted the 1972 Rookie of the Year, he appeared in 11 All-Star games, and won three Silver Sluggers

The Reds mounted another threat in the top of the 12th with two on, but failed to score. Nearly four hours into the game, with Pat Darcy on the mound, Fisk stepped up to the plate at 12:34 a.m. in the bottom of the 12th. On Darcy's second pitch, Fisk launched a shot down the left field line but the ball appeared to be foul. As Fisk headed down the first base line, he jumped and waved for the ball to

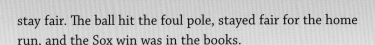

★ ★ ★ ★ ★ ★ ★ ★ ★ ★ ★

stay fair. The ball hit the foul pole, stayed fair for the home run, and the Sox win was in the books.

The Emmy winning film clip of Fisk coaxing the ball to stay fair was the first player reaction shot in televised baseball coverage. Interestingly, that footage was recorded by accident. The NBC cameraman positioned inside the left field wall got distracted when a large rat scurried by. He decided to keep the camera on Fisk because he lost the flight of the ball. By the way, the Red Sox lost Game Seven of the World Series 4–3, and the Boston drought continued until 2004, but Carlton Ernest Fisk was elected to the Hall of Fame in 2000.

Tales from Joe's Bat Rack

Like fellow Hall of Fame catcher Gary Carter, Carlton Fisk's career spanned three decades (1970s–1990s). As a result, Fisk bats are not scarce overall, but gamers that date to the 1970s are surprisingly tough to find. Fisk used three primary bat brands: H&B/Louisville Slugger, Adirondack, and Worth bats (which became somewhat popular by the mid-to-late 1980s). It is important to note that Fisk did not have an endorsement contract with H&B, which means the bats feature his name in block letters only. Fisk's Adirondack bats include his nickname "Pudge Fisk" in script.

There are a few distinct characteristics to be aware of when it comes to bats used by this Hall of Fame catcher. Fisk bats are often found with a circle around the knob and his uniform number located within the circle. This practice appears to be most prevalent during the first half of his career and subsides in the 1980s as a member of the Chicago White Sox. Nevertheless, you can still find plenty of Fisk photos

The Ultimate Season:					Career:				
Year/Team: 1977 BOS					Years: 24				
G:	152	HR:	26		G:	2499	HR:	376
AB:	536	RBI:	102		AB:	8756	RBI:	1330
R:	106	SB:	7		R:	1276	SB:	128
H:	169	BB:	75		H:	2356	BB:	849
2B:	26	OPS:	.922		2B:	421	OPS:	.797
3B:	3	BA:	.315		3B:	47	BA:	.269

documenting the presence of the circle. Gamers that date to his later years with the White Sox can be found with small dash marks around the "72" on the knob, although these additional marks are not always present.

Keep in mind that while his two primary uniform numbers were "27" (Boston) and "72" (Chicago), Fisk did wear number "40" during a very brief stint in 1969. Furthermore, you will occasionally see Fisk gamers with either a single ringlet of tape or a short, spiral taping pattern near the base of the handle. These taping patterns seem to be more common on bats from the post-1980 era, with the single ringlet application clearly the more common of the two taping methods. Finally, Fisk did use varying amounts of pine tar during his career. Most of his gamers show modest amounts of this substance, but you will find some Fisk bats with heavy applications from time to time.

> "He [Fisk] played the game the right way, both behind the plate and at the plate." – Carl Yastrzemski

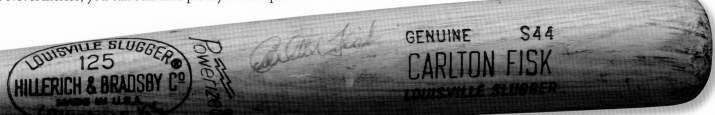

▲ Carlton Fisk's 1977–79 H&B bat.

Gabby Hartnett

★ ★ ★ ★ ★ ★ ★ ★ ★ ★ ★ ★

to Hall of Fame status was slow and steady. He did not bat .300 until his seventh season in the league (.302 in 1928). In 1930, he broke out with the greatest overall offensive output of his career. That season, the 6-foot, 1-inch, and 195 pound right-handed hitter smacked 37 homers, 122 RBI, batted .339 and slugged .630 with an OPS of 1.034. He batted .300 or better six times, hit over 20 homers three times, and his career numbers, .297 batting average, 236 home runs and 1,179 RBI, are impressive.

Four times, he helped the Cubbies make it to the World Series, and all four times, they lost (1929, 1932, 1935, 1938). In 1932 against the Yankees, he was terrific, batting .313 as the Baby Bears were bested by the Bronx Bombers in four games. By the way, Hartnett was behind the dish when Babe Ruth famously called his shot in Game Three of that Series. Hartnett's renowned at-bat, dubbed the "Homer in the Gloamin," helped the Cubs capture the 1938 pennant. On September 28, 1938, at 5:30 in the evening, before a packed house in Wrigley Field, with the Cubs and Pirates tied 5–5 going into the ninth inning, it was becoming hard to see the ball in the unlit stadium. With two out in the bottom of the ninth, player-manager Hartnett stepped up to the plate. Behind in the count 0-and-2, Hartnett connected with Pirates reliever Mace Brown's curveball, launching it high into the left-field bleachers. With that memorable walk-off home run, Hartnett put the Cubs a half-game ahead in the pennant race, but in the 1938 Fall Classic the Cubs again fell to the Yanks.

Still regarded as one of the greatest defensive catchers of all-time, the durable Hartnett battled injuries to catch 100 or more games 12 times in his career and he was adept at handling the Chicago pitching staff. A member of the

F**or 19 seasons, Gabby Hartnett** was a terrific catcher, doubles king, and RBI machine for the Chicago Cubs. He broke into the Bigs in 1922 and soon became a Windy City mainstay. Hartnett's climb

★ ★ ★ ★ ★ ★ ★ ★ ★ ★ ★ ★ ★

first six NL All-Star teams, and the 1935 NL MVP, his 24 homers in 1925 were a then-record for catchers. In 1937 he batted .354, a National League record for catchers for 60 years until it was bested by Mike Piazza. Hartnett saw his durability and numbers fall dramatically in both 1939 and 1940 while player-manager of the Cubs. He spent his final big league season with the Giants in 1941 as player-coach. In retirement, Hartnett managed in the minors, opened a successful recreation center outside Chicago, and served as a scout for the Kansas City A's. Elected to the Hall of Fame in 1955, Charles Leo Hartnett passed away at age 72 in Park Ridge, Illinois. He was, indeed, the embodiment of Chicago—tough, indefatigable, and reliable.

The Ultimate Season:
Year/Team: 1930 CHC

G:	141	HR:	37
AB:	508	RBI:	122
R:	84	SB:	0
H:	172	BB:	55
2B:	31	OPS:	1.034
3B:	3	BA:	.339

Career:
Years: 20

G:	1990	HR:	236
AB:	6432	RBI:	1179
R:	867	SB:	28
H:	1912	BB:	703
2B:	396	OPS:	.858
3B:	64	BA:	.297

majority feature Harnett's facsimile signature on the barrel. Like most players of the era, Harnett gradually reduced the weight of the bats he ordered from the 36–38-ounce range early on to the 32–34-ounce range during his last several seasons. Due to their scarcity and the popularity of the Chicago Cubs Hall of Famer, a player who led the team to four World Series appearances in the 1920s and 1930s, Harnett bats can sell for a premium.

Tales from Joe's Bat Rack

Like those used by other catching greats from the period, including Mickey Cochrane, Bill Dickey and Ernie Lombardi, Gabby Hartnett professional model bats are very scarce. In fact, there are only a handful of examples known to exist at this time. While most Hartnett bats do not possess any unique characteristics, you will occasionally see the 1935 National League MVP holding a bat with a spiral application of tape in vintage photographs. To this day, no bats have been found exhibiting this type of handle preparation, but you can see evidence of the pattern in some period images.

Hartnett did sign an endorsement contract with H&B, but the exact date is unknown. Of the few known gamers, the

" *I rated Gabby [Hartnett] the perfect catcher. He was super smart and nobody could throw with him. And he also was an outstanding clutch hitter." – Joe McCarthy*

▲ *Gabby Hartnett's 1938–40 H&B bat.*

Sandy Koufax

★ ★ ★ ★ ★ ★ ★ ★ ★ ★ ★ ★ ★

runs, 9 doubles, 2 home runs, 28 RBI, and 43 free passes in 776 career at-bats. So, why is he included in our *Top 100* list? Simply put, there are very few game-used Koufax bats in existence. Although his batting never improved, Koufax worked through six years of wildness and frustration on the mound to develop pinpoint control and set records for pitching excellence in the second half of his career.

The 19-year-old Brooklyn native joined his hometown Dodgers in 1955 but saw little action until 1958. He sat out the 1955 and 1956 World Series, and pitched only nine innings in the 1959 Series. Koufax finally broke out in 1961 after catcher Norm Sherry suggested he relax, ease up on his fastball and just try to get it over the plate. Koufax posted 18 wins, led the league with 269 strikeouts and never looked back. Over the next five years he won five National League pitching titles, three NL Triple Crowns and three Cy Young Awards. In that period, Koufax won 111 games and lost just 34. He led the league with 27 complete games in both 1965 and 1966, and with 11 shutouts in 1963. A strikeout king, he paced the league in Ks four times, with a career-high 382 Ks in 1965.

The six-time All-Star led the Los Angeles Dodgers to World Series wins in 1963 and 1965 and was Series MVP both years. He was named 1963 NL MVP and Major League Player of the Year in 1963 and 1965. In his relatively short career, Koufax pitched four no-hitters, a NL record. One of those no-no's was a perfect game. The list of his achievements goes on and on. In his last seasons, Koufax played through pain due to traumatic arthritis of his left elbow. After doctors told him continued

A **dominant mound presence,** Sanford "Sandy" Koufax was not exactly dominant at the plate. The famous lefty pitcher was a weak right-handed batter and, over his 12 Major League seasons, batted a miserable .097 with a grand total of 75 hits, 26

★ ★ ★ ★ ★ ★ ★ ★ ★ ★ ★ ★ ★

pitching might result in losing the use of his arm, the 30-year-old Koufax retired with a career 165-87 won-loss record, 2.76 ERA, and 2,396 strikeouts. In 1972, he became the youngest member to be elected to the Hall of Fame.

The Ultimate Season:				Career:			
Year/Team: 1965 LAD				Years: 12			
G:	43	HR:	0	G:	397	HR:	2
AB:	113	RBI:	7	AB:	776	RBI:	28
R:	4	SB:	0	R:	26	SB:	0
H:	20	BB:	10	H:	75	BB:	43
2B:	2	OPS:	.437	2B:	9	OPS:	.261
3B:	0	BA:	.177	3B:	0	BA:	.097

Tales from Joe's Bat Rack

Let's make this clear right out of the gate—Sandy Koufax was not a great hitter, even for a pitcher. That is not why this legendary lefty is on the list. First of all, let's remember, he's *Sandy Koufax*. The pitching icon is so popular that he would be included on an infinite number of top lists simply as a result of name recognition alone. He is the "James Dean" of baseball in some respects. Then there's that other thing about the guy being, arguably, the most dominant pitcher in the history of baseball. Just a small detail, but that is not the only or even the primary reason that Koufax would appear on a list of legendary lumber.

In every collectibles genre, there are what hobbyists refer to as Holy Grails. These are the items that are so desirable, yet so tough, that most collectors can only dream of owning them. Sometimes it's all about the money, as most of us have budget limitations. In other cases, it's about the sheer rarity of the item. In many instances, it's a little of both. Let me give you something to digest. During his entire career, Koufax had a grand total of 19 professional model H&B bats sent to him. We are not talking about 19 Koufax bats known at this time; there were only 19 made! To put this in perspective, his teammate Don Drysdale ordered 64 bats during the 1965 season alone and he was a pitcher. It is not

uncommon for position players, even during the era, to order 100 or more per year.

Today, there are a mere handful of known survivors, and the ones that have been discovered often have a similar appearance. The bats, while authentic, have no discernable use and feature his last name "Koufax" in block letters on the barrel end. So, why did Koufax order so few bats? Some experts believe that Koufax was a player who was so focused on pitching that he would often just grab whatever bat was available and felt good at the time, despite having the ability to custom order whatever model he wanted from the manufacturer. No matter what the reason was, Koufax professional model bats have become one of the great rarities in the bat world.

" *Hitting against him is like eating soup with a fork.*" – *Willie Stargell*

▲ *Sandy Koufax's 1966 H&B All-Star Game bat.*

Thurman Munson

★ ★ ★ ★ ★ ★ ★ ★ ★ ★ ★ ★

" *Of all the Yankee hitters, Munson was the one that scared me the most... He had that swing and that heart, he was just totally clutch.*" – Charlie Lau

and a product of Kent State University, Munson brought his Midwestern grit to the ballpark every day. His nicknames included Squatty Body, The Walrus, and Tugboat. They were all appropriate, but the last one rings most true. For whenever the Yankees were lost at sea, it was Munson who led them back to shore. Munson was the ultimate catcher, cut in the cloth of Berra, his Yankees backstop predecessor. He stood 5-foot, 11-inches, and weighed 190 pounds, and his stocky build, unkempt hair, eternal five o'clock shadow, and bushy moustache were Munson's trademarks.

From 1969 to 1979, he was a manager on the field for the Yankees, doing his job and assuring that his teammates did the same. It was not an easy task. The mid-1970s Yankees were a combustible bunch with characters such as Reggie Jackson, Sparky Lyle, Mickey Rivers, and Graig Nettles. The team hated each other perhaps more than they despised their opponents. Munson, himself, had a frosty relationship with Jackson from the moment the boisterous outfielder arrived as a free agent in 1977. If the roster seemed volatile, check out the manager's office. In Munson's 10-plus seasons in New York, he played for five different managers. Despite this, New York would win the

There have been many great leaders to don Yankees pinstripes. Names like Lou Gehrig, Yogi Berra, and Derek Jeter come to mind, but very few can match the sheer intensity, respect, and toughness of Thurman Lee Munson. Born in Akron, Ohio,

★ ★ ★ ★ ★ ★ ★ ★ ★ ★ ★

world championship in both 1977 and 1978, the latter after a torrid August and September comeback to vanquish the Red Sox in a memorable one-game playoff at Fenway Park. That 1978 postseason was Munson's high point. In the one-game playoff, he smacked a seventh-inning double that gave New York a crucial two-run lead. In the ALCS vs. Kansas City, Munson clubbed a key home run in the eighth inning of Game Three, and in the World Series against Los Angeles, he batted .320 with 8 hits and 7 RBI.

Munson was Rookie of the Year in 1970, a seven-time All-Star, three-time Gold Glove winner, and the 1976 American League MVP. Never a league leader offensively, Munson was consistent. In 1975, 1976, and 1977, he hit over .300 with 100-plus RBI. A tireless competitor, he had a vicious rivalry with Red Sox catcher Carlton Fisk and regularly fought through injuries to stay in the lineup. Alas, the story of Thurman Munson ended tragically on August 2, 1979, when, at age 32, he crashed his Cessna twin-engine jet just short of the runway at Akron-Canton Regional Airport. The entire baseball world was paralyzed with sadness. His number "15" was retired by the Yankees and a replica of his locker stands at the Baseball Hall of Fame in Cooperstown. Thurman Munson embodied everything good about being a ballplayer. He was a family man, a fighter, and a friend.

The Ultimate Season:				Career:			
Year/Team: 1976 NYY				Years: 11			
G:	152	HR:	17	G:	1423	HR:	113
AB:	616	RBI:	105	AB:	5344	RBI:	701
R:	79	SB:	14	R:	696	SB:	48
H:	186	BB:	29	H:	1558	BB:	438
2B:	27	OPS:	.769	2B:	229	OPS:	.756
3B:	1	BA:	.302	3B:	32	BA:	.292

Tales from Joe's Bat Rack

Thurman Munson may not be a Hall of Famer, but judging by his popularity and the value of his professional model bats, you would think he was. The combination of his excellent play, hard-nosed approach, Yankees affiliation, and tragic story creates a special kind of appeal. On average, Munson bats often sell for as much or more than any other player bats from the 1970s. In some cases, it's not even close. During his career, Munson used both H&B (endorsement contract) and Adirondack (block letter) bats. You will find his uniform number "15," one he wore his entire career, noted in black or red marker on the knobs of most of his well-used gamers. In some cases, you will also see his number marked on the barrel end.

Munson did use pine tar, and heavy applications can be found on known examples. Sometimes, the layer is a fairly consistent one from the base of the handle towards the center brand. Other times, you will find Munson gamers with a concentrated coating of tar on the upper handle, with sporadic remnants on the lower part towards the knob. In addition, cleat impressions along the barrel are often found on well-used gamers. Bicentennial H&B gamers from 1976 have always been popular with collectors, but with Munson they take on special significance because that was considered his best season—the season in which Munson was named the American League MVP. While autographed gamers are extremely rare, a handful of them do exist and a significant premium is attached as a result of their rarity.

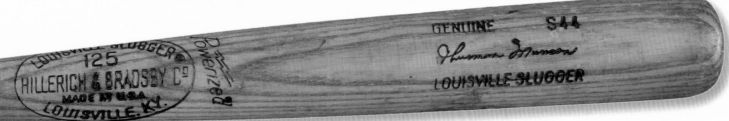

▲ *Thurman Munson's 1977–79 H&B bat.*

Mike Piazza

★ ★ ★ ★ ★ ★ ★ ★ ★ ★ ★ ★

Icon Sportswire

He was so crazy about baseball as a kid that his father had a batting cage built in his Pennsylvania back yard that he used year round. As a favor to a family friend, Ted Williams visited a teenaged Mike Piazza and was impressed by his batting ability. Interestingly, he was not a hot prospect, and was not picked until the 62nd round of the 1988 amateur draft. He was the last player chosen by the Dodgers, and that was only as a personal favor to Tommy Lasorda, a friend of Piazza's father. However, in 1993, his first full season with Los Angeles, Piazza catapulted into the spotlight batting .318 with 112 RBI and slamming 35 home runs to take Rookie of the Year honors. That year saw his first of 12 All-Star selections and his first of 10 Silver Slugger Awards.

The starting catcher for the Dodgers, Piazza was a force to be reckoned with at the plate, batting .331 with 177 home runs in his seven years with the team. After a brief stop with the Marlins in 1998, Piazza moved to the Mets where the 29-year-old superstar was so popular that attendance increased dramatically. The charismatic catcher helped drive the team to postseason play in 1999 and to the World Series in 2000. Piazza blasted another 220 home runs as a Met, hitting his most famous homer on September 21, 2001, in a game against the Braves. It was the first Mets home game after the 9/11 terrorist attack in New York City, and the team was determined to win for the fans. Behind 1–2 in the bottom of the eighth inning with one man on and one out, Piazza hit the go-ahead home run to center field for the 3–2 win. Another notable dinger was Piazza's number 352 on May 5, 2004, which broke Carleton Fisk's record for most home runs by a catcher. Over his 16-year career Piazza hit 396 home runs as catcher, the current record, and 427 total home runs.

Defensively, Piazza's arm was suspect, but he was very skilled at calling games and led the National League in games defended, putouts, and fielding percentage as catcher at various times in his career. After eight seasons as a Met, Piazza played briefly for the San Diego Padres and the Oakland Athletics before retiring at the end of the 2007 season at 38 years old. Interested in his Italian heritage,

★ ★ ★ ★ ★ ★ ★ ★ ★ ★ ★ ★

> "He's certainly the best hitting catcher of our era. And arguably the best hitting catcher of all time."
> – Tom Glavine

The Ultimate Season:				Career:			
Year/Team: 1997 LAD				Years: 16			
G:	152	HR:	40	G:	1912	HR:	427
AB:	556	RBI:	124	AB:	6911	RBI:	1335
R:	104	SB:	5	R:	1048	SB:	17
H:	201	BB:	69	H:	2127	BB:	759
2B:	32	OPS:	1.070	2B:	344	OPS:	.922
3B:	1	BA:	.362	3B:	8	BA:	.308

Piazza has been hitting coach for Team Italy in the European Championship and the World Baseball Classic, and was manager of the U.S. team in the 2011 Futures Game. In 2016, Michael Joseph Piazza, the kid who almost didn't make it to the majors, was elected to the Hall of Fame in his fourth year of eligibility.

Tales from Joe's Bat Rack

Any comprehensive bat collection would have to include a weapon from the greatest hitter to ever play at the catcher position. At his best, Piazza was a rare combination of precision and strength at the plate, with the kind of opposite field power rarely seen in the game. Through the years, Mike Piazza's professional model bat of choice was Mizuno, but he was known to use Rawlings/Adirondack bats on rare occasions towards the latter portion of his career. He also used Worth bats and Louisville Slugger bats at times during the first few years of his playing days. In fact, the Louisville Sluggers you will encounter are often of the cherry-colored variety. Piazza's

affinity for Mizuno bats resulted from an experiment with bats made for Jose Canseco. After homering twice against the Padres in San Diego in 1993 while using one of those Canseco models, Piazza decided to become, as he says, "a Mizuno man."

His primary uniform number "31" can often be found in black marker on both ends of his Mizuno gamers. He also wore "25" (early years with Los Angeles Dodgers) and "33" (San Diego Padres) during his career. Autographed gamers are extremely difficult to find because Piazza was not a very active signer while he was a player, although more autographed/game-used equipment has become available post retirement as a result of a deal with KLF Sports Investments. Many of his well-used bats have a light coating of concentrated pine tar on the upper handle area in addition to clusters of cleat marks on the back barrel. These are key Piazza game-use characteristics.

▲ Mike Piazza's 1999 Mizuno bat.

Jorge Posada

★ ★ ★ ★ ★ ★ ★ ★ ★ ★ ★

Icon Sportswire

seen postseason play since 1981 but during Posada's 17 seasons in pinstripes (1995–2011), the Yankees took seven pennants and won five World Series championships.

A native of Santurce, Puerto Rico, Jorge Rafael Posada was trained by his father to switch hit. His father had fled Castro's Cuba in 1968 and made Puerto Rico his home. Noticed by scouts while attending Calhoun Community College in Decatur, Alabama, he was drafted in 1990. A second baseman, Posada spent several years in the Yankees farm system learning the catcher position before making his debut in 1995. Although he did not have a strong throwing arm initially, Posada developed into one of the premier catchers of his time because of his focus, dedication, and leadership. The batterymate of David Wells and Roger Clemens, Posada was behind the dish on May 17, 1998, for Wells' perfect game vs. the Twins and caught Clemens' 15-strikeout, one-hit shutout of the Mariners in Game Four of the 2000 ALCS. He also caught Mike Mussina's near-perfect game vs. the Red Sox on September 2, 2001. As catcher, he led the American League in games defended three times, putouts three times, and assists twice. Over his career, he played the most postseason games as catcher (125) and started every Yankees postseason game in both 2000 and 2001.

A five-time All-Star with five Silver Slugger Awards, Posada could hit for power, blasting 20-plus home runs in eight seasons, slamming a career-high 30 homers in 2003. One of the best-hitting Yankees catchers ever, he was the first to notch a home run in the new Yankee Stadium in 2009 and on June 12–13 of 2010, Posada hit grand slams in consecutive games to tie the MLB record. However, in a 2015 interview, Posada's pick for his favorite at-bat was his two-run bloop double off Red Sox

The starting catcher for the dynastic Yankees of the late 1990s and early 2000s, Jorge Posada, along with "Core Four" members Derek Jeter, Mariano Rivera, and Andy Pettitte, became the heart and soul of the Bronx Bombers. The Yankees had not

pitcher Pedro Martinez in the eighth inning of Game Seven of the 2003 ALCS to tie the game.

After catching 1,574 games for the Yankees, Posada was switched to designated hitter in his final seasons. He retired in January 2012 with a career .273 batting average, 275 home runs, 1,065 RBI and 1,664 hits. He authored several books, including *The Journey Home: My Life in Pinstripes,* and launched the Jorge Posada Foundation to raise awareness of craniosynostosis, a condition his son was born with. Poseda's uniform number "20" was retired in 2015 and a plaque honoring him was placed in the Yankees' Monument Park.

The Ultimate Season:				Career:			
Year/Team: 2003 NYY				Years: 17			
G:	142	HR:	30	G:	1829	HR:	275
AB:	481	RBI:	101	AB:	6092	RBI:	1065
R:	83	SB:	2	R:	900	SB:	20
H:	135	BB:	93	H:	1664	BB:	936
2B:	24	OPS:	.922	2B:	379	OPS:	.848
3B:	0	BA:	.281	3B:	10	BA:	.273

Tales from Joe's Bat Rack

As a member of the vaunted "Core Four" that helped the New York Yankees to countless wins and numerous postseason appearances over a 20-year period, Jorge Posada is a name with a very loyal following in the hobby. When it comes to character and eye appeal, it is hard to compete with well-used Posada gamers. There is no question that Posada preferred Louisville Slugger professional model bats throughout

> " *Every time I go out on the field, I take a lot of pride in what I do at the plate, but I take a lot more pride in what I do behind the plate.*"
> – Jorge Posada

his career, even though he did try other brands on rare occasions, such as Rawlings/Adirondack and Marucci. Collectors may encounter Louisville Sluggers that feature Posada's name in block letters from his early years with the Yankees, but the overwhelming majority of the gamers made for the former All-Star possess his facsimile signature on the barrel.

Posada would often place a relatively short crisscross tape application along the handles of his bats along with a heavy coating of concentrated pine tar on the upper handle area, towards the center brand. As a result, his heavily-used bats have the appearance of a battle-scared war club. Some of his gamers feature a more traditional-looking tape application on the handle, but the crisscross method became his signature style.

Collectors might also notice some cleat marks on the barrel area. Keep in mind that the vast majority of Posada bats do not exhibit his primary uniform number "20" on the knob or barrel end. Earlier in his career, prior to 1997, Posada wore various numbers including "62," "41," "55," and "22" before settling on "20" in 1997. Like Derek Jeter gamers, Posada bats were available for years through Steiner Sports direct from the team.

▲ *Jorge Posada's 2010 Louisville Slugger bat.*

Buster Posey

★ ★ ★ ★ ★ ★ ★ ★ ★ ★

Icon Sportswire

fibula and tearing ligaments in his ankle in a serious collision at home plate resulting in season-ending surgery.

He came back strong in 2012 with 103 RBI and 24 home runs to win the National League Most Valuable Player Award, the first NL catcher to earn that honor in 40 years. That year, he batted .336 to become the first catcher to win the NL batting crown since Ernie Lombardi in 1942. Oh yeah, the Giants won another World Series title that year, too. In 2014, Posey batted .311 with 170 hits and the Giants once again were World

Like an artist working on an unfinished masterpiece, Buster Posey is painting a picture of what will likely be a great baseball odyssey. Thus far, the affable Posey has accomplished what most catchers only dream of. A bonus baby out of Florida State University, Gerald Dempsey "Buster" Posey signed with the San Francisco Giants in 2008 as a "can't miss," and did not disappoint. A good defensive catcher who can hit for power and average, Posey won the National League Rookie of the Year Award in 2010, batting .305 with 124 hits and 67 RBI. Moreover, Posey caught every inning of the World Series vs. the Texas Rangers, helping the Giants to their first championship title since 1954. During the early part of the 2011 season, Posey suffered a major setback, fracturing his

Series champs. According to Brian Sabean, Giants general manager, the organization "turned on a dime" when Posey joined the team. Over his relatively brief eight MLB seasons, Posey has been recognized with a plethora of awards. A four-time All-Star and three-time Silver Slugger Award winner so far, Posey won the 2012 Hank Aaron Award, the 2012 National League Comeback Player of the Year Award, and the 2015 Wilson Defensive Player of the Year Award.

Among Posey's memorable at-bats would be his four hits in Game Four of the 2010 National League Championship Series vs. Philly. Also, in the fifth inning of Game Five of the 2012 NLDS vs. Cincinnati, Posey hit a grand slam off Mat Latos; and in 2016 he hit two, three-run homers in a game

★ ★ ★ ★ ★ ★ ★ ★ ★ ★ ★ ★

> "*Buster's work ethic, leadership skills and extraordinary talent represent all that is great about our game and what it means to be a San Francisco Giant.*" – Larry Baer, president and CEO

The Ultimate Season:				Career To Date:			
Year/Team: 2012 SFG				Years: 8			
G:	148	HR:	24	G:	899	HR:	116
AB:	530	RBI:	103	AB:	3278	RBI:	527
R:	78	SB:	1	R:	443	SB:	14
H:	178	BB:	69	H:	1005	BB:	344
2B:	39	OPS:	.957	2B:	190	OPS:	.848
3B:	1	BA:	.336	3B:	8	BA:	.307

against the Rockies. Posey signed an eight-year extension on his contract in 2013 for a whopping $167 million, a record for a player with that level of experience in the majors. To go along with his offensive accomplishments, Posey caught three no-hitters so far in his career. He was behind the dish for Matt Cains in 2012, Tim Lincecum in 2013, and Chris Heston in 2015. It may be too soon to place Posey in the same category as Bench, Fisk, Campanella, or Berra but, barring any major obstacles, he is certainly on the right path.

Tales from Joe's Bat Rack

Buster Posey has established himself as one of the premier catchers in baseball. After playing a key role on the 2010 San Francisco Giants championship team, he suffered a horrific leg injury in 2011. Posey proved he was back and, perhaps, better than ever in 2012. At the time of this writing, Posey had already been named Rookie of the Year (2010) and National League MVP (2012), the same year he won the batting title. Along with

his offensive excellence, Posey has already played a key role on three World Series championship teams: in 2010, 2012, and 2014.

During his brief career, Posey has mostly used Louisville Slugger bats, but the All-Star catcher has started using more Marucci brand bats in recent times. Posey has used both ash and maple bats while in the major leagues. On Louisville Slugger bats, collectors can often tell them apart by the large *M* added near the center brand, which signifies that the bat was made out of maple versus ash.

You will sometimes find evidence of gripping substances like pine tar and Mota stick built up on the lower handle on well-used Posey gamers. Just recently, Posey has begun to apply Lizard Skins, which is a form of gripping tape, to the handles of some gamers. Posey has been known to occasionally inscribe his bats with "GU" (Game Used) along with the year, such as "10" (2010). These Posey gamers usually sell for a premium. You will not find many Posey bats with his number marked on the knob, outside of pre-stamped numbers on some bats. This is not a practice Posey has been known to employ.

▲ *Buster Posey's 2012 Louisville Slugger MVP Season bat.*

Joe Torre

★ ★ ★ ★ ★ ★ ★ ★ ★ ★ ★ ★

Icon Sportswire

his 29 years as manager of the Mets, Braves, Cardinals, Yankees, and Dodgers, Torre posted a 2,326–1,997 won-loss record, making him fifth on the all-time wins list. He was the American League Manager of the Year in 1996 and 1998 and managed six All-Star games.

As a player, Torre established himself as a very good catcher, first baseman, and third baseman playing for the Milwaukee/Atlanta Braves, St. Louis Cardinals, and New York Mets. During his first eight years with the Braves, Torre was a steady, dependable offensive force and also won his only Gold Glove in 1965. After a salary dispute, he was traded in 1969 to St. Louis, where he had his best offensive years. Switching to third base actually helped him offensively, and in 1971 he hit a lofty .363 for the batting crown, led the league with 230 hits and 137 RBI to go along with 24 bombs, and was named NL MVP. At the age of 34, Torre was traded to the New York Mets in 1975 where he played out the string for two seasons and finally retired as a player in 1977. Interestingly, his most memorable bat moment took place on July 21, 1975, when he hit into four double plays in one game. Felix Millan was hitting in front of him, and Torre kept his sense of humor in the after-game press conference saying, "I'd like to thank Felix Millan for making this possible."

When it comes to very good baseball players who became very good managers, Joe Torre is near the top of the list. Here was a player that had a lifetime batting average of .297, accumulated 2,342 hits, smacked 252 home runs, was a nine-time All-Star, National League Most Valuable Player and National League batting champ, yet is probably better known for his great managerial skills. Torre won four World Series championships with the Yankees (1996, 1998, 1999, and 2000). The Yanks were in the hunt for Torre's entire tenure as skipper, winning a total of six pennants from 1996 through 2007. Torre also won 13 division championships between the Atlanta Braves, Yankees, and Los Angeles Dodgers. In

★ ★ ★ ★ ★ ★ ★ ★ ★ ★

Joe Torre accomplished great things as a player, manager, and later as an MLB executive. When you look at players that eventually became managers, Joe Torre can be mentioned in the same breath as John McGraw, Tony La Russa, and the rest. In 2014, Joseph Paul Torre was elected to the Hall of Fame by the Expansion Era Committee with 100% of the vote.

The Ultimate Season:			Career:		
Year/Team: 1971 STL			Years: 18		
G:	161	HR: 24	G:	2209	HR: 252
AB:	634	RBI: 137	AB:	7874	RBI: 1185
R:	97	SB: 4	R:	996	SB: 23
H:	230	BB: 63	H:	2342	BB: 779
2B:	34	OPS: .976	2B:	344	OPS: .817
3B:	8	BA: .363	3B:	59	BA: .297

Tales from Joe's Bat Rack

Many baseball fans and collectors realize that Joe Torre is a Hall of Famer as a result of his excellent managerial record. What many people forget is what a terrific hitter Torre was when he was playing. In fact, some experts feel that Torre was the best catcher in the National League during the 1960s. Well, that is, before Johnny Bench came along. No man in the history of the game has been inducted into the Baseball Hall of Fame as a player *and* a manager in separate fashion, but the case for Torre is as strong as they come for those who have donned both kinds of caps. As a player, this nine-time All-Star was a fine all-around hitter, culminating with a National League MVP and batting title in 1971.

Torre was a big fan of the U1 model H&B and Adirondack professional model bats, which some people refer to as flared-knob bats. This was the preferred model of Roberto Clemente for a number of years. In addition, Torre was one of the rare players of the era that had signature models produced with both major manufacturers. Over time, Torre started to use pine tar more and more to enhance his grip

as evidenced by various period images. In fact, some of the well-used Torre bats that you see from his days with the St. Louis Cardinals and New York Mets are absolutely coated in the substance.

Torre's two primary uniform numbers, "15" (Milwaukee/Atlanta Braves) and "9" (St. Louis Cardinals and New York Mets), are often marked on the knob or barrel end. Bats that date to Torre's years with the Milwaukee Braves (1960–1965) tend to sell for a premium.

" *When you're in a slump, you do something different, just to try it... One time I borrowed one of Henry Aaron's bats and hit two homers... I just needed a change." – Joe Torre*

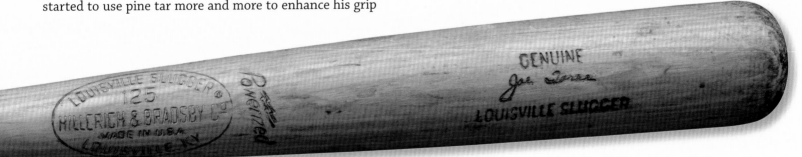

▲ *Joe Torre's 1965 H&B bat.*

The Infield

★ ★ ★ ★ ★ ★ ★ ★ ★ ★ ★ ★ ★ ★ ★ ★ ★ ★

This chapter discusses the bats owned by some of the greatest infielders that ever played in between the lines. Each one of these players was a magician with his stick. From the size, shape, and type of bat they used, each had particular likes and dislikes. Nap Lajoie's bat was certainly different from the bat used by Frank Thomas, yet they both did some incredible things offensively. From the Deadball Era to today's modern game, these are the infielders, and the bats they used.

▲ *This side-written Hank Greenberg bat was returned in 1937 after suffering a minor handle crack.*

Ernie Banks

★ ★ ★ ★ ★ ★ ★ ★ ★ ★ ★ ★

Louis Requena/Major League Baseball Collection/Getty Images

games. In 1954, he finished second in Rookie of the Year voting with 19 homers and 79 RBI. He played in all 154 games for the Cubbies that year, a feat that became commonplace for Banks. In 1955, Banks broke out in a big way with 44 home runs, 117 RBI, and 29 doubles. He hit more than 40 homers each season from 1957 to 1960, registering RBI totals of 102, 129, 143, and 117, respectively. In both 1958 and 1959, he won the NL MVP award.

A Gold Glove shortstop who eventually moved to first base, Banks played for only one team for his entire 19-year career. Since that team was the Cubs, this means Banks never saw the bright lights of the postseason. Still, he was an 11-time All-Star, including eight straight Midsummer Classic selections from 1955 to 1962. While he never had the opportunity to shine in World Series play, Banks' career was filled

The man known as "Mr. Cub" embodied everything that is good about a ballplayer. Ernie Banks played the game with an effervescent joy and a true passion. Famous for happily spouting, "Let's play two!" Banks was a throwback to a simpler time for baseball, when players and fans were closer and dollars did not dominate. The Chicago Cubs and their fans have had some huge disappointments over the decades, but they also had Ernie Banks, a fact that more than compensates for a few tough losses. Banks' jovial, welcoming demeanor often masked the tremendous competitor that he was. The Dallas, Texas, native joined the Cubs in 1953, batting .314 in ten

with great moments at the plate. In 1962, his first year playing at first base, Banks clubbed his 300th career home run on April 18, an extra innings walk-off blast. Just three years later, Banks registered home run number 400 against the Cardinals, a three-run tater scoring fellow Cub legends Billy Williams and Ron Santo. Banks ultimately joined the hallowed 500 Home Run Club on May 12, 1970, at the "Friendly Confines" of Wrigley Field, becoming the ninth player to reach that mark. Ernest Banks was inducted into the Hall of Fame in 1977. The fabled number "14" passed away in 2015. The man they called "Mr. Sunshine" brought light to his beloved Cubbies and his memory serves as a baseball beacon of joy and enthusiasm.

Tales from Joe's Bat Rack

The Ultimate Season:		Career:	
Year/Team: 1958 CHC		**Years: 19**	
G: 154	HR: 47	G: 2528	HR: 512
AB: 617	RBI: 129	AB: 9421	RBI: 1636
R: 119	SB: 4	R: 1305	SB: 50
H: 193	BB: 52	H: 2583	BB: 763
2B: 23	OPS: .980	2B: 407	OPS: .830
3B: 11	BA: .313	3B: 90	BA: .274

Ernie Banks is a player whose professional model bats rank high on the list of collector demand based on his popularity with fans and his inclusion in the 500 Home Run Club. Like the charismatic Cub himself, Banks' bats can have the kind of personality that endear them to collectors. In the spring of 1954, Banks signed an endorsement contract with H&B. Banks did make his debut in 1953, but he had less than 40 plate appearances that season, so virtually all of the bats made for Banks featured his facsimile signature on the barrel. Over the course of his career, Banks clearly preferred bats made by Hillerich & Bradsby versus rival Adirondack.

When it comes to Banks' gamers, there are a few keys that collectors should be made aware of. First, as with most players of his era, such as Roberto Clemente and Willie Mays, examples from the 1950s are much more difficult to locate than examples from later in his career. While you may encounter fewer bats from this period with Banks' uniform number "14" on the knob, they do exist. The uniform number is often noted in black marker and, like many other Cubs player bats from the 1950s–1970s, it is small in nature compared to most other knob uniform markings from the period.

Second, you will often find "Yosh" marks on his bats. These are small notations, usually found on the right side of the center brand, made by the Chicago's equipment manager Yosh Kawano during the 1960s/1970s era. In black marker, Kawano would often write the model number and length just to the right of "Powerized." This was a team practice that was not limited to Banks' gamers; his teammates—such as Ron

Santo—had their bats marked in this fashion as well. Not all of Banks' bats were marked in this way, but it is important to note.

Finally, most Banks' gamers do not exhibit an evident application of pine tar; however, you will find a small percentage of examples that do. Banks' bats that possess this characteristic often date to the latter stages of his career, when pine tar use became more common throughout the league.

> "*His wrists are the secret of Ernie [Banks] success...he swings his bat as if it were a buggy whip, striking at the ball with the reflexive swiftness of a serpent's tongue.*"
> – Bill Furlong, Baseball Stars of 1959

▲ *Ernie Banks' 1971 H&B bat used to hit his final career home run #512.*

Craig Biggio

Icon Sportswire

teammates Jeff Bagwell and Lance Berkman, Biggio led the Astros to the playoffs on six different occasions. As a matter of fact, Houston's Minute Maid Park was nicknamed "The House That Biggio and Bagwell Built."

A solid hitter with some pop in his bat, Biggio became the first Houston Astros player to reach the coveted 3,000-hit milestone on the evening of June 28, 2007. That memorable night, with a festive crowd of 42,537 on hand at Minute Maid Park, the Astros played the Colorado Rockies

At the time of this writing, nearly 19,000 players have come through the doors of Major League Baseball. Of those 19,000 players, only 30 have reached the 3,000-hit plateau. Craig Biggio is one of those 30 exceptional players. Granted, Biggio was no Ty Cobb, Stan Musial, or Honus Wagner, but he was a solid, hard-working, team player.

Considered by many to be the greatest all-around player in Houston Astros history, Craig Biggio was a great teammate, leader, and community servant. In addition to seven All-Star appearances and five Silver Sluggers, Biggio was recognized with the prestigious Roberto Clemente award in 2007 for his work helping kids with cancer through The Sunshine Kids Foundation. Loyal to Houston for his entire 20-year career, Biggio was the heart and soul of the Astros. As part of the offensive nucleus known as the "Killer Bs," along with

in a circus-like atmosphere. With balloons and banners, the Astro faithful were there for Craig Biggio. Entering the game batting only .238 with 2,997 hits, Biggio's chances of reaching the magic goal seemed slim, but he started off on the right foot with a single to center in the third. In his second at-bat, he hit another single, setting the stage for some good old fashioned baseball drama.

Aaron Cook was on the mound for the Rockies when Biggio stepped up to the plate in the seventh inning. He got ahead in the count 2–0 and ripped a single into center field. In typical Biggio fashion, he tried to stretch the single into a double and was thrown out at second, but the 3,000th hit was in the books. With the crowd in a frenzy, the game was stopped. Biggio asked his good friend, Jeff Bagwell, to join him on the field. After 15 years together in Houston, a shoulder injury had forced Bagwell into retirement in

★ ★ ★ ★ ★ ★ ★ ★ ★ ★ ★

> "*When I am in the zone, I feel prepared and I just go moment to moment—from one doing to another. It is simple. No thinking involved. I don't think ahead. All of a sudden, I just find myself on second base and the runners have been driven in.*" – Craig Biggio

The Ultimate Season:			
Year/Team: 1998 HOU			
G:	160	HR:	20
AB:	646	RBI:	88
R:	123	SB:	50
H:	210	BB:	64
2B:	51	OPS:	.906
3B:	2	BA:	.325

Career:			
Years: 20			
G:	2850	HR:	291
AB:	10876	RBI:	1175
R:	1844	SB:	414
H:	3060	BB:	1160
2B:	668	OPS:	.796
3B:	55	BA:	.281

2006. The two friends enjoyed the moment before the game resumed and the 41-year-old Biggio got two more hits, ending the night going 5-for-6. Less than a month later, he announced his retirement at the end of the season. In 2015, Craig Alan Biggio became the first Astro to be elected to the Hall of Fame. A solid player and a great guy, Biggio was loyal to his team, loyal to his friends, and worked to make a difference in his community.

Tales from Joe's Bat Rack

Once Craig Biggio became a member of the 3,000 Hit Club, his professional model bats were taken to a new level in the marketplace. As a result of his inclusion, bats used by the All-Star second baseman have become increasingly coveted by collectors. Aside from his accomplishments, well-used Biggio bats tend to have great character and eye appeal, thus adding to their popularity. Over the course of his career, there is no doubt that Biggio preferred using natural-colored Louisville Slugger bats. He was also one of the few players to use a bat with a flared knob, similar to the knob style of some Roberto Clemente bats, during the post-1980 era. Not all of his bats were manufactured that way, but many of them were— especially during the second half of his career.

Biggio would often prepare the handles of his bats with a very heavy, overlapping wrap of tape, which would extend to the upper-handle area and can reach up to nearly a foot in length. Biggio was also an avid user of Mota stick and pine tar. Some of his well-used gamers are coated in the gripping substance. It is important to note, however, that Biggio did not prepare his bats in the same manner during the early stages of his career, so most of the bats collectors will encounter have a relatively clean appearance in comparison. You will often find Biggio's primary uniform number "7" on the knob or barrel end of his gamers. Keep in mind that Biggio wore the number "4" at the start of his career, but it was only for a very brief period of time.

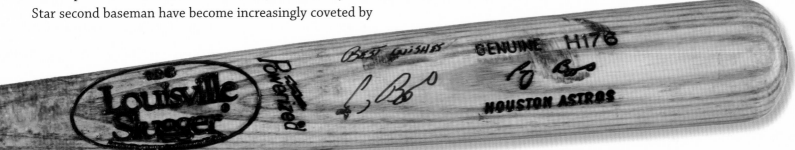

▲ *Craig Biggio's 1992–97 Louisville Slugger bat.*

Wade Boggs

★ ★ ★ ★ ★ ★ ★ ★ ★ ★ ★ ★

Rich Pilling/Getty Images Sport Collection/Getty Images

12-time All-Star and won eight Silver Slugger awards. Boggs finished his 18-year career with a .328 lifetime batting average. With the Boston Red Sox for the bulk of his career, Boggs holds the record for the highest career batting average at Fenway Park with .369, which is 8 points higher than Ted Williams.

After 11 years in Boston, the accomplished third baseman played for the Yankees from 1993 to 1997 and helped the Pinstripes win the championship in 1996. Who can forget the sight of Boggs on horseback, behind a mounted policeman, riding around Yankee Stadium to celebrate that World Series win? He finished out his career with the Tampa Bay Devil Rays from 1998 to 1999, where he attained his 3,000th hit and retired at 41 years old.

To say that Wade Anthony Boggs was a bit eccentric is an extreme understatement. It has been reported that Boggs once drank 107 beers in a day, a claim that he acknowledges to this day. One of his teammates swore that on a one-hour plane flight, Boggs consumed an entire case of beer, did not get drunk, and never got up to use the restroom. Likely the most superstitious player in baseball, Boggs ate chicken before every game, which earned him the nickname "Chicken Man." His reason for consuming the bird before every game? In the minor leagues, chicken was what he could afford, and Boggs found it to be a light, easy-to-digest pregame meal. As his batting average began to rise, he attributed it to his pregame chicken meals. Boggs continued this ritual for his entire career, and even came out with a chicken cookbook entitled *Fowl Tips*.

The prototypical contact hitter, Hall of Famer Wade Boggs could certainly put the bat on the ball. A member of the exclusive 3,000 Hit Club, the five-time American League Batting Champ was a

It gets even more interesting. In addition to the chicken, Boggs' pregame routine was legendary. It is said that before every game he would field exactly 150 ground balls, never more or less. He would begin batting practice at exactly 5:17

★ ★ ★ ★ ★ ★ ★ ★ ★ ★ ★ ★

and would run wind sprints at exactly 7:17. Before each at-bat he would trace the Chai symbol in the dirt. Chai is the Hebrew symbol for life but, oh yeah, Boggs is not Jewish. He also asked the Red Sox home public address announcer, Sherm Feller, to announce just his name and not his number, when he came up to bat. Why? Apparently, Boggs broke out of a slump one day when Feller forgot to announce his number and just announced his name.

Superstitions aside, as a pure hitter, Boggs was as good as anyone, batting at least .350 for four consecutive years. Whether it was with a baseball bat or a drumstick, you could count on Boggs to do everything with gusto.

The Ultimate Season:				Career:			
Year/Team: 1987 BOS				Years: 18			
G:	147	HR:	24	G:	2440	HR:	118
AB:	551	RBI:	89	AB:	9180	RBI:	1014
R:	108	SB:	1	R:	1513	SB:	24
H:	200	BB:	105	H:	3010	BB:	1412
2B:	40	OPS:	1.049	2B:	578	OPS:	.858
3B:	6	BA:	.363	3B:	61	BA:	.328

Tales from Joe's Bat Rack

If you want to complete a 3,000 Hit Club run, you need a bat used by this man. Wade Boggs was a big fan of Louisville Slugger bats during his career, from his early days with the Boston Red Sox through the New York Yankees years and finally with the Tampa Bay Devil Rays; however, he did use Rawlings/Adirondack bats as well, with increasing frequency by the mid-1990s. Most of these bats were of the two-toned variety, featuring a black barrel with a natural-colored handle. With the exception of mixing in an occasional Cooper bat, Boggs used Louisville Slugger and Rawlings/Adirondack bats almost exclusively.

The majority of Boggs gamers exhibit his uniform number on the knob, but keep in mind that his number changed from "26" with the Red Sox to "12" for the remainder of his career. Likewise, you might see Boggs gamers with his initials (WB) on the knob in large black marker from time to time. This was a practice employed by Boggs in the minor leagues and during his early days with the Red Sox.

An avid user of pine tar, Boggs would sometimes cake the upper handle and center brand area in the substance, thereby leaving remnants from grip marks near the base of the handle. This specific pattern is often seen on Boggs' gamers from the late-1980s until the end of his career. Early on, Boggs applied pine tar to a larger surface area and spread the substance around in more liberal fashion. Finally, as is the case with many great hitters, the hitting zone on Boggs gamers is often defined by an extremely concentrated area of ball marks.

> "*Whether it was his legendary hand-eye coordination or the discipline of his highly superstitious routine, his ability to hit line drive after line drive was remarkable.*"
> – John Henry, Red Sox owner

▲ *Wade Boggs' 1990 Louisville Slugger bat.*

Miguel Cabrera

★ ★ ★ ★ ★ ★ ★ ★ ★ ★ ★ ★

Icon Sportswire

Besides the awards and titles, Jose Miguel Cabrera also happens to be a member of one of baseball's most exclusive clubs. In 2012, he led the league in home runs, batting average, and RBI to become the first new member of the Triple Crown club in 45 years. The last player to attain this milestone was Red Sox great Carl Yastrzemski, as a member of the 1967 "Impossible Dream" team. Only fifteen players in the history of the game have attained this coveted distinction. The "club" consists of Cabrera, Yaz, Frank Robinson, Mickey Mantle, Ted Williams, Lou Gehrig, Jimmie Foxx, Ty Cobb, Joe Medwick, Chuck Klein, Rogers Hornsby, Heinie Zimmerman, Nap Lajoie, Tip O'Neill, and Paul Hines. They are the best of the best.

At the time of this writing Miguel "Miggy" Cabrera continues to tear it up in the American League. A genuine superstar in every sense of the word, the Hall of Fame could very well be in his future. As a member of both the Florida Marlins and Detroit Tigers, the kid from Maracay, Venezuela, has wreaked havoc on both National League and American League pitchers since 2003. With six Silver Slugger Awards, ten All-Star appearances, two American League Most Valuable Player Awards, two American League Home Run titles, four American League Batting Titles and a World Series championship, what is left for him to accomplish?

In a heated battle with Josh Hamilton of the Rangers, Mike Trout of the Angels, and Curtis Granderson of the Yankees, the soft-spoken Cabrera really solidified his grasp on the Triple Crown on October 1, 2012, while playing against the Kansas City Royals in the first of a three-game series at Kauffman Stadium. Although there were still two games to be played, and with the American League Central Division clincher on the line, Cabrera went 4-for-5, smacking his 44th home run of the season in the sixth inning off Bruce Chen. With the last two games still to be played, the Triple Crown was not official, but this game really got Cabrera over the top. Even though Granderson managed to hit two home runs for

★ ★ ★ ★ ★ ★ ★ ★ ★ ★ ★

" *He's [Cabrera's] one of the greatest hitters of all time, maybe the greatest right-handed hitter of all time, quite frankly — you can make the argument. And he's not done yet." – Brad Ausmus*

The Ultimate Season:				Career To Date:			
Year/Team: 2013 DET				Years: 14			
G:	148	HR:	44	G:	2096	HR:	446
AB:	555	RBI:	137	AB:	7853	RBI:	1553
R:	103	SB:	3	R:	1321	SB:	38
H:	193	BB:	90	H:	2519	BB:	1011
2B:	26	OPS:	1.078	2B:	523	OPS:	.961
3B:	1	BA:	.348	3B:	17	BA:	.321

the Yanks in the last game of the season it only brought him to 43 home runs. Cabrera's 44 home runs, 139 RBI, and .330 batting average got him over the top and into the baseball history books.

The first Latin player to attain the prestigious Triple Crown, Miguel Cabrera continues to add to his already impressive resume with every passing season. Already considered by many to be one of the all-time Tigers greats, Cabrera should have quite a few more years in the game. When his career finally does come to an end, there is little doubt we will see Miggy in Cooperstown.

Tales from Joe's Bat Rack

As Miguel Cabrera has evolved into one of MLB's elite all-around hitters, his bats have become increasingly popular with collectors. One Triple Crown in 2012, two AL MVPs (2012 and 2013) and four American League Batting Titles can do that. Cabrera,

like many players from the post-1990 era, has used a variety of bat brands during his career. This includes, but is not limited to, Louisville Slugger, Marucci, Nokona, SAM, X, and Zinger bats. Most of his gamers are either brown or black-colored bats, with some being of the two-toned variety. When it comes to bat characteristics, Cabrera will often tape the handles of his bats. Yet, unlike most other players, that taping style can vary quite a bit.

Sometimes the tape application is fairly traditional, while other times Cabrera's bats are found with crisscross patterns or tape ringlets. Even the more traditional-looking, spiral tape applications can vary in length. Many well-used Cabrera gamers can also be found with either pine tar or Mota stick applications, which is sometimes heavy in nature, along the handle. Another noteworthy Cabrera bat characteristic is the fairly frequent presence of defined cleat impressions along the barrel.

Cabrera's primary uniform number "24" is often found marked on the knob or barrel end. As a reminder, Cabrera did wear number "20" during his first year with the Florida Marlins. Finally, Cabrera does occasionally sign and inscribe some of his gamers, confirming their use.

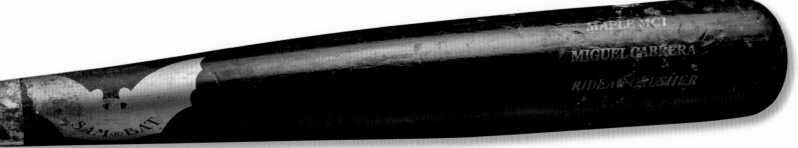

▲ *Miguel Cabrera's 2012 Triple Crown season SAM bat used to hit home run #s 33, 34, and 35 of the season.*

Rod Carew

★ ★ ★ ★ ★ ★ ★ ★ ★ ★ ★

Rich Pilling/Getty images Sport Classic Collection/Getty Images

contact hitter who could place the ball just about anywhere in the park. The only American League Latino player to have his jersey retired by two teams, the Panamanian-born Carew was voted AL Rookie of the Year in 1967 and AL Most Valuable Player in 1977. He batted .300 or better for 15 consecutive seasons and won the AL batting title seven times. Truly a fan favorite, Carew enjoyed 18 consecutive All-Star appearances and, as of this writing, he is the leading All-Star vote-getter in baseball history.

Carew developed a batting stance that was quite unique. A crouch-coil stance with a well-balanced base, he called it the "Carew Flex-Stance." Interestingly, Carew claims Hall of Fame pitcher, Nolan Ryan, was the inspiration for this unusual stance. During the early days of his career, Carew was overpowered by the famous Nolan Ryan fastball. The Ryan Express pitched Carew up in the strike zone, and struck him out on a fairly regular basis. Carew's strategy against Ryan was to change his stance by crouching down and widening more to force Ryan to get the ball down. He never moved his back foot but would adjust the placement of his front foot depending on who was on the mound. Carew believed that hitting the ball at the front end of the plate was the secret. The Flex-Stance worked for Carew, and he began making contact regularly. This strategy worked so well against Ryan that the great pitcher became aggravated and would yell out to Carew to "stand up like a man."

In 1985, his 19th and final season, 39-year-old Carew became the 16th MLB player to attain the 3,000-hits milestone. Still among the top offensive leaders in Twins history, Carew holds the highest career batting average for the Twins with .334, and the highest Twins career on-base percentage with .393. Rodney Cline Carew was a first ballot choice for the Hall of Fame in 1991. He is a national

One of the more respected players in the game, Rod Carew is a member of the 3,000 Hit Club who carved out his stellar Hall of Fame career with both the Minnesota Twins and California Angels. Never known for his power, Carew was a skilled

hero in Panama where, in 2004, Panama City's National Stadium was renamed Rod Carew Stadium. In 2016 MLB named the AL batting title the Rod Carew American League Batting Champion Award in his honor.

The Ultimate Season:				Career:			
Year/Team: 1977 MIN				Years: 19			
G:	155	HR:	14	G:	2469	HR:	92
AB:	616	RBI:	100	AB:	9315	RBI:	1015
R:	128	SB:	23	R:	1424	SB:	353
H:	239	BB:	69	H:	3053	BB:	1018
2B:	38	OPS:	1.019	2B:	445	OPS:	.822
3B:	16	BA:	.388	3B:	112	BA:	.328

Tales from Joe's Bat Rack

Rod Carew was always a good hitter, winning several batting titles along the way. That said, once he reached 3,000 career hits, Carew's professional model bats became an absolute necessity for those building a set devoted to collecting lumber from members of the exclusive club. When it comes to bats used by this Hall of Famer, there are a few interesting characteristics to note. First, while he did use Adirondack (block letter) bats at times, there is no question that Carew preferred H&B/Louisville Slugger bats.

The sweet-swinging lefty ordered a number of models from the manufacturer throughout his career, signing an endorsement contract in 1964, well in advance of his MLB debut. Carew would often apply a moderate amount of pine tar along the handles of his bats. He tended to use bat models that featured a thin handle/large barrel combination due to his hitting style: holding the bat very loosely in his hands prior to starting his swing.

Collectors may encounter some Carew gamers with his primary uniform number "29" in very small writing, but most of his bats exhibit a large uniform number noted in black marker on the knob and, sometimes, the barrel end as well. Carew did wear the number "21" for a brief period during his Rookie of the Year campaign in 1967, but he wore number "29" for the vast majority of his playing days. Finally, Carew gamers that date to his prime years with the Minnesota Twins tend to sell for a premium, which includes a stretch where he won six batting titles in seven seasons.

" *There is a special sensation in getting good wood on the ball and driving a double down the left-field line as the crowd in the ballpark rises to its feet and cheers. But, I also remember how much fun I had as a skinny barefoot kid hitting a tennis ball with a broomstick on a quiet, dusty street in Panama."*
– Rod Carew

▲ *Rod Carew's 1973–75 H&B bat.*

Eddie Collins

★ ★ ★ ★ ★ ★ ★ ★ ★ ★ ★ ★

Icon Sportswire

Nicknamed Cocky, Eddie Collins let his skill and knowledge do his bragging. In a Hall of Fame career that lasted a quarter century, he played a splendid second sack for the Philadelphia Athletics (1906–1914 and 1927–1930) and the Chicago White Sox (1915–1926). He also managed the ChiSox from 1924–1926. A member of the 1939 Hall of Fame class, Eddie Collins was one of the most influential figures in the game as baseball moved from the Deadball Era to a new age of power and popularity. Edward Trowbridge Collins, Sr., was born in Millerton, New York, in 1887. Although his name sounds more like a steel industrialist than a steal artist, Collins was just that, swiping 741 career bases and leading the league in

that category four times, highlighted by 81 in 1910.

The lefty batter hit to all fields and used his speed and smarts to make the most out of every swat. Most of all, he won baseball games. Playing for all-time managerial wins leader Connie Mack, Collins won three World Series with the Philadelphia A's (1910, 1911, 1913). While with the A's, he was part of Mack's famous "$100,000 Infield" alongside Home Run Baker, Jack Barry, and Stuffy McInnis. In 1917, Collins added another crown with the White Sox. Those World Series encompassed Collins' greatest hitting moments. In the 1910 Series, he batted .429, in the 1913 Fall Classic, he hit .421, and in the 1917 World Series, he batted .409. Three series, three times hitting over .400, three rings. Talk about clutch! Conversely, Collins was also part of two of the more historic World Series losses—his A's lost to the Miracle Braves in 1914, and his White Sox dropped the 1919 Series, although Collins was not implicated in the notorious fixing scandal.

Collins was all about getting on base and drawing walks was a specialty. He drew 1,499 free passes over his career, putting pitchers' pulses in perpetual panic with his patience. The numbers tell the story. The 1914 American League MVP had a lifetime OBP of .424 and a career OPS of .853. He was a sabermetrician's dream when sabermetrics were still just a dream. According to Hall of Fame records, Collins hit a single off the Tigers' Rip Collins on June 3, 1925, to collect his

3,000th hit, becoming the sixth player to reach that pinnacle. He hit .340 or better 10 seasons, and in his long career spanning from 1906 to 1930, he batted .333 with 3,315 hits, and 1,821 runs. The former Columbia University quarterback remained the ultimate field general as a player, manager, and later, when he was hired by Thomas Yawkey in 1933, as GM and Vice President of the Red Sox, a role he filled until his death in 1951. Eddie Collins surely saw all sides of the game in an extraordinary baseball life.

The Ultimate Season:			Career:		
Year/Team: 1920 CHW			Years: 25		
G:	153	HR: 3	G:	2826	HR: 47
AB:	602	RBI: 76	AB:	9949	RBI: 1300
R:	117	SB: 20	R:	1821	SB: 741
H:	224	BB: 69	H:	3315	BB: 1499
2B:	38	OPS: .932	2B:	438	OPS: .853
3B:	13	BA: .372	3B:	187	BA: .333

Tales from Joe's Bat Rack

Eddie Collins professional model bats are some of the toughest bats to find of any Hall of Famer in baseball history, and Collins was certainly one of the best hitters to ever patrol the second base position. Once Collins gained entry into the 3,000 Hit Club, finishing with 3,315 career knocks, he ensured that future hobbyists would make him a needed component for their collections built on the exclusive group. When you add the fact that Collins played for both the ultra-popular Philadelphia Athletics and the infamous Chicago White Sox (during the Black Sox era), his bats are elevated to another level of demand.

To the dismay of collectors, however, there are only a few Collins bats known today. Just a couple of examples have reached the auction block in the last 20 years, making it extremely difficult for bat enthusiasts to fill the void left by Collins. At the time of this writing, two of the scant few Collins professional model bats were fully documented, with each one exhibiting factory side writing and/or vault marks noting their return to the manufacturer. Collins did sign an endorsement contract with H&B in 1910, and the two documented bats do feature his facsimile signature on the barrel. One of those bats features slight scoring and a heavy application of a gripping substance similar to traditional pine tar on the handle to enhance Collins' grip.

> "Collins sustained a remarkable level of performance for a remarkably long time. He was past thirty when the lively ball era began, yet he adapted to it and continued to be one of the best players in baseball every year." – Bill James, historian & author

▲ Eddie Collins' 1915 J. F. Hillerich & Son factory side-written bat.

Charlie Gehringer

to churn out amazing numbers was remarkable. He batted over .300 in 13 of 14 seasons between 1927 and 1940. In that span, his only sub-.300 season was 1932, when he hit .298 with 19 home runs and 104 RBI—not bad for an "off" year. A six-time All-Star, Gehringer played in the first six Midsummer Classics and batted .500 as starting second baseman.

Gehringer was a Detroit Tigers institution, playing in Motown his entire career, from 1924 to 1942. Perhaps his most significant accomplishment as a hitter was the 1929 season—a campaign that truly put him on the baseball map. That season, Gehringer led the American League in hits with 215. He batted .339 and topped the junior circuit with 27 steals, 45 doubles and 131 runs scored. In addition, he had a league-high 19 triples. In 1934, Gehringer's 127 RBI and .356 batting clip propelled Detroit to a pennant but they lost the Fall Classic to St. Louis in a seven-game series. In defeat, Gehringer hit .379 with a home run and 11 hits. In 1935, he blasted 19 homers and 108 RBI while batting .330. Moreover, he led the Tigers to a world championship in a six-game victory over the Cubs. In the Series, Gehringer batted .375 with 9 hits and 4 RBI. Twice, he led the AL in two-baggers, highlighted by an amazing 60 in 1936. The following season, he had 209 hits and batted a career-high .371, winning the AL batting crown and MVP award.

The Fowlerville, Michigan, native was a hometown hero, playing at Fowlerville High School and the University of Michigan before joining the Tigers organization. It was manager Ty Cobb who ensconced Gehringer at second base. Gehringer last hit over .300 in 1940, and his plate prowess dwindled until his final season

With a .320 career batting average, and seven seasons in which he eclipsed the 200-hit mark, Charlie Gehringer was one of the most consistent hitters of his generation. Nicknamed "The Mechanical Man," Gehringer's seemingly robotic ability

The Mechanical Man

of 1942. He enlisted in the U.S. Navy, was assigned to the Navy's pre-flight school, St. Mary's College, as baseball coach, and rose to the rank of Lieutenant Commander. Gehringer returned to the Tigers as GM from 1951 to 1953 and served as Tigers VP until 1960. Inducted into the Hall of Fame in 1949, Gehringer later served on the HOF's Board of Directors until 1991. His number "2" was retired by the Tigers in 1983. Ten years later, Charlie Gehringer passed away at age 89. Ironically, as GM of the Tigers in 1953, Gehringer signed a kid named Al Kaline, who would play 22 years in Detroit and become known as Mr. Tiger. That title may have truly belonged to Charles Leonard Gehringer.

Tales from Joe's Bat Rack

Charlie Gehringer, a man who was an outstanding hitter for the Detroit Tigers, has one key characteristic to look for on some of his well-used professional model bats. Gehringer would occasionally apply a unique taping pattern along the handle of his bats. There are two styles that collectors may encounter: one has

"*You wind him up in the spring, turn him loose, he hits .330 or .340, and you shut him off at the end of the season.*" – Lefty Gomez

The Ultimate Season:			Career:		
Year/Team: 1934 DET			Years: 19		
G:	154	HR: 11	G:	2323	HR: 184
AB:	601	RBI: 127	AB:	8860	RBI: 1427
R:	135	SB: 11	R:	1775	SB: 181
H:	214	BB: 99	H:	2839	BB: 1186
2B:	50	OPS: .967	2B:	574	OPS: .884
3B:	7	BA: .356	3B:	146	BA: .320

a crisscross pattern and the other style, one that is clearly more prevalent in vintage images, is spiral in nature with slight gaps left along the continuous stretch of tape.

It is somewhat similar to the taping method seen on Carl Yastrzemski's bats decades later, only the gaps are even tighter on Gehringer's bats. The separation between each wrap is extremely thin—not even wide enough for a hitter to place a finger on the wood beneath it. It is important to note that Gehringer did not always prepare his bats with either of these taping methods, but evidence of the pattern does help place the bat directly into his hands.

Gehringer signed an endorsement contract with H&B during the middle of his first full season in 1926, but he did play several games in 1924 and 1925. While the overwhelming majority of Gehringer's gamers were manufactured with his facsimile signature, it is possible to find some containing his name in block letters made prior to the summer of 1926. Finally, Gehringer experimented with hickory bats early on, but he stayed loyal to ash bats from the spring of 1932 until the end of his career.

▲ *Charlie Gehringer's 1934–37 H&B bat.*

Hank Greenberg

★ ★ ★ ★ ★ ★ ★ ★ ★ ★ ★ ★

with his 331 home runs and 1,274 RBI, Greenberg led the Detroit Tigers to four World Series, winning the championship in 1935 and again, upon his return, in 1945. That year, his grand slam home run in ninth inning of the last game of the season clinched the pennant for the Tigers.

The four-time All-Star and two-time American League MVP dominated the league with 36 home runs in 1935, 40 homers in 1937, 41 in 1940, and 44 in 1946, but he captivated the attention of fans and foes alike with his 1938 run at the great Babe Ruth's record. Greenberg's 58 dingers that season were just two shy of the Babe's 60.

Very proud of his Jewish heritage, Henry Benjamin Greenberg had to deal with anti-Semitism displayed by players and fans alike. In the pre-war years, there was a vocal anti-Semitic element in Detroit and elsewhere in the country, but Greenberg took the high road and focused on playing to his potential. This all came to a head in September of 1934. With the Tigers and Yankees locked in a heated pennant race, Greenberg was torn about playing on the Jewish High Holidays of Rosh Hashanah and Yom Kippur. After consulting with family, friends, and his Rabbi, Greenberg decided to play on September 10, Rosh Hashanah, the Jewish New Year, as this was a day of celebration. That day he smacked

Had he not lost the better part of four seasons defending our country in World War II, Hank Greenberg's statistics would have rivaled the baseball greats. The "Hebrew Hammer" likely would have hit the 500 home run mark, and 1,800 RBI. Although he lost prime years to the war effort, the great right-handed hitter simply picked up where he left off when he returned to the diamond. With a .313 lifetime batting average to go along

two home runs in the Tigers 2–1 victory over the Red Sox. However, after much soul searching, he decided to sit out the contest against the Yankees on September 19, because it was Yom Kippur, the Jewish Day of Atonement. Instead of playing, he spent the day praying in the synagogue, and because of this decision, the congregation gave him a standing ovation when he arrived. Although the Tigers lost the game that day, they went on to win the pennant. However, they would have to wait one more year before they would finally win their first World Series championship.

Greenberg was traded to the Pittsburgh Pirates in 1947. He played out the season before leaving to serve as general manager of the Cleveland Indians, and later on, as part-owner and vice president of the White Sox. The Hebrew Hammer was elected to the Hall of Fame in 1956.

The Ultimate Season: Year/Team: 1937 DET				Career: Years: 13			
G:	154	HR:	40	G:	1394	HR:	331
AB:	594	RBI:	184	AB:	5193	RBI:	1274
R:	137	SB:	8	R:	1046	SB:	58
H:	200	BB:	102	H:	1628	BB:	852
2B:	49	OPS:	1.105	2B:	379	OPS:	1.017
3B:	14	BA:	.337	3B:	71	BA:	.313

Tales from Joe's Bat Rack

Hank Greenberg's career numbers may not stack up against some of the premier sluggers of the era he played in, but don't let that fool you. This gentle giant was one of the best power hitters of his time; and had Greenberg not lost so many plate appearances to military service, his career figures would be much gaudier than they are. As a result, his professional model bats are an easy addition to our exclusive list of lumber.

While Greenberg clearly preferred H&B bats during the course of his career, you will occasionally see other brands bearing his name, such as Spalding. Like many of his contemporaries, this slugger's H&B gamers were initially produced only with his last name "Greenberg" in block letters. That changed late in 1934 when he signed an endorsement contract with the company.

Greenberg's gamers can definitely exhibit character, as he would score the handle of his bats from time to time. Scoring of the handle is the act of carving lines into the wood in order to enhance the grip. In addition, Greenberg would occasionally use a pine-tar-like substance during an era when few batsmen used any concoction to enhance their grip. He would apply a thick layer near the base of the handle, about six to eight inches from the knob up. Keep in mind that he did not score all of his bats, nor did he apply large amounts of tar-like gripping substance on all of his gamers. The existence of either characteristic merely provides an additional link to Greenberg's use.

> " *I thought I was in good shape when I came out of the Army Air Corps. The toughest thing in being away so long is having to learn the peculiarities of opposing pitchers all over again. But that doesn't take long. You pick up a lot in one swing around the league.*"
> – Hank Greenberg

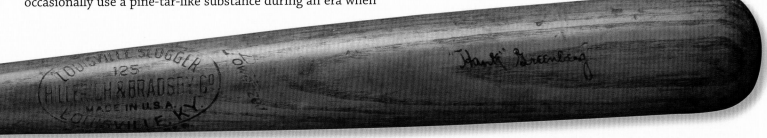

▲ *Hank Greenberg's 1937 H&B factory side-written bat.*

Gil Hodges

Robert Riger/Hulton Archive/Getty Images

more than 20 home runs in each of those seasons. He eclipsed the 100 RBI plateau from 1949 through 1955, compiling a career 1,274 RBI. His 370 career home runs were tops all-time for a National League right-handed batter until Willie Mays eclipsed the mark in 1963. The Gold Glove award was first established in 1957 and Hodges, a terrific first baseman, won the award in its first three seasons. The Dodgers became a National League dynasty, winning pennants in 1947, 1949, 1952, 1953, and 1956, and winning world championships in 1955 and 1959.

If the Dodgers were the heart and soul of Brooklyn, then Gil Hodges was the heart of soul of the Dodgers. After just two at-bats in the 1943 season, Hodges joined the Marines in 1944 and saw heavy combat action in World War II, earning the Bronze Star. He would return to Ebbets Field in 1947 and stake his claim as one of the all-time great Dodgers. Hodges did not have the flash of Jackie Robinson, the charm of Pee Wee Reese, the power of Roy Campanella, or the talent of Duke Snider, yet, among these great stars, Hodges was the ultimate leader.

While he spent the last two years of his playing career with the fledgling Mets (1962–1963), Hodges will forever be known as a Dodger. In an 11-year span from 1949 to 1959, he made the All-Star team eight times and smashed

Hodges was respected and revered by coaches and teammates, even in times of struggle. In the 1952 World Series, Hodges went 0–21. This slump continued into the 1953 season with Hodges hitting below .200 into May. In a career filled with memorable moments, this may have been Hodges' greatest. Despite his horrific failures at the plate, his beloved Brooklyn fans stayed loyal to Hodges. In his book, *The Game of Baseball,* Hodges recounts how Dodger fans actually prayed for him in church. Teammates swear that he was never so much as booed at Ebbets Field. This may be just the stuff of legend, but it worked. The resilient Hodges broke

★ ★ ★ ★ ★ ★ ★ ★ ★ ★ ★

out of his funk and ended up hitting .302 with 31 home runs, and 122 RBI in 1953, one of his best seasons.

Even after the team moved to Los Angeles in 1958, Hodges kept his Brooklyn home. He went on to a managerial career with the Senators and famously, the Mets, guiding them to their amazing 1969 World Series victory. Gilbert Raymond Hodges died tragically at the age of 47, suffering a heart attack after playing golf on Easter Sunday, 1972. Buried at Brooklyn's Holy Cross Cemetery, Gil Hodges has two baseball fields, a park, and two bridges named after him, one near his Princeton, Indiana, hometown and one in Brooklyn. This is fitting, for Hodges truly was the Brooklyn Bridge, connecting a team of special players with their adoring fans.

Tales from Joe's Bat Rack

As a former member of the Brooklyn Dodgers' core during their impressive run of World Series appearances in the 1940s and 1950s, Gil Hodges has remained popular with collectors,

The Ultimate Season:			Career:		
Year/Team: 1954 BRO			Years: 18		
G:	154	HR: 42	G:	2071	HR: 370
AB:	579	RBI: 130	AB:	7030	RBI: 1274
R:	106	SB: 3	R:	1105	SB: 63
H:	176	BB: 74	H:	1921	BB: 943
2B:	23	OPS: .952	2B:	295	OPS: .846
3B:	5	BA: .304	3B:	48	BA: .273

and that appeal extends to his professional model bats. The slugging first baseman used both H&B (block letter) and Adirondack (endorsement contract) bats during his career, a career that included a seven-year run of 100 RBI or more and an 11-year run of 20 or more home runs. With the exception of his extremely short MLB debut in 1943, a year when Hodges wore the number "4," his uniform number "14" remained the same for the entirety of his career.

You can often find his primary uniform number "14" noted in black marker on the knobs, and sometimes the barrel ends, of his post-1950 era gamers. On well-used Hodges gamers, it is not uncommon to find the bats coated in a heavy layer of pine tar on the lower-to-mid handle. Some of the handles of known examples have been blackened by the extent of the application. This is a key Hodges characteristic. As you might imagine, like his fellow teammate Duke Snider, bats used during his Brooklyn Dodgers playing days tend to sell for premium.

" *Hodges' combination of slugging as a player and success as a manager is unique in baseball history.*"
– Tom Verducci, Sports Illustrated

▲ *Gil Hodges' 1950s H&B bat.*

Chipper Jones

★ ★ ★ ★ ★ ★ ★ ★ ★ ★ ★ ★

Icon Sportswire

first full year of play, Jones finished second in the Rookie of the Year balloting. That year, the young third baseman hit a respectable .265 with 23 homers to help the Braves to the 1995 World Series championship.

Jones had a banner year in 1999 when he batted .319, slammed 45 home runs with 110 RBI and was voted the National League Most Valuable Player. Unfortunately, the Braves could not match the powerful Yankees and were swept in the 1999 World Series. An eight-time All-Star, Jones won two Silver Slugger Awards (1999, 2000) and was the 2008 National League batting champ with his .364 average. Extremely consistent hitting from both sides of the plate, Jones batted .304 as a left-handed hitter, and batted .305 as a righty. The only other switch hitter with 5,000 at-bats to hit over .300 from both sides of the plate was Frankie Frisch.

When it comes to the great third basemen, Chipper Jones is certainly in good company. Most baseball experts have Jones in the Top 10 list with the likes of Mike Schmidt, Eddie Matthews, George Brett, Wade Boggs, Brooks Robinson, and the rest.

As a ballplayer, Larry Wayne "Chipper" Jones was solid—solid offensively, solid defensively, and solid as a teammate. The Braves' first overall pick in the 1990 Major League draft, Jones carved out a brilliant 19-year career with Atlanta, finishing in 2012 with a lifetime .303 batting average, over 2,700 hits, and 468 home runs. The switch-hitting Jones' career 1,623 RBI is the most ever for a third baseman. In his

As injuries began to slow him down, Jones contemplated retiring a few times. He finally called it quits after the 2012 season. To top off a career filled with landmarks, Jones had many special moments during his last season. In his own words, here are some standouts: "My first five-hit game at home. I've never done that before. A couple of walk-offs at home. Man, that's the apex. Home run on my [40th] birthday. Home run in my first start of the season, with my parents in

the stands. Two homers on my bobblehead day. Just some really, really cool moments where, as the balls are flying out of the park, I'm running down to first, saying, 'You have got to be kidding me. Did that just happen?'"

In June of 2013, Chipper Jones was voted into the Braves Hall of Fame. Greater things will certainly happen when he becomes eligible for the hallowed halls of Cooperstown. If things fall into place the way some suspect they will, Chipper Jones should be a first ballot Hall of Famer.

The Ultimate Season:			Career:		
Year/Team: 1999 ATL			Years: 19		
G:	157	HR: 45	G:	2499	HR: 468
AB:	567	RBI: 110	AB:	8984	RBI: 1623
R:	116	SB: 25	R:	1619	SB: 150
H:	181	BB: 126	H:	2726	BB: 1512
2B:	41	OPS: 1.074	2B:	549	OPS: .930
3B:	1	BA: .319	3B:	38	BA: .303

Tales from Joe's Bat Rack

Like contemporary star Craig Biggio, Chipper Jones quietly put up terrific numbers over a long career, a career that has placed him amongst the best third basemen in MLB history. As a former batting title winner and National League MVP, hobbyists have plenty of reasons to add a Jones gamer to their collections. Jones used some different professional model bat brands throughout his career, including Louisville Slugger, Mizuno, Glomar and Rawlings/Adirondack, which was his preferred brand for most of his career. He did use some Louisville Slugger bats, especially early on, but he didn't appear to use many. Most of the Jones gamers that collectors will encounter are of the unfinished, natural color variety, which he normally used while hitting from the left side. The slugging third baseman would only occasionally order bats with a darker finish, which were used during most right-handed plate appearances. On occasion, Jones bats can be found with "LT" (left-handed) or "RT" (right-handed) marked on the knob.

Well-used Jones bats will often exhibit pine tar along the upper and lower handle, often appearing caked in spots towards the base. The presence of the heavy tar helps give his bats great eye appeal, which is a serious consideration for many collectors of top lumber. Since Jones seemed to prefer Adirondack bats, it is not uncommon for bats with substantial use to have wear near his name on the barrel. The stamped names on Adirondack bats can be susceptible to flaking and chipping (no pun intended), which does bother some collectors. His primary uniform number "10" can often be found noted in black marker on the knob or barrel end of his bats. Jones did wear number "16" during his debut season, but it was for a very brief period of time as he only had a total of four plate appearances.

" *As Don Baylor used to say, 'Don't take batting practice. Just show up, get dressed, stay loose and go out there, see it, hit it.'" – Chipper Jones*

▲ *Chipper Jones' 2010 Rawlings bat.*

Harmon Killebrew

★ ★ ★ ★ ★ ★ ★ ★ ★ ★ ★ ★

Louis Requena/Major League Baseball Collection/Getty Images

kind power and determination. He attacked the game and was never cheated at the plate. His swings were potent and, when he connected, it was as if an explosion occurred at home plate. A Minnesota Twins legend, Killebrew was a living, breathing home run derby, one of those guys fans would pay to simply see take batting practice. His robust and stocky frame, along with his tape measure blasts, harkened back to the likes of Babe Ruth and Hack Wilson.

Early in his career, Killebrew would not have been featured in the film, "Moneyball." Not one for patience at the plate, his mindset was to swing, swing often, and swing hard. In six consecutive seasons (1959–1964), Killebrew struck out over 100 times, including a league-leading 142 in 1962. Overall, he K'd 1,699 times, good (or bad) for 30th on the all-time list. Killebrew began his career in 1954 with the Washington Senators and moved to Minnesota with the club in 1961. He smacked 573 career homers and 1,584 RBI. His career batting average was a mere .256, but he led the American League in dingers six times and in RBI three times. Killebrew did evolve as a selective hitter. Over the course of his career, he actually led the league in walks four times. The 11-time All-Star was named American League MVP in 1969 with 49 homers, 140 RBI, and an incredible OBP of .427.

The 1927 New York Yankees were known as Murderers' Row, but in baseball history, there was only one "Killer." A polite gentleman from Idaho, Harmon Killebrew's off-field demeanor belied his violent nickname. On the field, however, it was most appropriate. Killebrew pounded the baseball with one-of-a-

Killebrew had numerous great moments at the plate, but two stand out prominently. On August 10, 1971, at home vs. Baltimore, he clouted a Mike Cuellar curveball into the left-field seats for his 500th career home run, becoming the 10th member of what, at that time, was a truly elite group. He added number 501 that same day. Three years later, the sturdy slugger hit a memorable game-winning tater against

Oakland. It was Killebrew's 559th career homer and, more significantly, his last as a member of the Twins organization. Killebrew had eight 40-plus home run seasons and a slew of multiple home run games. He played 22 seasons, finishing in 1975 with the Kansas City Royals. Nine years later, he became the first member of the Twins organization to be inducted into the Baseball Hall of Fame. Harmon Clayton Killebrew passed away in 2011, but his long ball legacy remains secure in the history of baseball.

The Ultimate Season: Year/Team: 1969 MIN				Career: Years: 22			
G:	162	HR:	49	G:	2435	HR:	573
AB:	555	RBI:	140	AB:	8147	RBI:	1584
R:	106	SB:	8	R:	1283	SB:	19
H:	153	BB:	145	H:	2086	BB:	1559
2B:	20	OPS:	1.011	2B:	290	OPS:	.884
3B:	2	BA:	.276	3B:	24	BA:	.256

Tales from Joe's Bat Rack

"The Killer's" professional model bats really can have a killer look when heavy use is present. In somewhat similar fashion to fellow Hall of Famer Johnny Bench, Harmon Killebrew would often apply a generous layer of pine tar to the handles of his bats, extending from the knob towards the center brand. In most cases, the tar doesn't reach quite as far up the bat as heavily-used Bench gamers, but the application itself is usually thick. While this appeared to be a consistent practice by Killebrew for the majority of his career, his early bats (1954–1957) often do not exhibit this characteristic. Furthermore, the knobs of Killebrew gamers will usually feature his primary uniform number "3" in either black paint or marker. Keep in mind that Killebrew did wear numbers "25" and "12" during his first couple of seasons with the Washington Senators.

In some cases, an additional number would be added to the knob alongside his uniform notation. For example, collectors will encounter Killebrew gamers that possess a smaller "1" or "2" to the immediate right of the larger "3." This single digit represented the second number for the weight of the bat in ounces. So, if a "2" is present, that would represent a bat that is approximately 32 ounces. This notation was helpful to Killebrew when selecting his gamer out of the bat rack. Killebrew signed an endorsement contract with H&B during his debut season in 1954. This was his bat of choice throughout his career.

It is important to note that Killebrew was one of the only star players of his era to keep many of his bats and jerseys. As a result, Killebrew bats tend to be slightly easier to find than bats used by other players during the period. In fact, Killebrew kept and eventually released a number of milestone and special event bats, including documented home run bats, over time.

" *Harmon has that graceful, fast swing, he swings up at the ball just a little bit and hits those high homers."*
– Bob Allison

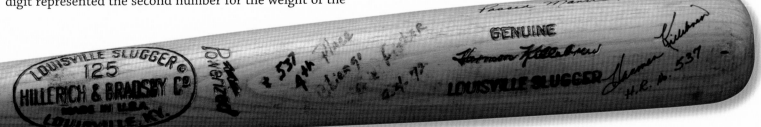

▲ *Harmon Killebrew's 1972 H&B bat used to hit career home run #537.*

Napoleon Lajoie

★ ★ ★ ★ ★ ★ ★ ★ ★ ★ ★ ★

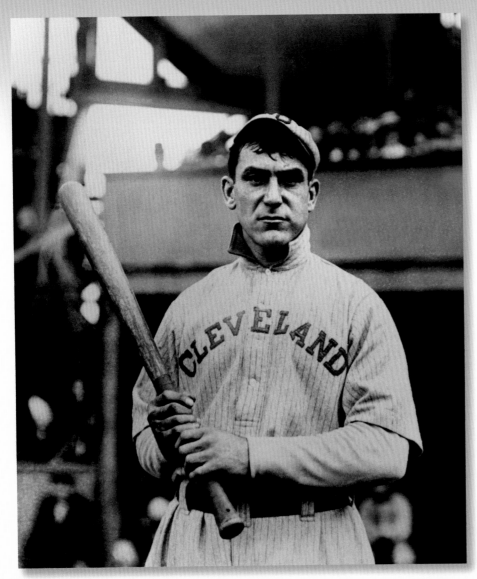

greatest bunters in baseball history. As a matter of fact, his bunting factors into the ultimate chase for an American League batting title.

On Monday, October 9, 1910, the lowly Cleveland Naps, with a record of 71–81, took on the last place St. Louis Browns, with an even more dismal record of 47–107, in a doubleheader to complete a very forgettable season for both teams. This contest would be long forgotten in the annals of baseball history had it not been for the greatest batting title duel in league history. Napoleon "Nap" Lajoie was locked into a heated race for the American League batting title with the greatest hitter of that era, Ty Cobb. Both players had tremendous seasons, battling head-to-head every step of the way. It would be an unbelievable finish, and the winner would receive a brand new Chalmers automobile.

In the lead going into the final day of the season, Cobb sat out the last two games to preserve that lead. It is an understatement to say Cobb was the most disliked player in the league. His surly attitude and rough style of play did not endear him to teammates or opponents. Because St. Louis manager, Jack O'Connor, had a particular dislike for Cobb, he instructed his rookie third baseman, Red Corriden, to play back on the edge of the infield grass, almost into shallow left field. Taking advantage of the charitable St. Louis team, Lajoie proceeded to lay down six bunt singles during the double header, while also hitting a triple and another routine single.

When the game ended Lajoie's line card read 8-for-8, and he was declared the batting title champ—until Cobb fans cried shenanigans. After review, AL President Ban Johnson

The man who perfected the "flat-to-down" technique used by Deadball Era hitters, Nap Lajoie used a bat with two knobs, giving him exceptional bat control with his split-handed grip. Known as "The Frenchman," Lajoie led the American League five times in batting, four times in hits, won the AL Triple Crown in 1901, and was a veritable RBI machine. He was such an offensive dynamo that his team, the Cleveland Bronchos, was renamed the Naps for him. Oh yes, he was also one of the

★ ★ ★ ★ ★ ★ ★ ★ ★ ★ ★

declared Lajoie the winner, but because *The Sporting News* proclaimed Cobb the winner, the Chalmers Company decided to give both players a car. Years later, it was discovered that one of Cobb's at-bats was counted twice so, in reality, Lajoie really did win the batting title with his .384 batting average to Cobb's adjusted .383. However, this is contested even to this day. Suffice it to say, Hall of Famer, Nap Lajoie was truly one of the original great stick magicians.

The Ultimate Season:				Career:			
Year/Team: 1901 PHA				Years: 21			
G:	131	HR:	14	G:	2480	HR:	82
AB:	544	RBI:	125	AB:	9589	RBI:	1599
R:	145	SB:	27	R:	1504	SB:	380
H:	232	BB:	24	H:	3243	BB:	516
2B:	48	OPS:	1.106	2B:	657	OPS:	.847
3B:	14	BA:	.426	3B:	163	BA:	.338

Tales from Joe's Bat Rack

The appeal of Napoleon Lajoie is obvious to those who appreciate the history of the game and offensive excellence. Lajoie is a 3,000 Hit Club member who won several batting titles over the course of his career, but the fact that he was such an outstanding hitter is only part of the reason his name remains a hot commodity in the bat marketplace. For collectors, the task of locating the genuine article is daunting, as Lajoie professional model bats are amongst the toughest to find in the entire hobby. In fact, at the time of this writing there were only a handful of authentic Lajoie gamers known. Of the scant few that exist, a couple of them are factory-documented examples, exhibiting remnants of side writing from being logged at the factory.

Since there are so few confirmed specimens to examine, with two side-written Lajoie gamers known today, the available physical evidence is limited. What we do know about Lajoie and his bats are mostly a product of studying the manufacturer records and vintage photography. Lajoie signed an endorsement contract with H&B on September 12, 1905, shortly after Honus Wagner became the first to

do so just days earlier. Lajoie, who was known for his upper body strength, was able to handle a hefty piece of lumber. He often used a bat that weighed close to, or more than, 40 ounces. Lajoie can be seen holding bats with a prominent, overlapping wrap of tape along a substantial portion of the handle in period images. While we cannot confirm how often Lajoie prepared his bats in this manner, it is clear that its presence can help place the bat in his hands.

" *[Nap] Lajoie quickly became one of the best hitters in the National League. His stance appeared lazy and nonchalant, but he was able to whip his bat through the strike zone with extraordinary quickness."*
– Eric Enders, Historian, MLB All-Star Program, 2001

▲ *Napoleon Lajoie's 1900–1905 J. F. Hillerich & Son bat factory side-written to 1912.*

Tony Lazzeri

Sporting News Archive/Sporting News Collection/Getty Images

and the Depression years, Lazzeri was the son of Italian immigrants and grew up in San Francisco's ethnic Italian neighborhood. At 16 years old, he started working as a boilermaker's helper, which developed his upper body strength. Although only 5-foot, 11-inches, and 170 pounds, he carried a big stick and the Yanks came calling after Lazzeri blasted 60 home runs and batted .355 in 1925 for Salt Lake City of the Pacific Coast League.

Coming out of the gate in 1926, Lazzeri batted .275 and whacked 18 home runs for the Pinstripes, finishing third in the league behind Ruth and Philadelphia's Al Simmons. That was the year of Lazzeri's infamous at-bat in the World Series vs. the Cardinals. The Series was even at three games apiece. In the seventh inning of Game Seven, with two outs, the bases loaded, and 22-year-old Lazzeri at the plate, the great Grover Alexander came in from the bullpen to preserve a 3–2 lead. By the way, the 38-year-old Alexander had pitched the win in Game Six and was under the weather from celebrating. Alexander had Lazzeri 1–2 when the crafty old-timer blew a curveball by him for strike three, essentially securing the win for the Cards. Years later, Lazzeri said people remembered him more for that strikeout than they remembered his great career.

One of the first Italian American baseball stars, Lazzeri's nickname "Poosh 'Em Up" came from his legion of Italian fans calling for him to hit one out of the park. Lazzeri played on five Yankees World Series champion teams (1927, 1928, 1932, 1936, 1937). A steady influence at

Part of the famous 1927 "Murderers' Row" Yankees, Tony Lazzeri carved out a great career playing with the likes of Babe Ruth, Lou Gehrig, Earle Combs, Bob Meusel, and the rest. One of the best second basemen of the Roaring Twenties

Poosh 'Em Up Tony

★ ★ ★ ★ ★ ★ ★ ★ ★ ★ ★ ★

> "When things get tough out there, the others don't look to Ruth or any of the veterans. They look to [Lazzeri], and he never fails them."
> – Tommy Connolly, umpire

The Ultimate Season:			Career:		
Year/Team: 1929 NYY			Years: 14		
G:	147	HR: 18	G:	1740	HR: 178
AB:	545	RBI: 106	AB:	6297	RBI: 1194
R:	101	SB: 9	R:	986	SB: 148
H:	193	BB: 68	H:	1840	BB: 869
2B:	37	OPS: .991	2B:	334	OPS: .846
3B:	11	BA: .354	3B:	115	BA: .292

second base, he was one of the silent leaders of the Yankees. Over his 14 seasons, Lazzeri had a .292 batting average. He hit .300-plus five times and 100-plus RBI seven times. In 1929, Lazzeri batted a lofty .354 while banging out 193 hits and, in 1933, he played in the first-ever All-Star game. On May 24, 1936, Lazzeri was the first MLB player to hit two grand slams in one game, and his 11 RBI that day still stands as the American League record. Released by the Yanks after the 1937 season, Lazzeri was player-coach for the 1938 AL pennant winning Chicago Cubs and briefly played for the Dodgers and Giants before retiring in 1939. He then managed and played in the minors and ran a tavern in San Francisco. Sadly, Tony Lazzeri died in 1946, at 42 years old, after suffering a seizure. Anthony Michael Lazzeri was elected to the Hall of Fame in 1991.

Tales from Joe's Bat Rack

Tony Lazzeri is not only a Hall of Famer but, as a key member of the fabled 1927 New York Yankees team, his professional model bats are a necessary component for collectors trying to build a complete team set. The lineup, one that opposing pitchers feared throughout the league, is still considered to be one of the most potent in baseball history. Referred to as "Murderers' Row," the first six batters in the order featured Earle Combs, Mark Koenig, Babe Ruth, Lou Gehrig, Bob Meusel, and Lazzeri.

Just one year earlier, Lazzeri made his debut and signed an endorsement contract with H&B around the middle of the season. This does leave the possibility of unearthing a gamer featuring Lazzeri's name in block letters, but the overwhelming majority of the bats made for him during his playing days featured his facsimile signature. In addition to ordering a number of ash bats, which was the norm for the time, Lazzeri requested many hickory, brown hickory, and white hickory bats from his rookie year (1926) all the way through his final season (1939).

As one would expect, Lazzeri gamers are very tough to locate as are most bats from the period. Lazzeri did play for a few other teams at the end of his career, including the Chicago Cubs, Brooklyn Dodgers, and New York Giants, but bats that date to his playing days with the Yankees sell for a major premium due to the legendary status of that team. Those years were also Lazzeri's most effective, by far, as a hitter.

▲ Tony Lazzeri's 1928–30 H&B bat.

Eddie Mathews

★ ★ ★ ★ ★ ★ ★ ★ ★ ★ ★ ★ ★ ★ ★

of the competing league. Mathews played for the Braves for 15 years from 1952 to 1966, the sole player to see action in Boston, Milwaukee, and Atlanta. One of the hottest prospects in 1949, Mathews was signed out of Santa Barbara High School by the Boston Braves. He blasted 25 home runs in 1952 as a rookie but that was just a sign of things to come. The next year, the 21-year-old left-handed slugger led the National League with 47 homers while batting .302 with 135 RBI and was the MVP runner up. Mathews had that universal appeal right away, appearing on the cover of the very first issue of *Sports Illustrated* in August 1954.

A nine-time All-Star, Mathews paced the league with 46 homers in 1959. He clouted 30-plus home runs for nine consecutive seasons and 40-plus dingers four times. Opposing teams would execute the "Mathews shift" on him, a practice that is very common today but was novel at the time. When Hank Aaron joined the Braves in 1954 they were the most dominant tandem in MLB, combining for an amazing 863 home runs in their 13 years as teammates. Powered by Mathews and Aaron, the Braves reached the World Series in 1957 and 1958, playing the Yankees both times. Mathews was a significant force in the 1957 World Series. He hit a towering 10th-inning blast off Bob Grim in Game Four to beat the New York Yankees 7–5. In Game Five, Mathews scored the only run for a 1–0 win and, in Game Seven, he hit a two-run double to give the Braves the lead. Wait, in the bottom of the ninth in that same game, with the bases loaded, he also made a great backhanded scoop on

On the short list of greatest third basemen, Eddie Mathews was a guy who could field and hit with power; huge power, to the tune of 512 home runs. In fact, he was often compared to Mickey Mantle, his Hall of Fame contemporary and the big stick

★ ★ ★ ★ ★ ★ ★ ★ ★ ★

a Moose Skowron shot to finish off the Yanks for the Series championship.

Mathews hit his 500th home run in 1967 after being traded to the Houston Astros, becoming the seventh player to achieve the 500 home run mark. With his career in its twilight, he was traded to Detroit and retired as a member of the 1968 World Series Championship Tigers. Also very good defensively, Eddie Mathews retired with MLB records for games, assists, and chances at the hot corner. After his playing days, Mathews briefly managed the Braves and coached for a time. He passed away at the age of 69 in 2001. Edwin Lee Mathews was elected to the Hall of Fame in 1978, and rightfully joined the great third basemen in the hallowed halls of Cooperstown.

Tales from Joe's Bat Rack

Eddie Mathews was a player who announced his presence early and with authority, hitting 25 home runs his very first year and then 40 or more homers in each of his next three seasons. Mathews became a premier power hitter in the 1950s and his scorching start helped put him well on his way to membership in the 500 Home Run Club, ending with 512 in 1968. Along with fellow third baseman and Hall of Famer Mike Schmidt, Mathews is considered one of the greatest sluggers to ever play the position. When it comes to Mathews gamers, there are a few key characteristics to observe.

Most Mathews gamers have his primary uniform number "41" noted on the knob in black marker, at least after the practice became more common in the late-1950s. Mathews did wear two other numbers—"11" (Houston Astros) and

The Ultimate Season:			Career:		
Year/Team: 1953 MLN			Years: 17		
G:	157	HR: 47	G:	2391	HR: 512
AB:	579	RBI: 135	AB:	8537	RBI: 1453
R:	110	SB: 1	R:	1509	SB: 68
H:	175	BB: 99	H:	2315	BB: 1444
2B:	31	OPS: 1.033	2B:	354	OPS: .885
3B:	8	BA: .302	3B:	72	BA: .271

"7" (Detroit Tigers)—after his time with the Braves. In addition, some of his gamers exhibit a spiral taping pattern along the handle, but the vast majority of his gamers do not feature this form of handle preparation.

Heavy cleat marks along the barrel are another fingerprint of well-used Mathews gamers. Keep in mind that Mathews did use both Adirondack (block letter) and H&B (endorsement contract) bats regularly. Mathews signed an endorsement contract with H&B in 1951, prior to making his Major League debut in 1952. After the spring of 1961, Mathews was shipped flame-burned finish bats from the company, which can really enhance the eye-appeal for collectors.

> " *I think he was one of the greatest third basemen of all time. He had one of the sweetest swings I ever saw. There was only one Eddie Mathews.*"
> – Johnny Logan

▲ *Eddie Mathews' 1965–66 H&B bat.*

Don Mattingly

★ ★ ★ ★ ★ ★ ★ ★ ★ ★ ★

Diamond Images/Diamond Images Collection/Getty Images

A career Yankee, "Donnie Baseball," also known as "The Hit Man," was a leader in the clubhouse, serving as the Yankees captain from 1991 through 1995. Selected in the 19th round by the New York Yankees, Donald Arthur Mattingly made his MLB debut on September 8, 1982, but didn't get productive playing time until the next year. He broke out in 1984, leading the American League with his .343 batting average, 207 hits and 44 doubles, while slamming 23 home runs and making his first All-Star appearance. Named 1985 AL MVP and MLB Player of the Year with 35 home runs, 211 hits, 145 RBI, and .324 BA, Mattingly actually had a better season in 1986 batting .352 and pacing the league with 238 hits and 53 doubles.

Although passed over by Cooperstown so far, with his .307 lifetime batting average, 222 home runs and 2,153 hits, he is hard to ignore. Defensively, at first base, Mattingly led the league in fielding percentage seven times. The six-time All-Star won nine Gold Gloves to go along with his three Silver Slugger Awards. For a large part of his career, Mattingly was dogged by back problems which impacted his at-bats periodically.

A favorite with Yankees fans, Mattingly gave them something to remember in the 1995 ALDS when the Yanks won the wild card. It was the last season of his career and Mattingly made the most of his only postseason appearance batting .417 with six RBI and one home run in the Series against the Seattle Mariners. That dinger was a dramatic go-ahead home run in the bottom of the sixth inning of Game Two. Yankees fans celebrated by littering the field with debris which prompted the Mariners to walk off the field until order was restored. The game resumed and was a real nailbiter, going 15 innings, but the Yankees prevailed.

After retiring as a player, Mattingly was an excellent batting coach and, later on, bench coach in the Yankees organization.

Donnie Baseball

★ ★ ★ ★ ★ ★ ★ ★ ★ ★

He took over the reins of the Los Angeles Dodgers in 2011 and led them to a winning record over five years before moving on to the Miami Marlins where, at the time of this writing, he is still managing.

The Ultimate Season:			Career:		
Year/Team: 1986 NYY			Years: 14		
G:	162	HR: 31	G:	1785	HR: 222
AB:	677	RBI: 113	AB:	7003	RBI: 1099
R:	117	SB: 0	R:	1007	SB: 14
H:	238	BB: 53	H:	2153	BB: 588
2B:	53	OPS: .967	2B:	442	OPS: .830
3B:	2	BA: .352	3B:	20	BA: .307

Tales from Joe's Bat Rack

Don Mattingly may not be a Hall of Famer, but he is certainly treated like royalty by the New York Yankees faithful and many collectors. For a time, Mattingly was one of the top all-around hitters in baseball, winning an American League batting title in 1984 and being named AL MVP in 1985. As a result, his professional model bats are very popular, with demand exceeding a number of Hall of Famers from the same era. Mattingly preferred Louisville Slugger bats, but he also occasionally used Rawlings/Adirondack, Cooper, and Worth bats. Most of his Louisville Sluggers are found with his facsimile signature as he signed an endorsement contract with the company, but some block letter examples do exist. Mattingly did order a decent amount of bats with darker finishes, but most of the bats collectors will see are of the natural color variety.

Well-used Mattingly gamers often have a fairly heavy coating of pine tar on the handle. However, it is not a consistent coating from the base of the handle towards the center brand; instead, you will find sporadic remnants clustered across the entire handle. Once in a while, you might also find a Mattingly gamer with a tape application, tape ring near the base of the handle, or shaved handle, but this was not an extremely common practice for him.

Mattingly's primary uniform number "23" is often marked on the knobs or barrel ends of many of his gamers, but keep in mind that he did wear number "46" during his first couple of seasons with the Yankees. One very interesting practice of Mattingly's was to intentionally mark the knobs of his bats with the wrong uniform number to help prevent his bats from being stolen from the clubhouse, which was happening quite a bit during his prime years. Occasionally, Mattingly would place retired Yankees numbers like "3" (Babe Ruth), "5" (Joe DiMaggio) and "7" (Mickey Mantle) on the knobs of his bats in part as a tribute to these legends and to also confuse those trying to acquire one of his true gamers.

> " *I'm glad I don't have to face that guy every day. He [Mattingly] has that look that few hitters have. I don't know if it's his stance, his eyes or what, but you can tell he means business.*" – Dwight Gooden

▲ Don Mattingly's 1985 Louisville Slugger bat.

Willie McCovey

★ ★ ★ ★ ★ ★ ★ ★ ★ ★ ★

In a career that spanned four decades (1959–1980), McCovey batted .270, with 1,555 RBI, and 2,211 hits. He led the National League in home runs three times, RBI twice, and he still holds the NL record for grand slams with 18. When he retired, his 521 career home runs were tops for left-handed power hitters in National League history. Defensively, "Stretch" McCovey was a very good first baseman. He never won a World Series but he did get to face the Yankees in the thrilling 1962 Fall Classic. In Game Seven, the score was 0–1 in the bottom of the ninth. There were two outs and two men on base when McCovey hit a rocket to second base that should have won the Series. Unfortunately, a great snag by second baseman Bobby Richardson preserved the win for the Yanks.

The original National League Bash Brothers, Willie McCovey and Willie Mays formed one of the most prolific offensive tandems in history. The 1-2 punch of McCovey and Mays was downright scary. Big, strong, and intimidating, McCovey caused many a National League pitcher to have a sleepless night before facing him. Signed by the Giants in 1955, the 17-year-old prospect was sent to the minors for seasoning. Willie Lee McCovey finally debuted at the end of July 1959 and did not disappoint, going 4-for-4 with two RBI right out of the gate. For the rest of the season he batted .354 and smacked 13 home runs in 192 at-bats, good for Rookie of the Year honors.

A six-time All-Star, McCovey clubbed two home runs in the 1969 midsummer classic for MVP honors. That year, he led the league with 45 homers and 126 RBI, while batting .320 to win the NL Most Valuable Player Award. McCovey spent most of his 22-year career in San Francisco. Traded to the San Diego Padres in 1974, he played briefly for Oakland in 1976 before returning to the Giants to hit .280 with 28 home runs in 1977, earning NL Comeback Player of the Year distinction. McCovey was always beloved in San Francisco. At the old Candlestick Park, fans stood behind the right-field bleachers in hopes of catching a Willie McCovey rocket. At the new AT&T Park, the body of water behind right field

was named McCovey Cove, and a statue of the slugger was placed nearby in 2003. On game day, fans wait in kayaks and boats, hoping to catch a home run ball. The Giants retired McCovey's uniform number "44" and instituted the Willie Mac Award in 1980. This annual award goes to the Giants' player, chosen by his teammates, who most emulates McCoveys "spirit and leadership." Inducted into the Hall of Fame in 1986, McCovey still works with the Giants in an advisory capacity.

The Ultimate Season:				Career:			
Year/Team: 1969 SFG				Years: 22			
G:	149	HR:	45	G:	2588	HR:	521
AB:	491	RBI:	126	AB:	8197	RBI:	1555
R:	101	SB:	0	R:	1229	SB:	26
H:	157	BB:	121	H:	2211	BB:	1345
2B:	26	OPS:	1.108	2B:	353	OPS:	.889
3B:	2	BA:	.320	3B:	46	BA:	.270

Tales from Joe's Bat Rack

Despite having immense raw power, finishing his career with 521 home runs, Willie McCovey's professional model bats are amongst the more affordable gamers on the 500 Home Run Club list. Perhaps this was a result of playing in the shadow of one of the true icons of the game—Willie Mays. Like his former teammate, McCovey used both H&B (block letter) and Adirondack (endorsement contract) bats during his

career, alternating between the two bat brands throughout his playing days. The H&B bats are found with his last name only, which date to the first half of his career, and with his full name in block letters from the latter stages of his playing days.

It is very common to find his uniform number "44" marked on the knobs of his gamers in black marker. Keep in mind that the intimidating slugger wore the same number his entire career. You may encounter McCovey bats that feature his nickname "Stretch" on the knob, but they are rare. In addition, McCovey had some of his bats manufactured with what is referred to as a flat knob instead of the more typical round-edge knobs ordered by most other players.

For H&B bats, this ordering pattern started in the spring of 1972 and lasted until the end of his career. The special knob request was not made on every order, but a substantial number of McCovey bats were manufactured with this distinct trait. The slugging first baseman was known for using moderate amounts of pine tar in preparing his bats for use, but usually the application was not heavy.

> *"McCovey didn't hit any cheap ones. When he belts a home run, he does it with such authority it seems like an act of God. You can't cry about it."*
> *– Walter Alston*

▲ *Willie McCovey's 1969–72 H&B bat.*

Mark McGwire

★ ★ ★ ★ ★ ★ ★ ★ ★ ★ ★ ★

Icon Sportswire

tripper are etched in baseball lore. All season long, they chased history.

The road show came to a wondrous climax in St. Louis as the Cards hosted the Cubbies, with McGwire and Sosa on the same field battling for legendary status. On September 7, McGwire hit his 61st home run while Sosa stood at 58 dingers. On September 8, 1998, in the fourth inning, McGwire hit a 341-foot laser beam line drive that just cleared the left-

Mark McGwire, the brawny, redheaded Oakland A's and St. Louis Cardinals super slugger, was one of the most entertaining baseball players to watch—and that was before the game even started. His tape measure batting practice blasts thrilled fans of all ages and skyrocketed him to 1987 Rookie of the Year honors and, eleven years later, to the single-season home run record. It was in 1998 that McGwire, playing for St. Louis, and Sammy Sosa, the incredibly popular Cub, took fans on a home run joy ride chasing Roger Maris' hallowed record of 61 home runs set in 1961. McGwire and Sosa were not only great power hitters. They were true ambassadors of the game. The images of Sosa joyously leaping after a home run and McGwire lovingly hugging his son after a round-

field fence. He had done it, home run number 62. McGwire's exuberant trot and hug-fest at home plate was silver screen worthy. He then took it to another level, going into the seats and sharing the moment with the family of Roger Maris, as if to give the great Number "9" the credit and joy that eluded him during his bittersweet chase of Babe Ruth's record 37 years earlier.

McGwire finished that 1998 season with 70 home runs, but the record would last just three seasons as Barry Bonds clubbed 73 in 2001. Mark McGwire's link to the use of performance enhancing drugs is the subject of debate, but his numbers make him one of the elite sluggers in baseball history. In 16 seasons (1986–2001), McGwire hit 583

★ ★ ★ ★ ★ ★ ★ ★ ★ ★ ★ ★

home runs and drove in 1,414 runs. His career slugging percentage was .588 and his fielding percentage was .993. He was a World Series champion, 12-time All-Star, and three-time Silver Slugger. Mark David McGwire led his league in slugging four times, home runs four times, and at-bats per home run seven times. He brought fans into the ballpark and entertained them with a prodigiously powerful performance.

The Ultimate Season:				Career:			
Year/Team: 1998 STL				Years: 16			
G:	155	HR:	70	G:	1874	HR:	583
AB:	509	RBI:	147	AB:	6187	RBI:	1414
R:	130	SB:	1	R:	1167	SB:	12
H:	152	BB:	162	H:	1626	BB:	1317
2B:	21	OPS:	1.222	2B:	252	OPS:	.982
3B:	0	BA:	.299	3B:	6	BA:	.263

Tales from Joe's Bat Rack

During the late 1990s and early 2000s, there was no professional model bat from the modern era more desirable than one used by Mark McGwire. While the demand for his bats has softened a bit, McGwire gamers are still an important piece of a comprehensive bat collection. McGwire was one of the most consistent players in baseball when it came to the bats he used. Early in his career, McGwire did use some Louisville Sluggers (block letter), but he clearly preferred Rawlings/Adirondack bats for the majority of his career—he used them from his rookie-era until his playing days were over.

McGwire wore number "25" for his entire career; however, it is important to note that while it is not uncommon to find his uniform number noted on bats used during his Oakland A's days, the knobs of his bats were not marked with his number as a member of the St. Louis Cardinals. You may also see "MAC" written on some of his early A's gamers.

McGwire did use pine tar and the pattern is fairly unique. On well-used gamers, particularly from his last few seasons with

Oakland and well into his St. Louis days, you will often see a concentrated coating of tar on the upper handle, towards the center brand. You will also see remnants of tar and grip marks from his batting gloves near the lower portion of the handle. Even though his single-season home run record was broken, bats used during the historic 1998 home run chase tend to sell for a premium. It is important to note, however, that a lot of unused bats escaped from the clubhouse during that time. They are real, professional model bats but often do not possess the proper characteristics for well-used McGwire gamers.

"When he hits line drives, get the family of four out of the left-field seats before they get killed."
– Craig Biggio

▲ Mark McGwire's 1998 Rawlings bat.

Johnny Mize

★ ★ ★ ★ ★ ★ ★ ★ ★ ★ ★

Icon Sportswire

Piedmont College while attending high school. The 17-year-old phenom was signed in 1930 by Branch Rickey's St. Louis Cardinals but languished in the minors until 1936. In his six seasons with the Cards, Mize batted .336 and slammed 158 home runs. He won the batting title in 1939 with his .349 average, and led the National League in 1940 with 137 RBI and 43 dingers, a St. Louis record that stood until Mark McGwire broke it in 1998.

Rickey traded Mize to the New York Giants where he batted .305 with a league-leading 110 RBI in 1942. He missed three seasons while serving in the U.S. Navy in World War II but returned in good form in 1946, batting .337 and losing the home run title to Pittsburgh's Ralph Kiner by one homer. In an epic rivalry, Mize and Kiner both swatted 51 homers in 1947, tying for the crown and, in 1948, they tied again with 40 homers apiece. Sold to the Yankees in August 1949, the 36-year-old Mize contributed to their World Series win over Brooklyn. Although a part-time first baseman and pinch hitter, Mize was an integral part of four more Yankees championships (1950–1953) and batted .400 with six RBI and three home runs in the 1952 Fall Classic.

Even though he missed three prime years to the war effort, Mize carved out impressive statistics over his 15-year career. The 10-time All-Star and four-time National League home run champ batted a lifetime .312 with 2,011 hits and 359 homers. A skilled hitter, Mize never stepped out of the box between pitches and is said to be the first to smear mud under his eyes to cut glare. His outstanding accomplishments include hitting

Affectionately known as "The Big Cat," Johnny Mize had a terrific run as a power hitter and slick-fielding first baseman. Interestingly, Mize was a distant cousin of Ty Cobb, and his second cousin married Babe Ruth. The big lefty with the sweet swing from Demorest, Georgia, actually played varsity baseball for

★ ★ ★ ★ ★ ★ ★ ★ ★ ★ ★ ★ ★

> "Remember how he reacted when brushed back? He'd just lean back on his left foot, bend his body back and let the pitch go by. Then he'd lean back into the batter's box and resume his stance, as graceful as a big cat."
> – Stan Musial

The Ultimate Season:			
Year/Team: 1947 NYG			
G:	154	HR:	51
AB:	586	RBI:	138
R:	137	SB:	2
H:	177	BB:	74
2B:	26	OPS:	.998
3B:	2	BA:	.302

Career:			
Years: 15			
G:	1884	HR:	359
AB:	6443	RBI:	1337
R:	1118	SB:	28
H:	2011	BB:	856
2B:	367	OPS:	.959
3B:	83	BA:	.312

three home runs in a game six times, a Major League record. Mize made MLB history with those 51 dingers in 1947. He was the first player to hit 50 or more home runs in a season while striking out less than 50 times.

In addition to business interests, Mize coached in the major and minor leagues after retiring in 1953. Although overshadowed during his playing days by greats of his era like Williams and DiMaggio, Mize is still considered one of the best hitters of the 1940s. John Robert Mize was elected to Cooperstown in 1981 and to the St. Louis Cardinals Hall of Fame in 2014.

Tales from Joe's Bat Rack

When it comes to professional model bats used by "The Big Cat," Johnny Mize, there is one key characteristic to look for. Mize would often employ a spiral, overlapping taping application along the lower part of the handle to enhance his grip. The tape application does not extend beyond the portion of the handle where someone would place their hands, and evidence of this pattern can be seen in various vintage images of Mize with bat in hand. Mize's bat of choice was H&B, and the slugging first baseman signed an endorsement contract with the company prior to making his debut in 1936. This means that all of the bats Mize ordered at the Major League level featured his facsimile signature on the barrel. Most of the bats Mize ordered from the company were made of ash, but a few hickory bats were shipped to him over the years as well.

Mize changed teams three times and his uniform number on four separate occasions. He wore "10," "15," "3," and "36" during his career. Most of the known Mize gamers do not feature his uniform numbers on the knob, which is primarily due to the fact that he played during a period when that practice was not common. Bats used during his brief run with the New York Yankees (1949–1953) tend to sell for a premium since they won five consecutive World Series titles, even though his prime years were split between the St. Louis Cardinals and New York Giants. This is the period when Mize captured a batting title (1939) and four National League home run crowns. Had Mize not lost significant time serving in the military, his career numbers would look even more impressive.

▲ *Johnny Mize's 1939–42 H&B bat.*

Paul Molitor

★ ★ ★ ★ ★ ★ ★ ★ ★ ★ ★ ★

Jamie Squire/Getty Images Sport Collection/Getty Images

Although they lost the Series to the Cardinals, Molitor garnered a record five hits in Game One and batted .355 with 5 runs and 11 hits in the seven-game contest.

Plagued by injuries throughout his career, Molitor played third base, second base, and occasionally first base and shortstop. The Brewers used him as designated hitter when recovering from injury, and it was as DH that Molitor flirted with baseball history in 1987, exciting fans with his 39-game hitting streak, the fourth longest in American League history. That year, Molitor batted a career-high .353 with 45 steals and led the American League with 114 runs and 41 doubles.

A smooth swinging contact hitter with speed and savvy on the basepaths, Paul Leo Molitor crafted his Hall of Fame career primarily with the Milwaukee Brewers and later with the Toronto Blue Jays and the Minnesota Twins. The Brewers signed the young University of Minnesota phenom in 1977 and put him in the starting lineup in 1978. The right-handed leadoff hitter batted .273 with 142 hits, 45 RBI, and 30 steals, which was good for runner up in Rookie of the Year voting. Nicknamed "The Ignitor" for his skill at the leadoff position, Molitor batted .302 with 201 hits and a league-leading 136 runs in 1982 helping the "Harvey's Wallbangers" Brewers to their first-ever pennant win and World Series appearance.

After 15 years with the Brewers, Molitor was assigned to Toronto in 1993. The 36-year-old DH had an immediate impact batting .332 with 22 home runs and 22 stolen bases while leading the league with 211 hits. The Blue Jays won the World Series that year and Molitor batted .500 with 10 runs, 12 hits, 2 home runs, and 8 RBI for Series MVP honors.

The Minnesota native moved on to play out his career with his home team, the Twins. As DH he continued to play a key role batting .341 with a league-leading 225 hits in 1996 and .305 with 164 hits in 1997. It was as a Twin that Molitor slammed a fifth-inning triple off Kansas City's Jose Rosado on September 16, 1996, to join the exclusive 3,000 Hit Club.

★ ★ ★ ★ ★ ★ ★ ★ ★ ★ ★ ★ ★

He retired after the 1998 season with a career .306 batting average, 504 stolen bases, 605 doubles, and 3,319 hits. The seven-time All-Star garnered four Silver Slugger Awards and led the league in runs scored, singles, hits, triples, and doubles at various points in his 21-year career. Consistent and dependable, he batted .300 or better twelve seasons. After his playing days, Molitor stayed close to the game as bench coach and roving minor-league coach for the Twins and batting coach for the Mariners before assuming the reins as manager of the Twins in 2015. He was elected to the Hall of Fame in 2004, his first year of eligibility.

The Ultimate Season:			Career:		
Year/Team: 1993 TOR			Years: 21		
G:	160	HR: 22	G:	2683	HR: 234
AB:	636	RBI: 111	AB:	10835	RBI: 1307
R:	121	SB: 22	R:	1782	SB: 504
H:	211	BB: 77	H:	3319	BB: 1094
2B:	37	OPS: .911	2B:	605	OPS: .817
3B:	5	BA: .332	3B:	114	BA: .306

Tales from Joe's Bat Rack

Paul Molitor professional model bats remain relatively affordable compared to many of his fellow Hall of Famers who played during the same era. Part of that affordability is a product of Molitor never having the chance to play for a big market team. The other part is due to the nature of how this 3,000 Hit Club member slowly built his case for the Hall over time. Molitor may never have been regarded as the best player in the game in any one season, but his consistent excellence was evident during his 21-year career. Molitor did use H&B/Louisville Slugger bats after signing an endorsement contract with the company (1978) like most other players from the 1970s and 1980s, but later on he seemed to prefer Cooper bats more than any other brand. A large number of his bats were of the two-toned variety.

Sometimes, Molitor would order bats with flared knobs, a rarity in the post-1980 era. This is similar in style to many of the Roberto Clemente bats that you see from the 1960s until the end of his final playing days. One characteristic that seems to be fairly consistent throughout Molitor's career is the marking of his uniform number on the knobs of his bats. Keep in mind that while Molitor wore number "4" for his run with the Milwaukee Brewers, he also wore "19" during his time with the Toronto Blue Jays from 1993 to 1995 and later went back to "4" with the Minnesota Twins. You may also find a small number notation added to the knob, which Molitor applied to help track things such as bat quality and the order he wished to use his gamers in. Molitor was occasionally known for applying a moderate amount of pine tar on the handles of his bats; yet the application is rarely heavy.

> " *He had tremendous instincts and you could see right away he was a talented athlete. Not only physically, but mentally too.*" – George Bamberger

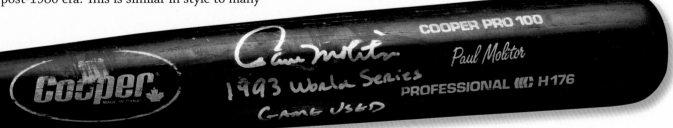

▲ *Paul Molitor's Cooper bat used in the 1993 World Series.*

Joe Morgan

★ ★ ★ ★ ★ ★ ★ ★ ★ ★ ★ ★

Joe Morgan may have been the most frightening 5-foot, 7-inch, and 160-pound man in the history of sports. With a body that should have been riding Triple Crown winners, Morgan played against them and won more often than he lost. The Oakland, California, product broke into the big leagues in 1963 with the Houston Colt .45s and remained with them for 10 years as they transitioned to the Astros. Morgan would return to Houston in 1980 and later played for the Giants, Phillies, and A's, but make no mistake, he was inducted into the Baseball Hall of Fame in 1990 because of his eight seasons as the head gasket in Cincinnati's "Big Red Machine" (1972–1979). His Cincy stint tallied 152 home runs, 612 RBI, 220 doubles, 1,155 hits, 406 steals, a .288 batting average, eight consecutive All-Star appearances, and MVP awards in 1975 and 1976.

Morgan hit over .300 only twice in his 22-year career, but he led his league in OBP four times and was a pitcher's nightmare. He led the National League in walks four times and drew over 100 free passes eight times—fouling off good pitches and using his keen eye to lay off bad pitches. Morgan was all business, holding his bat high over his left shoulder and then violently pumping his left arm as if loading a lethal weapon. He was also a terrific second baseman, winning five consecutive Gold Gloves from 1973 to 1977. Morgan had blinding speed on the basepaths and the intelligence to know how to use it. He stole no less than 40 bases each year from 1969 to 1977 and 689 for his career. For a guy who usually hit near the top of the order, Morgan's 1,133 RBI are outstanding. Of course, it did not hurt that, many times, the guy hitting in front of him was Pete Rose, the all-time hits leader.

Morgan played in 50 postseason games and four World Series, none bigger than the seminal 1975 tilt with the Red Sox. While Game Six of that series is viewed as an all-time classic, it was the Reds' Game Seven win that gave the Queen City its first world title since 1940.

★ ★ ★ ★ ★ ★ ★ ★ ★ ★ ★ ★

"Pitchers don't mind me stealing a base or driving in a run with a single or a double. But I see it in their eyes when I'm circling the bases on a home run. They don't like a little man taking them downtown."
– Joe Morgan

The Ultimate Season:				Career:			
Year/Team: 1976 CIN				Years: 22			
G:	141	HR:	27	G:	2649	HR:	268
AB:	472	RBI:	111	AB:	9277	RBI:	1133
R:	113	SB:	60	R:	1650	SB:	689
H:	151	BB:	114	H:	2517	BB:	1865
2B:	30	OPS:	1.020	2B:	449	OPS:	.819
3B:	5	BA:	.320	3B:	96	BA:	.271

Boston jumped out to a lead in that final game, but the Reds rallied and the man they call "Little Joe" stepped to the plate in the top of the ninth. Boston's rookie pitcher Jim Burton looked scared and justifiably so. Morgan pumped that left arm and delivered the Series-winning single.

The 10-time All-Star wrapped up his career in Oakland in 1984 and soon started a second career as a popular sports broadcaster on ABC, NBC, and ESPN. Joe Leonard Morgan also became involved in numerous charitable organizations including the Baseball Assistance Team which helps former ballplayers with financial and medical needs.

Tales from Joe's Bat Rack

Based upon his all-time ranking at the second base position, you could argue that Joe Morgan professional model bats are amongst the most undervalued on the entire Hall of Fame list. They are not only some of the most affordable gamers from his era, they are some of the most inexpensive Hall of Famer bats of all time. While bats used during his Houston Colt .45s and Astros days are very scarce, Morgan gamers used during the "Big Red Machine" era usually sell for a premium. It is not uncommon to find Morgan bats with his uniform number marked on the knob or the barrel end in either black or red marker from his Cincinnati Reds days.

Some Morgan bats feature a large, more traditionally-sized uniform number that virtually covers the surface area of the knob, but collectors will often encounter other gamers that possess a relatively small one. Keep in mind that while his uniform number was "8" for most of his career, Morgan did wear numbers "12," "35," and "18" during the early portion of his career with Houston.

On well-used gamers, you will frequently see a concentrated application of pine tar near the upper handle and center brand area, but Morgan's overall use of the gripping substance was rarely heavy in nature. Finally, it was very apparent that Morgan's bat of choice was H&B/Louisville Slugger. Morgan signed an endorsement contract with the company in his very first year, 1963, which continued through 1984, his last year.

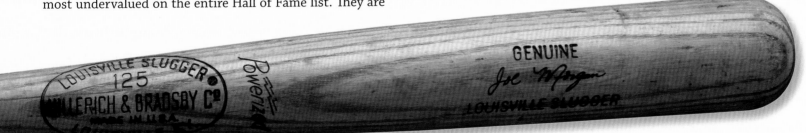

▲ *Joe Morgan's 1965–68 H&B bat.*

Eddie Murray

★ ★ ★ ★ ★ ★ ★ ★ ★ ★ ★

Ronald C. Modra/Sports Imagery/Getty Images Sport Collection/Getty Images

If ever there was a player who followed the Teddy Roosevelt credo of "Speak softly and carry a big stick," it was Eddie Murray. Definitely more action than words, the silent slugger and longtime Oriole crushed the baseball consistently. A 1973 third-round draft pick, Murray was a star almost immediately, winning the American League Rookie of the Year award in 1977 with 27 homers, 88 RBI, and a .283 batting average. Murray struck out 104 times that season and 97 times in 1978, but he developed into a patient hitter, never striking out more than 90 times in a season again.

The switch-hitting Murray led the league in homers just once, hitting 22 in the strike-shortened 1981 season, but he hit over 20 dingers sixteen times, the last at age 40 in 1996. All told, Murray hit 504 home runs and added an impressive 1,917 RBI, good for 10th all time. His 19 grand slams are fourth on the all-time list. In addition to his immense power, Murray was an excellent hitter. Seven times he batted over .300, including a career best .330 with the Dodgers in 1990. The eight-time All-Star, three-time Silver Slugger winner, and three-time Gold Glove winner at first base never won an MVP award, but he finished in the top five in voting six times.

Inducted into the Hall of Fame in 2003, Eddie Clarence Murray's magical moments are many. He played on some terrific teams in Baltimore, but won just one World Series. In Game Five of that 1983 Fall Classic vs. Philadelphia, Murray put on a show for the ages. He smacked two home runs off Charlie Hudson, the first a solo shot that gave the Orioles a 1–0 lead, and the second, a fourth-inning, 425-foot, two-run blast that hit the Veterans Stadium scoreboard and sealed the victory and the Series in five games.

After 12 years and a productive 1988 season, Murray was unceremoniously traded to his native Los Angeles. He continued to put up impressive numbers with the Dodgers, Mets, and Indians into his early 40s. In 1995, he powered the Indians to the World Series with three postseason home runs and, in a brief return to Baltimore in 1996, he batted .400 in the ALDS. Murray left the game in 1997 having collected

★ ★ ★ ★ ★ ★ ★ ★ ★ ★ ★ ★ ★

> "*For a long time in his career, his average was almost the same right or left. You'd look at the numbers and say, 'Damn, there's a reason why they call him 'Steady Eddie.''*"
> – *Elrod Hendricks*

The Ultimate Season:				Career:			
Year/Team: 1982 BAL				Years: 21			
G:	151	HR:	32	G:	3026	HR:	504
AB:	550	RBI:	110	AB:	11336	RBI:	1917
R:	87	SB:	7	R:	1627	SB:	110
H:	174	BB:	70	H:	3255	BB:	1333
2B:	30	OPS:	.940	2B:	560	OPS:	.836
3B:	1	BA:	.316	3B:	35	BA:	.287

3,255 hits—the third player to reach both the 3,000-hit and 500-home run milestones. He also retired as the all-time leader in sacrifice flies. Over his 21-year career, he played 2,413 games at first base, more than anyone in history. A Baltimore legend, Eddie Murray will be remembered as one of the great hitters in baseball history.

Tales from Joe's Bat Rack

Eddie Murray professional model bats can certainly have their share of character. For most of his career, Murray used H&B/Louisville Slugger bats after signing an endorsement contract with the company long before making his Major League debut, with early MLB gamers dating to the H&B labeling period of 1977–1979. That said, he occasionally used other bat brands such as Rawlings/Adirondack and Cooper bats as well.

The knobs on Murray gamers will usually feature his uniform number "33," but often times, the style is very distinct. Some Murray gamers have his number noted with a bright-colored marker, while outlined in black. On other bats, Murray's uniform number is marked in a more traditional manner. Collectors may encounter Murray gamers with the uniform number also marked on the barrel end, but bats with this feature are less common.

In addition, Murray would often employ a very identifiable taping pattern to the handle for grip. Murray would place several very small, thick ringlets of tape along the handle with slight gaps in between. Collectors will usually see between four to six ringlets applied, slightly spread apart in varying formations. This taping application is very unique to Murray, and while he did not use this method all the time, the existence of the pattern provides a fingerprint of his use.

Keep in mind that, like fellow switch-hitting Hall of Famer Mickey Mantle, most of the contact marks are often located on the right barrel where a left-handed hitter would usually strike the ball. This is simply because there are more right-handed pitchers in the league, which causes switch-hitters to bat from the left side. Finally, large amounts of cleat marks are often found along the barrel of heavily-used Murray gamers. As one of the few members of both the 500 Home Run Club and 3,000 Hit Club, Murray bats are highly collectible.

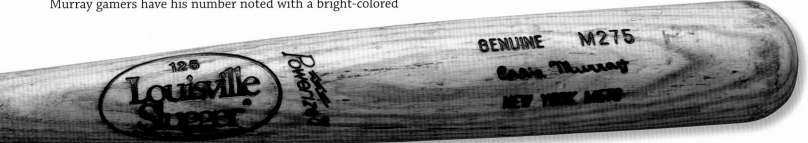

▲ *Eddie Murray's 1992–93 Louisville Slugger bat.*

David Ortiz

★ ★ ★ ★ ★ ★ ★ ★ ★ ★ ★ ★

Icon Sportswire

walk-off single in Game Five to earn the ALCS MVP Award. He went on to bat .308 in the World Series against the St. Louis Cardinals, helping the Red Sox to their first championship in 86 years. In 2007, the powerful slugger batted .332 with 35 home runs during the season and batted .333 in the World Series vs. the Colorado Rockies. In 2013, "Big Papi" was a one-man wrecking crew, batting .385

Some baseball purists argue there is no such thing as a clutch hitter. Bobby Thomson's "Shot Heard 'Round the World," Carleton Fisk's iconic 1975 World Series home run, Joe Carter's 1993 Series walk-off homer. Were they clutch hitters? Some argue yes, some argue no. If the whole concept of a clutch hitter is real, look no further than David Ortiz as the greatest of them all.

After six seasons with the Minnesota Twins, Dominican Republic native David Americo Ortiz joined the Boston Red Sox in 2003 and quickly became an integral part of the team. The designated hitter and occasional first baseman had a slew of game-winning hits during the 2004 season and slammed a 10th-inning walk-off home run in the ALDS over the Anaheim Angels to propel the Sox to the American League Championship Series. In the ALCS vs. the Yankees, Ortiz blasted a two-run walk-off homer in Game Four and a

and socking two home runs in the ALDS and, in Game Two of the ALCS, Ortiz hit a grand slam off Detroit's Joaquin Benoit in the bottom of the eighth inning that propelled the Red Sox to a dramatic come from behind victory. Against the Cardinals in the World Series he batted an amazing .688 with two home runs to win the Series MVP Award.

In 2005, Red Sox owner John Henry called Ortiz the greatest clutch hitter in the team's history. That year alone, he hammered 20 home runs that either put the Red Sox ahead or tied a game. A 10-time All-Star, three-time World Series Champ, six-time Silver Slugger Award winner, and member of the 500 Home Run Club, Ortiz has become the face of the Red Sox. With his gregarious personality and charitable work, Ortiz is a true ambassador for the game. He spends many hours overseeing his David Ortiz Children's

★ ★ ★ ★ ★ ★ ★ ★ ★ ★

Fund and is a frequent presence at Boston's Jimmy Fund Clinic, visiting children with cancer. Beloved in Boston, Ortiz will be remembered for his inspirational pregame speech that brought the city of Boston together after the Boston Marathon bombing in April 2013. He said, "Boston is our [expletive] city. Nobody is going to dictate our freedom. Stay strong." Popular throughout baseball, Ortiz announced his retirement in late 2015 and, at 40 years old, put up one of his best career seasons in his 2016 farewell year, batting .315 with 38 homers, 48 doubles, and 127 RBI.

The Ultimate Season: Year/Team: 2006 BOS		Career: Years: 20	
G: 151	HR: 54	G: 2408	HR: 541
AB: 558	RBI: 137	AB: 8640	RBI: 1768
R: 115	SB: 1	R: 1419	SB: 17
H: 160	BB: 119	H: 2472	BB: 1319
2B: 29	OPS: 1.049	2B: 632	OPS: 1.021
3B: 2	BA: .287	3B: 19	BA: .286

Tales from Joe's Bat Rack

David Ortiz professional model bats, like the man himself, have become a collector favorite over the years. As "Big Papi" rose to stardom, putting up monster power numbers as a member of the Boston Red Sox, his bats became a hot commodity. Ortiz may go down in history as the greatest Designated Hitter of all time, giving him the chance to possibly become the first DH to enter the Hall of Fame. Once he became a member of the 500 Home Run Club in 2015, the gregarious slugger became a necessary component to any collection founded on the exclusive group. Sprinkle in the fact that Ortiz helped break the "Curse of the Bambino" by helping bring three World Series titles to Boston, and one could say that his gamers have a lot going for them.

Ortiz used various bat brands during his career such as Louisville Slugger and Marucci, but he seems to have used Rawlings/Adirondack bats more than any other brand. On well-used Ortiz gamers, it is not uncommon to find a host of different tape applications placed along the handles of his bats. The tape used can vary in color and style. Ortiz was also an avid user of pine tar and Mota stick, sometimes using a combination of both to enhance his grip. His primary uniform number "34" is usually found noted or stamped on the knob. Sometimes, Ortiz's number appears on the barrel end as well. Keep in mind that for several seasons, as a member of the Minnesota Twins, Ortiz's number was "27."

"He's bulletproof, as far as I'm concerned. Whether there's a left-hander on the mound or a right-hander on the mound, he beats us up pretty good."
– Joe Torre, Yankees manager

▲ David Ortiz's 2014 Marucci bat used for career home run #443.

Pee Wee Reese

★ ★ ★ ★ ★ ★ ★ ★ ★ ★ ★

Rogers Photo Archive/Getty Images Sport Collection/Getty Images

Dodgers known as "Dem Bums." He joined the team in 1940 and, amazingly, the "Lovable Losers" won the National League pennant in 1941, their first flag in 21 years. However, the team struggled while Reese and several teammates served Uncle Sam in World War II for three years. Branch Rickey came on board as manager bringing new talent to the team including Duke Snider and Gil Hodges. In 1947, Rickey turned baseball upside down when he brought in Jackie Robinson, the first African-American player in MLB.

Raised in Louisville, Kentucky, "The Little Colonel" rose above his segregated southern upbringing to lead by example and befriend Jackie Robinson. Besides helping to smooth Robinson's entry into the all-white MLB, Reese and Robinson bonded into a stellar double-play tandem with Reese at shortstop and Robinson on second. The team jelled and soon became the contenders known as the Boys of Summer, winning six pennants in a 10-year span. Each time, they dueled the dreaded crosstown Yankees for the title and finally thrilled loyal fans with a World Series win in 1955.

A 10-time All-Star, Reese was a skilled bunter and hit-and-run guy. He led the league with 104 walks in 1947, 132 runs in 1949, 30 steals in 1952, and 15 sacrifice hits in 1953.

Reese made history on May 21, 1952. He actually had three at-bats in the first inning. With a walk, a single, and a second walk, Reese reached base safely three times in one inning which set a National League record. The Dodgers pummeled the Reds with 15 runs that inning and finished with a 19–1 win. Defensively, Reese's top years were in the 1940s when he led the league in assists, putouts, double plays turned, range factor, and fielding percentage.

The slick-fielding shortstop and beloved captain of the remarkable "Boys of Summer" Brooklyn Dodgers teams of the 1950s, Pee Wee Reese was known for his leadership. Drafted by the Red Sox in 1939, Reese was quickly traded to the perennial cellar dweller

The Little Colonel

★ ★ ★ ★ ★ ★ ★ ★ ★ ★ ★ ★

> *"If I had my career to play over, one thing I'd do differently is swing more. Those 1,200 walks I got, nobody remembers them."* – Pee Wee Reese

The Ultimate Season:				Career:			
Year/Team: 1954 BRO				Years: 16			
G:	141	HR:	10	G:	2166	HR:	126
AB:	554	RBI:	69	AB:	8058	RBI:	885
R:	98	SB:	8	R:	1338	SB:	232
H:	171	BB:	90	H:	2170	BB:	1210
2B:	35	OPS:	1.049	2B:	330	OPS:	.932
3B:	8	BA:	.309	3B:	80	BA:	.269

Reese moved to the West Coast with the Dodgers in 1958 but retired after that season at age 40 with a career .269 batting average, 2,170 hits, and 1,210 walks. He stayed on as coach and then worked on CBS with Dizzy Dean and later on NBC with Curt Gowdy. After a stint as broadcaster for the Cincinnati Reds, Reese went back to Louisville to work for Hillerich & Bradsby. He was inducted into the Hall of Fame by the Veterans Committee in 1984 and his uniform number "1" was retired by the Dodgers that same year. Harold Henry Reese died in 1999 at the age of 81.

Tales from Joe's Bat Rack

As a key component to the strong Brooklyn Dodger teams of the 1940s and 1950s, Pee Wee Reese professional model bats are very popular. They are also fairly scarce. Reese may not have carried the biggest bat on the squad, but he was part of an iconic core that featured the likes of Roy Campanella, Gil Hodges, Jackie Robinson, and Duke Snider. While Reese did use some Adirondack bats during his career, it was clear that he preferred H&B bats like most players during the period. Reese signed an endorsement contract with the company prior to his MLB debut in 1940, which means all of the bats made for the Hall of Famer's use at the Major League level featured his facsimile signature. However, that signature brand did change over time. Early on, his bats were branded "Hal Reese" and later the brand changed to "Pee Wee Reese" in the 1950s.

Well-used Reese gamers will often have remnants of gripping substances, such as pine tar, along the handle. The application is often far from heavy but visible upon close inspection. Collectors may also see evidence of his uniform number "1" in black paint on some of his bats, which was a common practice of the Dodgers and some other teams during the era. Reese's relationship with the bat company would ultimately go much further than most players of the era.

It is important to keep in mind that Reese worked as a coach after he retired as a player, so post-career Reese bats do exist. Bats of this nature are sometimes mistakenly represented as Reese gamers. Well after his playing career was over, Reese would eventually work for H&B in a few different capacities, including acting as a sales representative with Major League teams. Reese worked for the manufacturer until his death in 1999.

▲ *Pee Wee Reese's 1954–56 H&B bat.*

Phil Rizzuto

★ ★ ★ ★ ★ ★ ★ ★ ★ ★ ★ ★

Icon Sportswire

"*He [Rizzuto] was as good a shortstop as ever played the game.*"
– *Jerry Coleman*

made a name for himself with his bunting ability, speed on the basepaths, and excellent fielding.

Born in Brooklyn to hard-working, blue-collar Italian parents, Philip Francis Rizzuto grew up in Queens and was captain of the Richmond Hill High School baseball team. Although the Giants thought he was too small to play in the majors, the Yanks took a chance on the young Rizzuto, signing him in 1937. He earned a starting slot with the Yankees after batting .347 with 201 hits in 1940 for Kansas City of the American Association, winning Minor League Player of the Year and American Association MVP honors. Except for three years serving in the U.S. Navy during World War II, Rizzuto was the Yankees shortstop until the mid-1950s. During that time, the Yankees won nine pennants and seven World Series championships.

In 1950, a *New York Times* article called Rizzuto "the dashing little shortstop, widely hailed as the 'indispensable man' of the world champion Bombers." That was the year Rizzuto batted a career-high .324 with 200 hits and was named both American League Most Valuable Player and the 1950 Major League Player of the Year.

An integral part of the great Yankees dynasty teams of the late 1940s and early 1950s, Phil Rizzuto wore the pinstripes for his entire career. Popular with teammates and fans alike, the diminutive 5-foot, 6-inch, and 150-pound scrappy shortstop

Rizzuto never hit for power but he hit the ball to all fields and was a skilled bunter who led the league in sacrifice hits four times in his career. The five-time All-Star shortstop also led the league in putouts, assists, double plays turned, range factor, and fielding percentage at various times.

Years later, Rizzuto told the *New York Daily News* that his proudest moment at-bat was his walk-off suicide squeeze on September 17, 1951, off Cleveland's Bob Lemon. It was the bottom of the ninth during the pennant race. The score was tied 1–1. Joe DiMaggio was on third base and Gene Woodling was on second. Rizzuto bunted and DiMaggio scored easily for a 2–1 Yankees win. According to Rizzuto, "Lemon was so mad. He'd thrown the pitch right at my head and I'm sure he couldn't believe I was able to make contact with it."

After 11 years, Rizzuto saw his playing time diminish in 1955 and 1956. He was unceremoniously released in August 1956, but very soon after, he moved to the Yankees' broadcast booth and for nearly 40 years entertained new generations of fans with his homespun humor, rambling commentary, and signature "Holy Cow!" shouts at amazing plays. The Yankees retired his uniform number "10" in 1985 and he was elected to the Hall of Fame by the Veterans Committee in 1994. The voice of the Yankees passed away in 2007 at the ripe old age of 89.

The Ultimate Season:				Career:			
Year/Team: 1950 NYY				Years: 13			
G:	155	HR:	7	G:	1661	HR:	38
AB:	617	RBI:	66	AB:	5816	RBI:	563
R:	125	SB:	12	R:	877	SB:	149
H:	200	BB:	92	H:	1588	BB:	651
2B:	36	OPS:	.857	2B:	239	OPS:	.706
3B:	7	BA:	.324	3B:	62	BA:	.273

Tales from Joe's Bat Rack

Often overshadowed by the likes of Joe DiMaggio, Yogi Berra, and Mickey Mantle, Rizzuto's popularity as a player and broadcaster helps keep his bats on many collector wish lists, beyond their challenging scarcity. To the surprise of many, professional model Rizzuto bats are amongst the toughest Hall of Fame gamers to find from the 1940s–1950s era. In fact, at the time of this writing, there are only several of them known to exist.

It's not often that a bat used by a prolific bunter and someone known mainly for their defense can rise to the upper echelon of period bats, but Rizzuto has an appeal that goes well beyond offensive statistics. He was extremely likable and a winner, capturing nine American League titles and seven World Series championships during his 13-year run with the powerful New York Yankees.

Rizzuto signed an endorsement contract with H&B prior to his debut in 1941, which means that all of the bats made for "Scooter's" use at the Major League level were manufactured with his facsimile signature. Rizzuto gamers are usually not defined by especially noteworthy characteristics such as unique handle preparation. That said, Rizzuto did order a good quantity of bats that were manufactured with a small knob, much like fellow Hall of Famer Richie Ashburn who played during the same era. Most of the known Rizzuto gamers do not possess his uniform number "10" marked on the knob, but that was not a common practice by the team or in the league for a good portion of his career.

▲ *Phil Rizzuto's 1955-56 H&B bat.*

Brooks Robinson

★ ★ ★ ★ ★ ★ ★ ★ ★ ★ ★

The Human Vacuum Cleaner, Mr. Impossible—these names, while colorful, do not paint a glorious enough portrait of perhaps the greatest defensive third baseman in baseball history, Brooks Calbert Robinson. A career Baltimore Oriole (1955–1977), Robinson won a mind-boggling 16 consecutive Gold Gloves beginning in 1960. In fact, they should have just created a separate honor for the hot corner and called it "The Brooksie." For more than a decade, he teamed with shortstop Mark Belanger in what might have been the best left side of an infield ever. His sweet music helped power the Orioles to two world championships (1966, 1970) and four American League flags. Robinson's longtime manager Earl Weaver built his empire on fielding, pitching, and the three-run home run. If Weaver was the Emperor, Robinson was surely the Minister of Defense.

While Robinson was elected to the Hall of Fame in 1983 based on throwing the leather around, he was pretty darn successful with the wood as well. He smashed 268 home runs and knocked in 1,357 runs in his career. He also batted .303 in nine postseason series, including .583 in the 1970 ALCS and .429 in the 1970 World Series in which he was named MVP. It was in that Series that Robinson had perhaps his greatest offensive moments. With that short-brimmed batting helmet and ferocious swing, he delivered a game-winning homer in Game One, two doubles in Game Three, and a homer plus a clutch single in Game Four. Robinson also made one amazing defensive play after another as Baltimore beat Cincinnati's "Big Red Machine" in five games.

The Little Rock, Arkansas, native brought small-town humility to big city baseball and dashed the hopes of his rivals. He was the kind of a player who could go 0-for-4 and still win a game for his team. As a young player, Robinson was the quintessential "good field, no hit" prospect. While never an offensive juggernaut, Robinson, the 1964 American League MVP, worked himself into a solid hitter, surpassing the 20-home-run plateau six times, twice hitting above .300 and twice knocking in over 100 runs. His career .267 average was plenty enough in a powerful Oriole lineup that, over the years, included the likes of Frank Robinson, Don Baylor, and Boog Powell.

★ ★ ★ ★ ★ ★ ★ ★ ★ ★ ★ ★

> *"It's a pretty sure thing that the player's bat is what speaks loudest when it's contract time, but there are moments when the glove has the last word."* – Brooks Robinson, *Third Base is My Home*

The Ultimate Season:				Career:			
Year/Team: 1964 BAL				Years: 23			
G:	163	HR:	28	G:	2896	HR:	268
AB:	612	RBI:	118	AB:	10654	RBI:	1357
R:	82	SB:	1	R:	1232	SB:	28
H:	194	BB:	51	H:	2848	BB:	860
2B:	35	OPS:	.889	2B:	482	OPS:	.723
3B:	3	BA:	.317	3B:	68	BA:	.267

Robinson was not blessed with great size, strength, or speed, but he was born to play baseball and possessed tremendous anticipation, instinct, and reflexes. Brooks Robinson was, on the baseball field, an artist.

Tales from Joe's Bat Rack

Considered perhaps the best defensive third baseman ever, Brooks Robinson was certainly better known for his handiwork with the glove, but the perennial Gold Glove winner was no slouch with the bat either. Over his 23-year career, Brooks Robinson ordered a lot of H&B and Adirondack professional model bats, but the bats he used are defined by different characteristics depending on the period in which they were manufactured.

You will find some early Robinson gamers with barrel grooving, similar to the style seen on some later Roberto Clemente bats, where Robinson would carve straight lines into the hitting surface in order to generate more spin on the ball upon contact. Most of his bats, however, do not possess this feature. In addition, Robinson would occasionally tape the handles of his bats using a fairly standard tape wrap to enhance his grip.

While some of his bats do have very light remnants of pine tar, Robinson did not use heavy amounts often. The result is that most of his bats have a relatively clean look around the handle. Robinson's primary uniform number "5" can often be found on the knobs of his gamers. A fair number of examples from the 1950s, 1960s, and 1970s exist with his number written in black marker. Robinson did wear "40," "6," and "34" very early in his career but wore "5" for the vast majority of his playing days (from a portion of the 1957 season to the end of his career in 1977). Some of Robinson's bat knobs showcase a "5" along with solid black lines on each side of the number.

Finally, while his Adirondack bats always featured Robinson's name in block letters, collectors will encounter Robinson H&B bats that feature his facsimile signature or his name in block letters from different periods during the 1960s and 1970s. The variance in the appearance of his name exists despite initially signing an endorsement contract with the company in 1955, prior to making his Major League debut.

▲ *Brooks Robinson's 1958 H&B bat.*

Alex Rodriguez

★ ★ ★ ★ ★ ★ ★ ★ ★ ★ ★

Icon Sportswire

Rodriguez became a matinee idol and fan favorite. By the year 2000, he had already produced four All-Star appearances, three seasons of 40-plus home runs, and four 100-plus RBI seasons. He was a doubles machine and registered 215 hits in 1996 followed by 213 in 1998.

Rodriguez became a free agent after the 2000 season and, in a surprise move, signed with the Texas Rangers for a record $252 million. He spent just three seasons in Texas, all last place finishes, but set baseball on its ear with earth-shattering numbers. 2001: 52 HR, 135 RBI, .318 BA, 133 runs. 2002: 57 HR, 142 RBI, .300 BA. 2003: 47 HR, 118 RBI, 124 runs, .600 SLG, AL MVP. Nearly dealt to the Red Sox after the 2003 season, Rodriguez was acquired by the Yankees. He moved to third base and racked up MVP awards in 2005 and 2007, eventually leading the Yankees to a championship in 2009. Despite being embroiled in baseball's PED woes, Rodriguez continued with New York, surpassing 3,000 hits and 600 home runs as a Yankee. When released as a player in August 2016 to finish his contract as special advisor and instructor for the Yankees, Rodriguez was just four home runs short of the 700 mark.

Born in New York City and schooled in Miami, Alexander Enmanuel Rodriguez was one of the most polarizing figures in baseball history. He broke into the majors with the Seattle Mariners in 1994 and achieved superstar status in 1996, clouting 36 home runs and 123 RBI. At age 20, he won the American League batting crown with a .358 average and led the league with 141 runs and 54 doubles. It was non-stop production from there. Long, lean, and blessed with classic good looks,

His most memorable at-bat may have been his most embarrassing. It was October 19, 2004, Game Six of the 2004 ALCS with the Yankees leading Boston in the series 3–2. With Derek Jeter on first and the Yanks trailing 4–2,

★ ★ ★ ★ ★ ★ ★ ★ ★ ★ ★ ★

> "*I'm looking at 600 like first base. You want to run right through it and use it as a springboard for more to come.*"
> – Alex Rodriguez

The Ultimate Season:			Career:		
Year/Team: 2007 NYY			Years: 22		
G:	158	HR: 54	G:	2784	HR: 696
AB:	583	RBI: 156	AB:	10566	RBI: 2086
R:	143	SB: 24	R:	2021	SB: 329
H:	183	BB: 95	H:	3115	BB: 1338
2B:	31	OPS: 1.067	2B:	548	OPS: .930
3B:	0	BA: .314	3B:	31	BA: .295

Rodriguez hit a weak grounder toward first base. Red Sox pitcher Bronson Arroyo fielded it and moved toward Rodriguez to make the tag. A-Rod slapped at Arroyo's glove knocking the ball toward right field. Jeter scored and Rodriguez stood at second base. Boston manager Terry Francona argued that Rodriguez interfered with Arroyo and the umps agreed. Jeter was sent back to second and Rodriguez was called out, all the while standing at second with a "What did I do wrong?" look on his face. Boston won the game and, eventually, the series, erasing a 3–0 deficit to win the pennant. Like him or not, Alex Rodriguez is an unforgettable personality who consistently courted controversy off the field and history on it.

Tales from Joe's Bat Rack

While there may be little doubt that Alex Rodriguez became a polarizing figure during the last several years of his career, the slugger's numbers put him in special company, which makes it hard for many collectors of prized lumber to ignore. The slugging infielder was almost entirely loyal to Louisville Slugger bats. There have been exceptions, such as Cooper bats early on, but Rodriguez clearly preferred both natural-colored and black Louisville Slugger bats. Most of his gamers were of the solid black variety. Rodriguez's well-used bats are characterized by heavy amounts of Mota stick and pine tar along the handle. In some cases, clusters of the gripping substances extend into the center brand area as well.

Collectors will often find a fair amount of cleat marks on the barrel from Rodriguez constantly banging his cleats with his bat while at the plate. You will not, however, find many Rodriguez bats with his uniform number (either "3" with the Seattle Mariners and Texas Rangers or "13" with the New York Yankees) marked on the knob. Occasionally, hobbyists may encounter gamers that feature "A Rod" in block letters on the barrel end, but most of Rodriguez's bats were manufactured with his facsimile signature or his real name in block letters, not his nickname.

In his early playing days, along with teammate Ken Griffey, Jr., Rodriguez provided game-used bats and other equipment to the public through Mill Creek Sports in the Seattle area. This included documented home run bats amongst other items. In fact, Rodriguez has documented a number of home run bats over time and has often been willing to add the inscription "Game Used" along with the year. After becoming a member of the New York Yankees, a large number of bats became available through Steiner Sports, a company that acquires game-used equipment directly from the team.

▲ *Alex Rodriguez's 2003 MVP Louisville Slugger bat used to hit home run #12 of the season.*

Ryne Sandberg

★ ★ ★ ★ ★ ★ ★ ★ ★ ★ ★ ★

Focus On Sport/Getty Images Sport Collection/Getty Images

With power and speed, it seemed that Ryne Sandberg could do it all. An all-around talent, he excelled both offensively and defensively. The 10-time All-Star garnered seven Silver Slugger Awards, led the National League in runs scored three times and logged 20-plus steals nine times. He also won nine Gold Glove Awards and led the league in assists at second base seven times, and fielding percentage four times.

A three-sport star and All-American quarterback at Spokane's North Central High School, Sandberg was recruited to play football and baseball for Washington State University, but opted to sign with the Philadelphia Phillies in 1978 instead. After a few seasons in the minors, he played for the Phillies briefly at the end of the 1981 season before he was traded to the Chicago Cubs. Assigned to third base in 1982, Sandberg batted .271 with 32 stolen bases and finished sixth in Rookie of the Year voting. Everything started to come together for

Sandberg in 1983 after he was switched to second base. In 1984, Sandberg led the league with 114 runs and 19 triples. He batted a career-high .314 and swiped 32 bases while helping the Cubs to the National League East title, their first postseason berth in 39 years.

That was also the year of "The Sandberg Game." It was the nationally televised "Game of the Week" between the Cubs and the Cardinals on June 23, 1984, at Wrigley Field. The Cubs had come back from a 9–3 deficit and were within one run going into the ninth inning. Sandberg blasted a home run off the Cards' Bruce Sutter into left-center field to take the game into extra innings. The Cardinals scored two runs in the 10th to take the lead again. In the bottom of the 10th, with two outs and Bobby Dernier on first, Sandberg launched another shot off Sutter to the same spot, left-center field, to tie the game again. The Cubs won the game in the 11th inning, and Sandberg secured his place in baseball history. His performance that day was outstanding—five hits in six at-bats with seven RBI, two homers, and a .332 batting average. Sandberg was named National League Most Valuable Player and the 1984 Major League Player of the Year.

Known for his professionalism, Sandberg played for the Cubs for 15 years. They won the NL East title again in 1989 and Sandberg powered out a career-high 40 home runs in 1990. He retired in 1997, at 38 years old, with a .285 batting

★ ★ ★ ★ ★ ★ ★ ★ ★ ★ ★

average, 1,061 RBI, 282 homers, 2,386 hits, 403 doubles, and 344 stolen bases. Sandberg managed in the minors for the Cubs organization before managing the Phillies from 2013 through 2015, after which he returned to the Cubs as ambassador. Ryne Dee Sandberg was elected to the Hall of Fame in 2005.

The Ultimate Season:				Career:			
Year/Team: 1990 CHC				Years: 16			
G:	155	HR:	40	G:	2164	HR:	282
AB:	615	RBI:	100	AB:	8385	RBI:	1061
R:	116	SB:	25	R:	1318	SB:	344
H:	188	BB:	50	H:	2386	BB:	761
2B:	30	OPS:	.913	2B:	403	OPS:	.795
3B:	3	BA:	.306	3B:	76	BA:	.285

Tales from Joe's Bat Rack

Ryne Sandberg ordered many Rawlings/Adirondack and Louisville Slugger professional model bats during his career, but he seemed to prefer Adirondacks, especially during his prime years. The largest orders Sandberg placed for Louisville Slugger bats came in 1984 and 1985 after signing an endorsement contract in the summer of 1982. After 1985, the size of each order dropped substantially as he drifted more towards Adirondack.

In classic Chicago Cubs fashion, his primary uniform number "23" is often marked on the knob in smaller numbers and usually in black or blue marker. The Chicago Cubs' team practice of writing the uniform number in small print dates back to the days of Ernie Banks and Ron Santo. Collectors may also encounter Sandberg gamers with a "23" on the barrel end. While Sandberg did sign an endorsement contract with Louisville Slugger that summer, some bats were produced with "Sandberg" in block letters.

Many people forget but Sandberg did start his career with the Philadelphia Phillies in 1981, but he only had a total of six plate appearances. Sandberg wore "37" during that lone summer, but it would be extremely challenging to locate a gamer from his debut season. Sandberg bats are typically found with light-to-moderate amounts of pine tar along the handle, but gamers do exist with noticeably heavier applications. Despite playing for such a popular franchise and having the reputation as a fan favorite, Sandberg bats remain amongst the more affordable gamers on the Hall of Fame list.

"*Ryne Sandberg worked harder than any player I've ever seen. A lot of guys with his athletic ability get by on that and have a nice career. Sandberg worked his butt off because he knew it was wrong not to.*" – Pete Rose

▲ *Ryne Sandberg's 1987–89 Rawlings/Adirondack bat.*

Ron Santo

★ ★ ★ ★ ★ ★ ★ ★ ★ ★ ★

Icon Sportswire

He covered the hot corner with aplomb for 14 years and is probably the best third baseman to never get a shot at the postseason, because Ronald Edward Santo was a Cubbie through and

through. The nine-time All-Star, slammed 20-plus home runs in nine consecutive seasons and led the National League in walks, triples, and OBP at various times during the 1960s. Stellar defensively, Santo won five Gold Gloves, led the league in putouts seven times, assists seven times, and double plays turned six times.

Santo joined the Chicago Cubs in 1960 but the 20-year-old Seattle native was playing with a secret—Type 1 Diabetes. Santo wanted his accomplishments or failures on the field to be on his own merits and did not want the focus to be on his medical condition. He became a force at the plate and on the field, and many consider Santo to be the premier third sacker of the 1960s, even though the Cubs never made it to the postseason during that time. With 342 career home runs, Santo certainly had his share of memorable at-bats. He slammed six career walk-off home runs and the Braves definitely felt the heat of his bat in 1966. On May 28, Santo blasted a 12th-inning walk-off dinger for an 8–5 win over the Atlanta Braves. He followed that on the next day with a walk-off homer in the 10th inning for a 3–2 Cubs-Braves finish. Just a month later, on June 26, 1966, Santo fractured his left cheekbone in a beaning by Jack Fisher of the Mets and he became one of the early advocates of wearing batting helmets with an ear flap.

On the Cub's Ron Santo Day in August 1971, Santo finally went public about his diabetic condition. After that, he became very active in fundraising for the Juvenile Diabetes Research Foundation. In 1974, Santo moved to the crosstown White Sox and retired after that season with a career .277 batting average, 342 home runs, 2,254 hits, and 1,331 RBI. He went on to some successful business ventures

★ ★ ★ ★ ★ ★ ★ ★ ★ ★ ★ ★

> " *When it comes to all-around work, nobody is close to him. Ron is the best in the league, both offensively and defensively. He's one of the most aggressive players in the league—a born leader." – Leo Durocher*

The Ultimate Season:				Career:			
Year/Team: 1964 CHC				Years: 15			
G:	161	HR:	30	G:	2243	HR:	342
AB:	592	RBI:	114	AB:	8143	RBI:	1331
R:	94	SB:	3	R:	1138	SB:	35
H:	185	BB:	86	H:	2254	BB:	1108
2B:	33	OPS:	.962	2B:	365	OPS:	.826
3B:	13	BA:	.313	3B:	67	BA:	.277

but came back to the Cubs in 1990 as broadcaster. Santo was the voice of the Cubs for 20 years. His uniform number "10" was retired by the Cubs in 2003. Santo died of complications from diabetes and cancer in 2010 at 70 years old. He was inducted into the Hall of Fame by the Golden Era Committee in 2012.

Tales from Joe's Bat Rack

Ron Santo was always a popular player in the Chicago area, but once he was enshrined in the Hall of Fame in 2012, his professional model bats reached another level of demand on a national scale. Santo used both H&B (block letter) and Adirondack (endorsement contract) bats over the course of his career while he was with the Chicago Cubs and during his last season with the Chicago White Sox.

With the exception of his very first season, when he wore the number "15" for a portion of the year as a rookie, Santo wore the uniform number "10" for his entire career. This is important to note as a good portion of the Santo gamers in circulation have "10" marked on the knob, and a fair number of those bats showcase his uniform number in relatively small numerals (as was the norm with the Cubs).

Collectors will often find "Yosh" marks near the center brand of his bats. These are small notations, usually found on the right side of the center brand, made by the Cubs' equipment manager Yosh Kawano during the 1960s/1970s era. In black marker, Kawano would often write the model number and length just to the right of "Powerized." Santo was an avid user of pine tar, and you will see many of his gamers with some measure of coating on the handle, but it is usually a relatively light coating. Occasionally, you will also see a Santo gamer with handle tape added for grip, but this was not a regular practice. Santo bats that date to the 1960s are noticeably tougher than, and sell for a premium over, those ordered in the 1970s.

▲ *Ron Santo's 1969–72 H&B bat.*

George Sisler

★ ★ ★ ★ ★ ★ ★ ★ ★ ★ ★ ★

Icon Sportswire

The legendary Jackie Robinson's epitaph reads, "A life is not important except in the impact it has on other lives." George Sisler's baseball legacy fits this bill. After a magnificent career of his own, Sisler instructed the talented likes Bill Mazeroski, Roberto Clemente, Willie Stargell, and Donn Clendenon.

Sisler scouted Robinson for the Dodgers and taught him the nuances of playing first base. In addition, Sisler's sons, Dick and Dave, had respectable big league careers. There is no doubt that George Sisler paid his baseball acumen forward.

Sisler and Robinson had something else in common. Both men's lives were positively affected by Branch Rickey. Sisler and Rickey first met when the former was a player and the latter a coach at the University of Michigan in 1912. As smart as he was skilled, Sisler graduated from Michigan with a degree in mechanical engineering. The ever-wily Rickey saw Sisler's skill and brought him to the St. Louis Browns in 1915, where Rickey had joined as manager. One of the greatest first sackers of all time, Sisler was the best thing that ever happened to the woeful Browns. He started as a promising southpaw pitcher, but soon abandoned the mound in favor of his rich hitting skills.

The man they called "Gorgeous George" played 15 years and hit over .300 in 13 of those seasons. His career .340 batting average is tied with Lou Gehrig for 16th all time. He won two batting crowns, hitting .407 in 1920 and .420 in 1922, the only man in American League lore not named Ty Cobb to post two .400-plus seasons. In that 1920 season, he enjoyed the signature hitting moment of his career, smacking 257 hits, a record that stood until 2004 when Ichiro Suzuki had 262. Sisler led the American League in steals four times with a high of 51 in 1922. He also set the pace in runs, hits, and triples in 1922, garnering the first MVP trophy in American League history. That year, Sisler had a 41-game hitting streak, which stood as the MLB record until DiMaggio's 56-game streak in 1941.

However, bad luck soon hit Sisler the way Sisler hit pitches.

★ ★ ★ ★ ★ ★ ★ ★ ★ ★ ★ ★

"*Except when I cut loose at the ball, I always try to place my hits. At the plate, you must stand in such a way that you can hit to either right or left field with equal ease.*"
– George Sisler

The Ultimate Season:			Career:		
Year/Team: 1920 SLB			Years: 15		
G:	154	HR: 19	G:	2055	HR: 102
AB:	631	RBI: 122	AB:	8267	RBI: 1178
R:	137	SB: 42	R:	1284	SB: 375
H:	257	BB: 46	H:	2812	BB: 472
2B:	49	OPS: 1.082	2B:	425	OPS: .847
3B:	18	BA: .407	3B:	164	BA: .340

He missed the entire 1923 season with sinus and vision problems. In 1924, he rejoined St. Louis as player-manager, and would hit over .300 six more times but never flirted with the .400 mark again. 1927 was Sisler's final season with the Brownies and he left on a high note—97 RBI, a .327 average, and 27 steals. He played until 1930 with the Boston Braves, hitting over .300 into his late 30s. Eventually, Rickey hired Sisler as a scout and instructor with both the Dodgers and Pirates. George Harold Sisler was inducted into the Hall of Fame in 1939 and passed away in 1973. In all aspects of the game, Gorgeous George was one beauty of a ballplayer.

Tales from Joe's Bat Rack

George Sisler, a .340 career hitter who twice hit .400 or better, is a key figure for collectors who value the weapons of great batsmen. In fact, the bat used by Sisler for hit #257 of the 1920 season sold for $152,647 at auction in 2010. While that single-season hit record has since been broken by Ichiro Suzuki with 262 hits in 2004, it remains the highest total for any hitter who played during the 154-game schedule. The record-setting bat certainly sold for a massive premium versus regular Sisler professional model bats, but collectors have plenty of reasons to make this former batting champion's gamers part of their collections.

On some occasions, collectors might encounter a Spalding Sisler bat. However, as is the case with most players from the period, H&B gamers were the preferred brand. They are also preferred by most collectors. Sisler signed an endorsement contract with H&B in the spring of 1916, just one year after his rookie campaign. So, while most of the bats ordered by this fine hitter featured his facsimile signature, it is possible to come across a rare gamer with Sisler's name in block letters. Many of the bats Sisler ordered from H&B were substantial pieces of lumber, weighing in at 40 ounces or more. Some of his bats tipped the scales at 44–45-ounces. Bats that date to his earlier playing days with the St. Louis Browns are considered more desirable than those made during his last few seasons with the Washington Senators and Boston Braves.

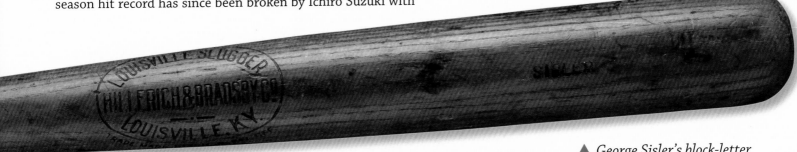

▲ *George Sisler's block-letter (rookie era) H&B bat.*

Frank Thomas

★ ★ ★ ★ ★ ★ ★ ★ ★ ★ ★

Icon Sportswire

to tear up the American League for 19 years, playing all but four seasons with Chicago. An unassuming superstar, Thomas played scandal-free baseball, separating himself from the names associated with performance enhancing drugs and was one of the early proponents of constant drug testing.

Over the course of his exceptional career, Thomas maintained a .301 average while walloping 521 home runs. The five-time All-Star and four-time Silver Slugger Award winner won back-to-back American League Most Valuable Player Awards in 1993 and in the strike-shortened 1994 season. One of only seven players to win two consecutive AL MVP awards, Thomas won the 1995 Home Run Derby and batted .347 in 1997 to win the AL batting title. Although no standout defensively, Thomas played first base before making the switch to designated hitter. A broken ankle kept him from playing in the 2005 World Series and, after that season, Thomas was unceremoniously dumped by Chicago after 16 years. He had a few more productive seasons with the Oakland A's and Toronto Blue Jays, playing his last game in 2008 at age 40. Thomas hit two homers in a game 31 times in his career, perhaps most memorably in 2006. Oakland was scoreless in the first game of the 2006 ALDS vs. the Twins when 38-year-old Thomas homered off a Johan Santana fly ball in the second inning and, in the ninth, he homered again off

Called the "Big Hurt," Frank

Edward Thomas certainly put the big hurt on many a pitcher over his great career. The 6-foot, 5-inch, and 240-pound Columbus, Georgia, native was signed out of Auburn University by the White Sox in 1989 and proceeded

a Jesse Crain fly ball to win the game. Oakland proceeded to win the ALDS in a three-game sweep.

When all was said and done, the Big Hurt left his mark. Thomas was the only player in MLB history to hit over

★ ★ ★ ★ ★ ★ ★ ★ ★ ★ ★

.300, drive in at least 100 runs, score 100 runs, walk at least 100 times, and hit at least 20 home runs for seven straight seasons (1991–1997). In those seven seasons, he averaged 36 home runs, 118 RBI, and a .330 batting average. One of the great White Sox hitters, Thomas still holds team records in on-base percentage (.427), slugging (.568), walks (1,466), extra base hits (906), home runs (448), RBI (1,465), and runs (1,327). The White Sox retired his uniform number "35" in 2010 and unveiled a bronze statue of Thomas at U.S. Cellular Field in 2011. He was inducted into the Baseball Hall of Fame with 83.7% of the vote in 2014, the first player elected primarily as a designated hitter. Today, Thomas is a special consultant and broadcaster for the White Sox and an analyst for Fox Sports.

The Ultimate Season:			Career:		
Year/Team: 2000 CHW			Years: 19		
G:	159	HR: 43	G:	2322	HR: 521
AB:	582	RBI: 143	AB:	8199	RBI: 1704
R:	115	SB: 1	R:	1494	SB: 32
H:	191	BB: 112	H:	2468	BB: 1667
2B:	44	OPS: 1.061	2B:	495	OPS: .974
3B:	0	BA: .328	3B:	12	BA: .301

Tales from Joe's Bat Rack

Frank Thomas used a variety of professional model bat brands during his career, including Louisville Slugger, Rawlings/Adirondack, Worth, and Hoosier to name a few. The Louisville Sluggers are found with his last name only and full name in block

> *It's so much fun watching him [Thomas] from the on-deck circle. I just sit back and become a fan just like everybody else." – Eric Chavez*

letters. The "Big Hurt" also used a combination of natural-colored, solid black, and two-toned bats during his playing days. Collectors will tend to see more natural-colored bats during Thomas' early years, but he gradually moved on to bats with darker finishes for the majority of his time in the majors. For a very brief period of time, Thomas provided game-used bats to the public, which included documented home run bats. These home run bats are inscribed by Thomas as such on the barrel of the bats and are fairly scarce.

While you will occasionally find bats used early in his career with heavy amounts of pine tar, Thomas did not often use an excessive amount of tar for the majority of his career. Most of the Thomas bat handles you will see have a relatively clean look to them. In addition to his sporadic use of tar, Thomas was not known for employing the use of tape either. You will find Thomas bats with and without his primary uniform number "35" marked on the knob or barrel end. Keep in mind that Thomas did wear "15" for a very brief period of time during his rookie season in 1990. Bats that date to the early-to-mid 1990s tend to sell for a premium as a result of Thomas winning consecutive American League MVPs (1993/1994) and his lone AL Batting Title (1997) during that time.

▲ *Frank Thomas' 2007 Hoosier bat used to hit career home run #493.*

Jim Thome

★ ★ ★ ★ ★ ★ ★ ★ ★ ★ ★

Icon Sportswire

right hand, pointing to right field, was copied from the fictional character Roy Hobbs in the movie "The Natural."

After 12 seasons in Cleveland and three in Philly, Thome was traded to the While Sox. In his first season with Chicago, he slammed 42 homers, with 141 hits, while batting .288 to earn the 2006 American League Comeback Player of the Year Award. On September 16, 2007, Thome hit his 500th home run off Los Angeles

At 6-foot, 4-inches, and 250 pounds, James Howard Thome was a menacing figure at the plate but one of the most likeable, friendly players in the game. Voted the most popular athlete in Cleveland history in a 2003 fan poll, Thome was a kind, gentle man who did his talking with his stick. In his long, distinguished career he amassed 2,328 hits and smashed 612 home runs, the eighth player to attain the 600-home-run pinnacle. He played for six different teams in 22 seasons, with return trips to the Indians and the Phillies, and was the model of consistency. The five-time All-Star and 1996 Silver Slugger Award winner was a prolific power hitter, banging out 40 or more homers in six different seasons. Interestingly, Thome's unique batting stance of holding the bat out with his

pitcher Dustin Moseley. Not only number 500, it was also a walk-off home run to win the game. Thome currently holds the MLB record for career walk-off home runs with 13. The White Sox "blackout" game on September 30, 2008, was another opportunity for Thome to shine. In a one-game playoff with the Twins for a postseason berth, Thome blasted a 461-foot homer off Nick Blackburn for the only run of the game, advancing the Sox to the ALDS.

Although slowed down periodically by back woes, Thome posted consistent power numbers, topping out in 2002 with 52 home runs. Unlike some of his contemporaries, Thome was never linked to steroid use. True to his blue-collar roots, he dedicated himself to improving his skills through

The Thomenator

★ ★ ★ ★ ★ ★ ★ ★ ★ ★ ★ ★

hard physical work. Popular in every city he played for, he never refused autograph requests and spent countless hours accommodating fans. From a philanthropic standpoint, Jim Thome is involved in many non-profit organizations including the Children's Hospital of Illinois. He is the recipient of the 2002 Roberto Clemente Award and the 2004 Lou Gehrig Award, among others. Considered a can't miss for Cooperstown, Jim Thome was claimed by the Indians as an "afterthought" in the 13th round of the 1989 amateur draft, and worked hard to become a MLB power force to be reckoned with. After his unofficial retirement in 2012, Thome joined the White Sox in an administrative capacity. In 2014 he signed a one-day contract with Cleveland so he could officially retire as a member of his original team. He was inducted into the Indians Hall of Fame in 2016 and his statue now stands outside Progressive Park.

The Ultimate Season:			
Year/Team: 2002 CLE			
G:	147	HR:	52
AB:	480	RBI:	118
R:	101	SB:	1
H:	146	BB:	122
2B:	19	OPS:	1.122
3B:	2	BA:	.304

Career:			
Years: 22			
G:	2543	HR:	612
AB:	8422	RBI:	1699
R:	1583	SB:	19
H:	2328	BB:	1747
2B:	451	OPS:	.956
3B:	26	BA:	.276

Tales from Joe's Bat Rack

After Jim Thome became a member of the elite 600 Home Run Club, his professional model bats became a hot commodity in the hobby. Throughout his career, Thome used a variety of bats including

" I just try to be consistent, have good at-bats and good things happen."
– Jim Thome

Louisville Slugger, Rawlings/Adirondack, Worth, Mizuno, and some brands that came into prominence in the 2000s (such as Marucci). Thome did sign an endorsement contract with Louisville Slugger, so many of the bats collectors will encounter possess the slugger's facsimile signature on the barrel, but block letter bats do exist. Thome also used bats with a variety of finishes as well, such as natural-colored, two-toned, and solid black bats during his playing days.

As far as player characteristics are concerned, there are a few key features to note. First, Thome was known for placing a distinct wrap of tape, which was sometimes padded, around the base of the handle and knob area. Second, you will frequently see pine tar remnants in a concentrated area near the upper handle and towards the center brand. Finally, you will see Thome gamers with his primary uniform number marked on the knob or barrel end. Do keep in mind, however, that many times the knob is partially or totally covered as a result of the tape wrap being near the knob. Thome wore number "25" for the vast majority of his career, but he did also wear "59" and "6" during his very first season with the Cleveland Indians.

▲ *Jim Thome's 1997 Louisville Slugger bat.*

Robin Yount

★ ★ ★ ★ ★ ★ ★ ★ ★ ★ ★ ★

Rich Pilling/Getty Images Sport Collection/Getty Images

MLB games played as a teenager and, over the next 20 seasons, would mature into a 3,000-hit man and Hall of Famer. A lifetime Brewer, Yount was the face of the Milwaukee franchise and remains a role model for any young ballplayer who strives for consistency and performance. In that 1974 season, the precocious Yount played in 107 games and showed leadership and fight that belied his young age. The Brewers struggled for team success in his early years, but Yount put up steady, if unspectacular, numbers over his first six seasons. In 1980, Yount broke out with season that saw him hit 23 homers with 87 RBI and a .293 batting average. His 49 doubles led the league, he was selected to his first of three All-Star games, and he won the first of three Silver Slugger Awards.

Two years later, both Yount and the Brewers escaped obscurity for good. The 1982 season saw a managerial change with Harvey Kuenn replacing Buck Rodgers after 47 games. Yount had a league-high 210 hits in 1982 while also pacing the junior circuit with 46 doubles, a .578 slugging percentage, and .957 OPS. He smashed 29 homers and 114 RBI and was named AL MVP while winning a Gold Glove at shortstop. With Yount, Paul Molitor, Ben Oglivie, Gorman Thomas, Cecil Cooper, Jim Gantner, and Ted Simmons in their potent lineup, the Brewers clouted 216 home runs and became known as "Harvey's Wallbangers." The team sped past traditional American League East powers to win their first-ever division title. They then dispatched the Angels and faced the St. Louis Cardinals in a thrilling seven-game World Series. While his Brewers came up just short in the Fall Classic, Yount's

Recognized as one of the greatest Milwaukee Brewers of all-time, Illinois native Robin Yount joined the Brew Crew in 1974 as an 18-year-old. He would break Mel Ott's big league record for most

performance was his greatest yet, batting .414 with 12 hits, a home run, 6 RBI, and a gaudy 1.072 OPS in the seven-game contest.

Amazingly, seven years later, as a 33-year-old converted centerfielder, Yount would snag another MVP award with 21 home runs, a .318 batting average, and 103 RBI. His ability to overcome injury and age, and transition from shortstop to centerfield only confirmed his tremendous acumen and athleticism. Throughout his career, Yount was speedy and smart, using guile and quickness to stretch doubles into triples and steal bases. He surpassed the 3,000-hit mark on September 9, 1992, with a single into right field off Cleveland Indian Jose Mesa. At 36 years old, he was the third youngest player, after Hank Aaron and Ty Cobb, to reach that milestone. He retired in 1993, his number "19" was retired by the Brewers in 1994 and he was inducted into the Hall of Fame in 1999. In short or, for that matter, in center, Robin Yount could do it all, and did just that for two decades.

The Ultimate Season:				Career:			
Year/Team: 1982 MIL				Years: 20			
G:	156	HR:	29	G:	2856	HR:	251
AB:	635	RBI:	114	AB:	11008	RBI:	1406
R:	129	SB:	14	R:	1632	SB:	271
H:	210	BB:	54	H:	3142	BB:	966
2B:	46	OPS:	.957	2B:	583	OPS:	.772
3B:	12	BA:	.331	3B:	126	BA:	.285

variety of models for 20 years, including bats with traditional and cupped ends.

In terms of bat preparation, the Milwaukee staple would often place a concentrated application of pine tar on the upper-handle area. If heavy in nature, the pattern is somewhat similar to the one seen on well-used Mickey Mantle bats from a generation earlier. Other times, you will see a more even application of the gripping substance along the length of the lower-to-mid handle on Yount gamers. In addition, most Yount bats contain his uniform number "19" in large black marker on the knob. You can frequently find his uniform number marked on the barrel end as well. This was the only uniform number Yount wore during his entire MLB career.

Tales from Joe's Bat Rack

Robin Yount professional model bats became even more desirable once the two-time American League MVP gained entry into the 3,000 Hit Club in 1992, but as a result of playing for a small market team, his gamers remain relatively affordable considering his significant accomplishments. Throughout his career, Yount was very consistent about the brand of bats he preferred (H&B/Louisville Slugger) and the way he prepared his bats for battle. Yount signed an endorsement contract with H&B in the spring of his rookie season (1974), and he ordered a

" *He could do everything. He never stopped hustling. He was what a ballplayer is supposed to be.*"
– Bob Uecker

▲ *Robin Yount's 1976 Bicentennial H&B bat.*

6

The Outfield

★ ★ ★ ★ ★ ★ ★ ★ ★ ★ ★

Some of the outfielders featured in this chapter used bats the size of redwoods and some used bats as light as possible. Some used globs of pine tar and some used none. Some even inserted a little bit of cork inside their bat to give them a little extra advantage. We can still picture Yaz holding that big bat very high over his head and following through with that vicious swing, or Vlad Guererro with that exaggerated flailing of his bat standing at the plate. In any event, these are the men that patrolled the outfield, and the bats they used.

▲ *Here's a shot of Paul O'Neill's cleat marks embedded on the barrel.*

▲ *Roger Maris gamers are often found with his first or last name written on the knob instead of his uniform number.*

Richie Ashburn

★ ★ ★ ★ ★ ★ ★ ★ ★ ★ ★

In baseball, you have to show up to win. Well, Hall of Famer Richie Ashburn did just that. During the years 1948 to 1960, when baseball still had a 154-game season, Ashburn played in over 150 games 11 times. He led the National League in plate appearances four times, topping the 700 mark in eight seasons. Seven times, he registered over 600 at-bats. A Nebraska native, Ashburn brought a Midwestern work ethic to the ballpark every day of his 15-year career. An All-Star as a rookie, he grabbed his lunch pail, laced up his cleats, and played hard—win or lose. More often than not, it was lose. Ashburn spent the bulk of his career with the Phillies (1948–1959), often playing for truly hapless teams. During Ashburn's tenure, the Phils finished higher than fourth just three times. Their only trip to the World Series came in 1950, a year that saw Ashburn bat .303 with 180 hits, 25 doubles, and 14 triples. The "Whiz Kids" ended that glorious season on a sour note as Philadelphia was swept by the powerful New York Yankees. The 23-year-old Ashburn suffered with a .176 average in that Series.

A quintessential leadoff hitter and center fielder, Ashburn bounced back big time in 1951. He batted .344 with 31 doubles and a career-high of 221 hits, and he got the second of his five All-Star selections. The phrase home run was not in Ashburn's vocabulary, but he topped the 200-hit plateau three times, leading the National League in that category in 1951, 1953, and 1958. Overall, Ashburn collected 2,574 career hits. He was indeed a throwback to baseball's Deadball Era, eschewing the long ball for using the entire field and taking the extra base. He led the National League in walks four times, topping the century mark three times. What Ashburn did better

★ ★ ★ ★ ★ ★ ★ ★ ★ ★ ★ ★ ★

"*Anybody who saw him play loves him because he was a bust-tail ballplayer who hated to lose.*"
– Harry Kalas, broadcast partner

The Ultimate Season:				Career:			
Year/Team: 1955 PHI				Years: 15			
G:	140	HR:	3	G:	2189	HR:	29
AB:	533	RBI:	42	AB:	8365	RBI:	586
R:	91	SB:	12	R:	1322	SB:	234
H:	180	BB:	105	H:	2574	BB:	1198
2B:	32	OPS:	.897	2B:	317	OPS:	.778
3B:	9	BA:	.338	3B:	109	BA:	.308

than almost anyone was to get on base. A career .308 hitter, he batted over .300 nine times, won two batting crowns, stole 234 bases, and led the league in OBP four times. Ashburn played for the Cubs in 1960 and 1961. He joined the expansion New York Mets in 1962 for what would be his final season. There he performed what may have been the greatest of his many offensive feats. On probably the worst team in baseball history, losers of 120 games, Ashburn was an All-Star, batting .306 with a .424 OBP, and 119 hits. The popular Ashburn began his lengthy career as television and radio broadcaster for the Phillies in 1963. His commentary and wit as color man entertained fans for nearly 35 years. Don Richard Ashburn was elected to the Hall of Fame by the Veterans Committee in 1995 and passed away two years later at the age of 70. He will always be remembered as a great table setter who feasted on pitching.

with either a small knob or no knob at all—the flared-knob bats (U1 models) made popular later by Roberto Clemente in the 1960s. It is also clear that throughout his career he preferred H&B brand bats. Ashburn signed an endorsement contract with the company prior to the 1948 season, which means that all of the gamers he used at the MLB level feature his facsimile signature on the barrel.

While most Ashburn bats do not exhibit his uniform number "1" on the knob, you might see other characteristics such as evidence of green paint streaks from the dugout and bat rack at Shibe Park on bats that date to his Philadelphia Phillies days (1948–1959) when he was most effective as a hitter. When it comes to player characteristics, Ashburn was not known for preparing his bats with tape, using heavy amounts of pine tar or modifying them by scoring or grooving the handles. Finally, despite ordering a healthy number of bats during his career, Ashburn gamers are one of the tougher bats to find from the era.

Tales from Joe's Bat Rack

Richie Ashburn, the player who collected more hits in the 1950s than any other player in the league and winner of two National League batting titles, often used professional model bats

▲ *Richie Ashburn's 1956 H&B bat.*

Barry Bonds

★ ★ ★ ★ ★ ★ ★ ★ ★ ★ ★

Icon Sportswire

the Pirates, he hit 34 homers, but also led the NL in runs and walks. The following year, as a San Francisco Giant, he registered a then career-high 46 dingers and 123 RBI. For the next five years, Bonds continued to hit home runs and steal bases, making a mockery of the 30-30 and 40-40 clubs. Comparable to his godfather, Barry Bonds was a complete player and his career stats prior to 1999 were Hall of Fame worthy.

In the aftermath of Mark McGwire's and

The son of All-Star Bobby Bonds and godson of Willie Mays, Barry Bonds starred at Arizona State before joining the Pittsburgh Pirates in 1986. Bonds brought an attitude of confidence to the game and, almost immediately, staked his claim as a superstar, excelling in all facets of the game. He could play the outfield with precision, run the bases like a gazelle, hit for power and average, and he could make mincemeat out of any mound master. Very focused on being the best player he could be, Bonds was never popular with the media or his teammates. He won his first of seven National League MVP Awards in 1990, at the age of 25. That season, he hit 33 homers with 114 RBI, stole 52 bases, and slugged .565. In 1992 and 1993, he again was named MVP. In 1992, his last season with

Sammy Sosa's epic 1998 assault on Roger Maris' single-season home run record, Bonds added more muscle and became visibly and physically thicker than ever. Because of this, he would remain a focal point in baseball's blossoming PED struggles. He would also set records galore. From 2000 to 2004, Bonds recorded home run totals of 49, 73, 46, 45, and 45. The 73 taters in 2001 shattered McGwire's three-year-old record of 70. He led the league in walks, many of them intentional, seven out of eight seasons between 2000 and 2007. He also won four straight MVP Awards (2001–2004). This barrage of production in his late 30s and early 40s put him on the brink of history and, on August 7, 2007, he did what most thought was impossible. In the most incredible moment of his storied career, Bonds shattered

★ ★ ★ ★ ★ ★ ★ ★ ★ ★ ★

Hank Aaron's record of 755 career home runs. Bonds would not play again after 2007, leaving the game with 762 home runs, 1,996 RBI, a .298 career average, and a record 2,558 walks. There will always be questions swirling around Barry Lamar Bonds.

The Ultimate Season:			Career:		
Year/Team: 2001 SFG			Years: 22		
G:	153	HR: 73	G:	2986	HR: 762
AB:	476	RBI: 137	AB:	9847	RBI: 1996
R:	129	SB: 13	R:	2227	SB: 514
H:	156	BB: 177	H:	2935	BB: 2558
2B:	32	OPS: 1.379	2B:	601	OPS: 1.051
3B:	2	BA: .328	3B:	77	BA: .298

Tales from Joe's Bat Rack

While there is no doubt that Barry Bonds is a controversial figure, his professional model bats are still desirable as a result of his remarkable offensive exploits. Aside from occasionally swinging a less popular bat brand such as Cooper early on, Bonds used Louisville Slugger bats almost exclusively during the first half of his career. These bats feature the slugger's name in block letters, with some possessing the last name only and others featuring his full name. Yet, by the late 1990s, Bonds started using other bat brands like the maple wood SAM bats, which he came to use predominantly. While the look and feel of his bats changed over time, Bonds was relatively consistent about his bat preparation habits for long stretches.

On earlier gamers, Bonds often placed a coating of pine tar, sometimes light and sometimes heavy, on the upper handle.

"You walk Barry. Just walk him."
– Greg Maddux

Grip marks from his batting gloves are commonly found near the base of the handle. After transitioning to SAM bats, Bonds applied a very unique taping pattern to the handles of his bats for grip. He used both a crisscross method and solid spiral taping application during his career. In some cases, it was a mixture of both. In addition, a fairly high percentage of Bonds gamers display most of the ball contact marks on the left barrel, which means he often hit with the label facing downward.

You will find Bonds bats, from the early part of his career, with his uniform number marked on the knob, either "7" or "24" (Pittsburgh Pirates) or "25" (San Francisco Giants). On occasion, collectors may encounter early Bonds gamers with "Bonds" written on the knob in marker. Once Bonds started using SAM bats in the late 1990s, however, that practice came to an end. Starting around 1997 or so, Bonds provided game-used equipment directly to the hobby with his own hologram and authentication system (Barry Bonds Authenticated). While early bats from his career are harder to find, many collectors prefer the visual appeal of the SAM bats that Bonds made famous during his record-setting run.

▲ *Barry Bonds' 2001 SAM bat used to hit career home run #558.*

Lou Brock

★ ★ ★ ★ ★ ★ ★ ★ ★ ★ ★ ★ ★

Louis Requena/Major League Baseball Collection/Getty Images

If you want a double-barreled offensive threat, look no further than Hall of Famer Lou Brock. One of the greatest base stealers in the history of the game, the speedster from El Dorado, Arkansas, was a 19-year headache for National League catchers. His aggressive base-running style made for some very exciting moments

on the basepaths, and if Brock didn't do it with his speed, he would do it with his stick, spraying balls all over the park to amass 3,023 hits over his brilliant career.

In one of the most lopsided trades in MLB history, Louis Clark Brock landed with the Cardinals in June of 1964. Along with a couple of other players, Brock was traded from the Chicago Cubs to the St Louis Cardinals for 18-game-winner Ernie Broglio and several other players. Broglio only won seven games over the next three years for the Cubbies and eventually called it quits. Brock, on the other hand, became a six-time All-Star, played on two World Series championship teams, led the league in stolen bases eight times, and hit a nifty .293 over his 19 seasons, but the most important factor was his speed.

On September 10, 1974, the 35-year-old "Running Redbird" broke the single-season stolen base record of 104, held by Dodger great Maury Wills. Brock surpassed it that day and ended the season with 118 steals, but his single-season record was really just a taste of things to come. Brock soon began his assault on the MLB record of 892 career stolen bases held by the legendary Ty Cobb. On August 29, 1977, Brock entered the game at San Diego stadium one base shy of Cobb's record. Right out of the gate, in the first inning, the 38-year-old Brock erased his deficit by drawing a walk off Padres pitcher Dave Freisleben. With the enemy San Diego fans screaming, Brock immediately bolted for second. Catcher Dave Roberts'

★ ★ ★ ★ ★ ★ ★ ★ ★ ★ ★ ★ ★

throw was wide and Brock got his first steal of the game to tie Cobb's record.

After a double and a groundout in his next two at-bats, Brock came up to the plate in the seventh. With a man on first, he hit into a fielder's choice and ended up on first base. Freisleben was still on the mound, and the San Diego faithfuls were on their feet. When Brock broke for second this time, he ended up in the history books. Lou Brock had broken Ty Cobb's record and was mobbed by his teammates. The game was stopped so Brock could thank the fans, as well as Cobb, and he was given the base that he swiped as a keepsake. Lou Brock finished his stellar career with 938 stolen bases. Another Hall of Famer, Ricky Henderson, finally eclipsed that record in 1991. Because of his exceptional speed and huge talent with the stick, Lou Brock made it into the hallowed halls of Cooperstown on the first ballot.

The Ultimate Season:				Career:			
Year/Team: 1971 STL				Years: 19			
G:	157	HR:	7	G:	2616	HR:	149
AB:	640	RBI:	61	AB:	10332	RBI:	900
R:	126	SB:	64	R:	1610	SB:	938
H:	200	BB:	76	H:	3023	BB:	761
2B:	37	OPS:	.810	2B:	486	OPS:	.753
3B:	7	BA:	.313	3B:	141	BA:	.293

Tales from Joe's Bat Rack

When you consider all of his accomplishments, including membership in the 3,000 Hit Club, it is no wonder Lou Brock professional model bats are in such high demand. Brock seemed to prefer Louisville Slugger (endorsement contract) bats, but collectors will see Adirondack (block letter) bats from time to time. He signed with the former in 1961, during his debut season. Well-used gamers are often characterized by either a heavy application of pine tar or tape along the handle to enhance Brock's grip. The tape application can be very distinct looking, with several thin ringlets of tape spread along the handle. This is somewhat similar to the ringlets

seen on certain Eddie Murray and Pete Rose gamers, but the ringlets are not quite as wide in most cases.

Scoring on the handle, while not nearly as prevalent, is another characteristic that may be present on well-used Brock gamers. You will often find the noting of Brock's primary uniform number "20" on the knob or barrel end in black marker. Early Chicago Cubs-era bats are considerably tougher to find compared to bats from his St. Louis Cardinals days, and keep in mind that Brock wore number "24" for his first few seasons with the Cubbies. As with most players, price premiums are often attached to bats that date to the early stages of his career, including the Cardinals championship period of the mid-to-late 1960s.

" *Your bat is your life. It's your weapon. You don't want to go into battle with anything that feels less than perfect."* – Lou Brock

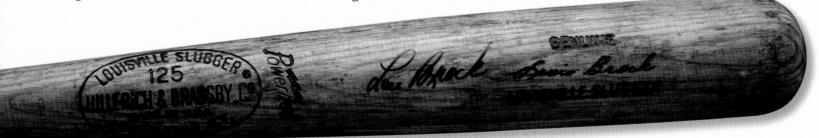

▲ *Lou Brock's 1969-71 H&B bat.*

Andre Dawson

★ ★ ★ ★ ★ ★ ★ ★ ★ ★ ★ ★

Ronald C. Modra/Sports Imagery/Getty Images Sport Collection/Getty Images

came out of the gate with a vengeance, winning Rookie of the Year honors batting .282, and smacking 19 home runs in 1977. In his 11 years and 1,443 games with the Expos, Dawson held many offensive records, some of which have since been broken. For a period of time he held the record for home runs, extra base hits, and sacrifice flies. He is also the only Expo to ever hit 200 home runs and steal 200 bases.

An outstanding outfielder, Dawson could effortlessly track down fly balls with grace and had a great arm. Over his career, he won four Silver Slugger Awards to go along with his eight Gold Gloves. As a matter of fact, Dawson was the second player in history to hit 400 home runs and steal 300 bases. Dawson struggled with knee problems throughout his career and worked with determination to

A quiet superstar who let his bat do his talking, Andre Nolan Dawson carried himself with dignity throughout a Major League career that spanned the mid-1970s to the mid-1990s. The Miami, Florida, native was known as "The Hawk," a nickname given to him by his uncle because Dawson had a "hawk eye" at the plate. In a career that spanned 21 seasons, Dawson excelled both offensively and defensively and possessed both speed and power. Drafted by the Montreal Expos in 1975, Dawson

come back after each of his 12 knee surgeries. His teammates believed that had he not had the knee problems, he could have reached 600 home runs and stolen 500 bases. Because the artificial turf at Montreal's Olympic Stadium contributed to his wheel problems, Dawson finally signed with the Cubs in 1987, in hopes that the natural grass turf at Wrigley Field would be more forgiving on his knees. Determined to revitalize his career, Dawson won the National League MVP Award that year and put together five of his eight All-Star seasons as a Cub.

★ ★ ★ ★ ★ ★ ★ ★ ★ ★ ★ ★

> *"Nobody played on sheer guts and bad knees longer than Hawk. He could have had a lot bigger numbers. He was a big-time player." – Dusty Baker, Chicago Cubs manager*

The Ultimate Season: Year/Team: 1987 CHC				Career: Years: 21			
G:	153	HR:	49	G:	2627	HR:	438
AB:	621	RBI:	137	AB:	9927	RBI:	1591
R:	90	SB:	11	R:	1373	SB:	314
H:	178	BB:	32	H:	2774	BB:	589
2B:	24	OPS:	.896	2B:	503	OPS:	.806
3B:	2	BA:	.287	3B:	98	BA:	.279

A fan favorite because of his unassuming nature, Dawson was one of the most respected players in the game. Don Zimmer, Dawson's manager in Chicago once said that he never managed a greater human being than Andre Dawson. He worked extremely hard to overcome his knee problems, but they finally caught up with him. Dawson was signed as a free agent by the Boston Red Sox in December 1992, and it was at Fenway Park that Dawson had one of his most memorable at-bats. As designated hitter on April 15, 1993, Dawson faced Cleveland's Jose Mesa and blasted a line shot over the left-field wall for career home run number 400, his first in a Boston uniform. He played for the Florida Marlins in 1995 and 1996, after which he went to work for the Marlins and is still employed by them today. In 2010, Dawson was elected to the Hall of Fame in his ninth year of eligibility.

Tales from Joe's Bat Rack

Even though Andre Dawson used professional model bat brands such as H&B/Louisville Slugger during the first half of his career, signing an endorsement contract very early on, the slugger became a fairly loyal user of Worth bats from the mid-1980s until the end of his career in 1996. Dawson did use modest amounts of pine tar from time to time, but most of his gamers do not exhibit a heavy coating. The examples that do exhibit pine tar usually have a concentrated area below the center brand or a modest, even coating spread across the handle.

Many of Dawson's gamers do feature his uniform number on the knob or barrel end; however, it is important to note that his number changed from "24" to "10" to "8" at various stages in his career. Dawson's Cubs-era bats will often showcase a slightly smaller uniform number "8" on the knob, which is typical for Cubs bats from various generations. Early Montreal Expos bats and bats that date to "The Hawk's" time with the Cubs, the period when Dawson was named National League MVP in 1987, tend to sell for a premium versus those used while playing with the Boston Red Sox and Florida Marlins. Finally, Dawson bats remain amongst the most affordable Hall of Famer bats in the hobby, from any era.

▲ *Andre Dawson's 1988-89 Worth bat.*

Ken Griffey, Jr.

★ ★ ★ ★ ★ ★ ★ ★ ★ ★ ★

Icon Sportswire

It seems that every generation produces a player who simply changes the game, and when it happens, it is beyond special. George Kenneth Griffey, Jr., was one of those players. Griffey had everything—a rocket arm, lightning speed, and one of the purest swings Major League Baseball has ever seen. What separated Griffey from other stars of his era was his undeniable charisma. Nicknamed "The Kid," his smile was

contagious, and he singlehandedly made wearing a baseball cap backwards cool. Griffey's unorthodox style connected with a new generation of fans and helped propel his popularity to new heights. Griffey, an Ohio native and the son of longtime Major Leaguer Ken Griffey, Sr., began his career with the Seattle Mariners, drafted first overall in the 1987 Amateur Draft. One of Griffey's best moments with the Mariners was when he scored the winning run in a winner-take-all game against the New York Yankees in the 1995 American League Division Series. Griffey's joyous slide into home and the celebration that ensued became an instant moment for the ages.

Griffey's most memorable moment at bat is a rare baseball gem that will likely never occur again. Near the end of the 1990 season, Ken Griffey, Sr., was signed by the Mariners. August 31, 1990, marked the first time in MLB history that a father and son duo stepped on the field as teammates. The Griffeys did not disappoint, hitting back-to-back singles in the first inning. Two weeks later, they outdid themselves by hitting back-to-back home runs against the Angels. Absolutely astonishing!

One of Seattle's most popular players, in his 11 years with the Mariners, Griffey was named to 10 consecutive AL All-Star teams (1990–1999), and won 10 Gold Gloves along with seven Silver Slugger Awards. In early 2000, Griffey was traded to his dad's old team, the Cincinnati Reds. With three more All-Star selections in his nine seasons with the Reds, Griffey finished his career with the White Sox and back with Seattle. Over his 22-year career (1989–2010), he smashed 630 homers and 1,836 RBI, all while missing hundreds of games due to injury. In short, Griffey played the game all out, all the time, sacrificing his body, and probably a few MLB all-time records,

★ ★ ★ ★ ★ ★ ★ ★ ★ ★ ★

in the process. A baseball savant and bona fide superstar, Ken Griffey, Jr., was elected to Hall of Fame in 2016, receiving a record 99.32 % of the vote.

The Ultimate Season:				Career:			
Year/Team: 1997 SEA				Years: 22			
G:	157	HR:	56	G:	2671	HR:	630
AB:	608	RBI:	147	AB:	9801	RBI:	1836
R:	125	SB:	15	R:	1662	SB:	184
H:	185	BB:	76	H:	2781	BB:	1312
2B:	34	OPS:	1.028	2B:	524	OPS:	.907
3B:	3	BA:	.304	3B:	38	BA:	.284

Tales from Joe's Bat Rack

Ken Griffey, Jr., professional model bats are amongst the most desirable bats of the post-1980 era. He was a slugger that put up tremendous numbers during a time when so many top sluggers were linked to PEDs, but Griffey was not one of them. Throughout his career, Griffey clearly preferred Louisville Slugger bats, although he did occasionally use other brands such as Cooper, Rawlings/Adirondack and even the very scarce Nike bats during the mid-1990s. Very early in his career, Griffey's bats had his name in block letters, but he quickly signed an endorsement contract in 1990. While the majority of his bats feature his facsimile signature on the barrel, some rare examples have "The Kid" or "Junior" in its

place. In other cases, either the acronym "C.M.B.-24" (Cash Money Brothers along with his uniform number) was added in place of his name or the nickname "SWINGMAN" can be found in block letters underneath his signature in all caps.

The one key characteristic that remained consistent throughout Griffey's career was the application of a unique taping method along the handles of his bats. Griffey would apply a very thin layer of tape, in a crisscross pattern, to enhance his grip. He would also use varying amounts of pine tar and Mota stick from time to time, but it is the distinct taping application that acts as a fingerprint for Griffey gamers.

Collectors might also notice cleat marks near the top or back barrel of his bats as a result of Griffey banging his cleats while at the plate. While some of his bats exhibit Griffey's uniform number in marker or pre-printed fashion, many of his gamers do not. Keep in mind that his uniform changed from "24" (Seattle Mariners) to "3" and "30" (Cincinnati Reds) to "17" (Chicago White Sox). For a period of time, Griffey provided game-used equipment to the public via Mill Creek Sports in the Seattle area. This included special game-used items such as documented home run bats, which often sell for large premiums since he ranks so high on the career home run list.

" *Griffey owned one of the smoothest strokes in recent baseball history, masking big-time power behind a short stride and an easy uppercut that put the nation's upper decks under assault." – Ted Berg, USA Today*

▲ *Ken Griffey, Jr.'s, 1995 Louisville Slugger bat used to hit home run #12 of the season.*

Vladimir Guerrero

★ ★ ★ ★ ★ ★ ★ ★ ★ ★

Icon Sportswire

The epitome of a great "bad ball" hitter, Vladimir Alvino Guerrero could hit it wherever the pitcher would put it—balls at eye level, balls in the dirt, it didn't matter. Legend has it that Guerrero once

hit a home run on a pitch that bounced off the dirt. Well, what we do know is that on August 14, 2009, he did, in fact, hit a pitch for a looping single that bounced before it came to the plate. There have been many great players that have come from the Dominican Republic. Like many of them, Guerrero grew up in poverty and baseball became his salvation. As a matter of fact, baseball was good to many members of the Guerrero family. His older brother played for the Montreal Expos, and cousins and nephews also played Major League baseball. In 2015, Guerrero's son, 16-year-old Vladimir, Jr., was signed as hot prospect by the Toronto Blue Jays.

Guerrero never wore batting gloves, attributing his calloused hands to tending cattle as a kid on the family farm. His batting helmet was always covered with pine tar and his hands were usually covered with the sticky substance. Over his 16-year career, Guerrero generated 449 home runs with a .318 lifetime batting average. He was a total pain in the neck for opposing pitchers as evidenced by his eight Silver Slugger Awards and nine All-Star appearances. The right-handed hitter had some excellent offensive years with the Montreal from 1996 to 2003 and is the Expos' career leader in home runs, slugging percentage and batting average.

Signed by the Anaheim Angels as a free agent in 2004, Guerrero batted .337 with 39 home runs and 126 RBI and was voted American League MVP that year. He was the Home Run Derby winner in 2007. If you had to pick his one biggest offensive moment, it would have to be in Game Three of the 2009 ALDS against the Boston Red Sox. Behind 4–6 in the top of the ninth inning, with three men on base, he lashed a line drive single to center field off Jonathan Papelbon

★ ★ ★ ★ ★ ★ ★ ★ ★ ★ ★

> " *I don't have to get a pitch down the middle. If I like the pitch—even if it's 15 inches off the plate, and that's the pitch I wanted—I'm swinging.*"
> – Vladimir Guerrero

The Ultimate Season:				Career:			
Year/Team: 2000 MON				Years: 16			
G:	154	HR:	44	G:	2147	HR:	449
AB:	571	RBI:	123	AB:	8155	RBI:	1496
R:	101	SB:	9	R:	1328	SB:	181
H:	197	BB:	58	H:	2590	BB:	737
2B:	28	OPS:	1.074	2B:	477	OPS:	.931
3B:	11	BA:	.345	3B:	46	BA:	.318

to beat the Sox for the first time in Angels postseason history and advance them to the American League Championship Series against the Yankees.

Guerrero played one season for the Texas Rangers in 2010. That year he batted .300, made his last All-Star appearance, and won his eighth Silver Slugger Award. At 36 years of age, he finished his MLB career with the Baltimore Orioles in 2011. However, in 2014 Anaheim signed him to a one-day contract so he could retire as an Angel. With his offensive numbers including over 2,500 hits, Guerrero's Hall of Fame chances are pretty good. Time will tell.

Tales from Joe's Bat Rack

Vladimir Guerrero was one of those players who seemed to use just about every professional model bat brand ever made, just like it appeared as if he could hit any type of pitch in any location. Guerrero was, in some respects, the anti-Griffey at the plate. Instead of possessing a smooth, effortless-looking swing, Guerrero swatted at baseballs like he was trying to prevent an angry bee from stinging him. A study in contrast,

no matter how unorthodox Guerrero's swing appeared, he finished his career with a higher batting average than many top stars of the era, including Griffey, Jr.

From Louisville Sluggers to Rawlings/Adirondacks, from SAM bats to X bats, Guerrero used a wide variety of bat brands and seemed to prefer maple bats for most of his career once this type of wood came into vogue. The combination of the maple wood and his violent, powerful swing caused a good number of his gamers to crack in dramatic fashion.

Some players prefer maple wood bats because of their durability, but when they crack, they have a tendency to *really* crack. You can often find his uniform number "27" marked on the knobs or barrel end of his bats, and this is the number he wore for the entirety of his playing days with four different teams. A number of his well-used gamers have a hefty coating of pine tar or Mota stick along the handle, and sometimes the gripping substance will extend into the center brand area. Guerrero was pretty active in signing a fair amount of his gamers, so if a collector exercises some patience, they should be able to locate a nice, autographed example. This includes a very limited number of home run bats.

▲ *Vladimir Guerrero's 2010 Louisville Slugger bat used in the All-Star Game.*

Tony Gwynn

★ ★ ★ ★ ★ ★ ★ ★ ★ ★ ★

Icon Sportswire

He was known as "Mr. Padre." We call him "Mr. Everything." A superb athlete for San Diego State University, Tony Gwynn was so good he was drafted by both the NBA and MLB in 1981. The 22-year-old Gwynn started with the Padres in 1982 and lit it up immediately. A prototypical contact hitter, Gwynn

had great bat skills and used the entire field to his advantage. After talking hitting with the legendary Ted Williams, Gwynn became the complete hitter, placing the ball all over the place.

How good was Tony Gwynn? A 15-time All-Star, with seven Silver Slugger Awards, and five Gold Gloves, Gwynn had a career .338 batting average and 3,141 hits. He holds the record for most seasons (7) leading the National League in hits and is tied with Honus Wagner for most NL batting titles (8). His 19 consecutive seasons batting at least .300 is a league record, and in the 1994 strike-shortened season, Gwynn batted .394, the closest any player has come to the magic .400 since Ted Williams nailed it in 1941.

Part of Gwynn's success was due to his amazing vision and ability to see pitches. An excellent bad ball hitter, he could identify what type of pitch was coming as soon as it left the pitcher's hand. One of the first to study video to refine his swing, Gwynn used thin handled, lightweight bats for more bat speed. His offensive output was overwhelming. The greatest Padre ever, Gwynn holds just about every Padre record, including batting average, at-bats, runs, hits, doubles, triples, RBI, stolen bases, walks, and total bases. He led the Padres to two NL pennants and, although they lost both contests, Gwynn batted a combined .371 in the 1984 and 1998 World Series. Off the field, Gwynn started the Tony Gwynn Foundation for charitable work. He was honored with the 1995 Branch Rickey Award, the 1998 Lou Gehrig Memorial Award, and the 1999 Roberto Clement Award.

A 20-year career Padre, Gwynn retired from baseball as one of the greatest contact hitters of all time. He returned to his alma mater as head baseball coach, compiling a .500 record and winning three Mountain West Championships in 12 years. The baseball facility at San Diego State University

Mr. Padre

★ ★ ★ ★ ★ ★ ★ ★ ★ ★ ★ ★ ★

is now named Tony Gwynn Stadium. Anthony Keith Gwynn was elected to the Hall of Fame in 2007 with almost 98% of the vote. Diagnosed with salivary gland cancer in 2010, Gwynn lost his valiant battle on June 16, 2014. Tony Gwynn is right up there with the baseball greats. As a matter of fact, the National League batting trophy is now known as the Tony Gwynn National League Batting Championship Award.

The Ultimate Season:				Career:			
Year/Team: 1994 SDP				Years: 20			
G:	110	HR:	12	G:	2440	HR:	135
AB:	419	RBI:	64	AB:	9288	RBI:	1138
R:	79	SB:	5	R:	1383	SB:	319
H:	165	BB:	48	H:	3141	BB:	790
2B:	35	OPS:	1.022	2B:	543	OPS:	.847
3B:	1	BA:	.394	3B:	85	BA:	.338

Tales from Joe's Bat Rack

Tony Gwynn professional model bats are certainly not as rare as some of the other wooden weapons used by the great hitters of the past, but the combination of his popularity as a player and the significance of his offensive achievements make his gamers a must for any comprehensive collection. In addition, some of his well-used gamers exhibit excellent character and visual appeal as a result of his distinct bat preparation. Bats from the latter part of his career, starting in the early 1990s, are often characterized by unique handle treatment in the form of thick tape near the base of the handle or other forms of grip enhancers, which often varied in color and design. Furthermore, well-used gamers often exhibit a light coating of pine tar on the upper handle.

Towards the end of his career, Gwynn provided game-used equipment to the hobby via his own company, which included equipment such as documented "hit" bats. These bats are autographed and inscribed (noting the particular hit) by Gwynn on the barrel. His bat of choice was certainly Louisville Slugger during his playing days, but Gwynn did use other brands along the way such as Rawlings/Adirondack and Hoosier bats.

Gwynn gamers are commonly found with his uniform number "19" noted on the knob or barrel end in black marker. This is the number Gwynn wore during his entire career. In some cases, you may see the specs of the gamer, such as the model number, length, or weight of the bat (ounces) noted as well. This practice started around 1990 and was added by the Padres' equipment manager.

Heavily-used Gwynn bats often possess a highly-concentrated area of ball marks located on the right barrel. Unlike some of the war clubs of the past, such as those ordered by the likes of Ty Cobb and Roberto Clemente, Gwynn bats are amongst the lightest gamers in baseball history. For Gwynn, the perennial National League batting champion, it was all about bat control.

" I love to hit. I can't wait until it's my turn. Sometimes, I think that's all baseball is. I root for the other team to go down 1-2-3 so I can hit again."
– Tony Gwynn

▲ *Tony Gwynn's 1999 Louisville Slugger bat.*

Rickey Henderson

★ ★ ★ ★ ★ ★ ★ ★ ★ ★ ★ ★

Mickey Pfleger/Sports Illustrated Collection/Getty Images

I t's a bird! It's a plane! No, it is the Man of Steal—Rickey Henderson. Drafted by the Oakland Athletics in 1976, Rickey Henderson was no Superman, but he was a superstar who could indeed fly like a bird and move with the speed of a 747. From the moment he debuted in 1979 at the age of 20 to the day he retired some 25 years later, Henderson scatted and swatted his way to baseball immortality. Upon his first ballot induction into the Hall of Fame in 2009, Henderson deservedly joined the likes of Ty Cobb, Jackie Robinson, and Willie Mays as men who employed speed as well as strength.

Henderson, baseball's all-time leader in runs scored, with 2,295, and stolen bases, with 1,406, was a thief of the highest magnitude. Twelve times, he led the league in steals, including his all-time best 130 in 1982. The Chicago native and Oakland wunderkind had power to go along with his pep. Henderson had an amazing 297 home runs, an impressive total for a man who, most often, served as the leadoff man. In fact, he had 81 leadoff homers, an all-time record. Henderson was all about stepping to the plate and making his way back there. He had 13 seasons with 100-plus runs scored including 146 in 1985. For a quarter-century, Henderson was a showman of the highest magnitude. The 10-time All-Star and 1990 American League MVP won World Series rings with the 1989 A's and the 1993 Blue Jays, and also made stops with the Yankees, Padres, Angels, Mets, Mariners, Red Sox, and Dodgers.

So what was the greatest hitting moment for a man who had 3,055 career hits? Why, of course, it was reaching base on an error on May 1, 1991. Well, there is a bit more to it than that. After a single moved him to second base, Henderson picked the right moment and sprinted for third base and history. Yankees catcher Matt Nokes had no shot and Henderson slid safely into the third sack with his all-time record 939th steal, breaking Lou Brock's long-held

★ ★ ★ ★ ★ ★ ★ ★ ★ ★ ★ ★

> " *Some way, I was going to scratch to get on base to steal that base. I steal that base, my day was good. My pride and joy was coming across the plate.*" – Rickey Henderson

The Ultimate Season:				Career:			
Year/Team: 1990 OAK				Years: 25			
G:	136	HR:	28	G:	3081	HR:	297
AB:	489	RBI:	61	AB:	10961	RBI:	1115
R:	119	SB:	65	R:	2295	SB:	1406
H:	159	BB:	97	H:	3055	BB:	2190
2B:	33	OPS:	1.016	2B:	510	OPS:	.820
3B:	3	BA:	.325	3B:	66	BA:	.279

record. Brock, the great St. Louis Cardinal, was present and congratulated Henderson. The ever-charismatic Henderson raised the base over his head and proclaimed himself "The greatest of all time!" He may not have been wrong. Henderson retired as the game's all-time leader in steals, runs, and walks—the latter number would be eventually surpassed by Barry Bonds. Baseball has been the backdrop for many a diamond dandy, but no man played the game with more verve, vitality, and vibrancy than Rickey Nelson Henley Henderson. Faster than a speeding bullet and more powerful than a locomotive? Yes, that was the Man of Steal.

Tales from Joe's Bat Rack

Rickey Henderson, the man that many consider the greatest leadoff hitter of all time, had a very long career. As a result, he used a lot of bats. While Henderson tried different professional model bat brands throughout his career, such as Rawlings/Adirondack, Carolina Club, and Mizuno, his bat of choice for most of it appeared to be Louisville Slugger. Moreover, he tended to use

a fairly light bat, much like contemporary Hall of Famer Tony Gwynn. Henderson also preferred using solid black bats for a good portion of his playing days versus the more common, natural-colored bats or two-toned gamers, though he did use all three types of bats at different stages of his career. To enhance his grip, Henderson did use pine tar and Mota stick at times, but he didn't use heavy amounts of either gripping substance very often.

It is not uncommon to find Henderson bats with various styles of taped handles too, especially towards the latter half of his career. Furthermore, Henderson would occasionally shave the handles of his bats to make them thinner, but this was a rare practice for him. It is important to note that Henderson's uniform number changed several times during his career, and you can find a number of his gamers with his uniform number noted on the knob or barrel end. While his primary uniform number was "24" with various teams, Henderson wore other numbers like "39" and "35" (Oakland A's, Seattle Mariners and Boston Red Sox), "22" (A's), "14" (Toronto Blue Jays), and "25" (Los Angeles Dodgers). Keep in mind that Henderson did produce a limited number of documented hit bats in the early 2000s.

▲ *Rickey Henderson's 2000 Louisville Slugger bat used to register career hit #3,001.*

Monte Irvin

★ ★ ★ ★ ★ ★ ★ ★ ★ ★ ★

Bettmann/Bettmann Collection/Getty Images

Between prime years lost to
segregated baseball and service in World War II,
Monte Irvin never got to show his best stuff in the
Major Leagues. The first African-American to play for the
New York Giants, Monford Merrill Irvin starred for 10 years
in the Negro National League, Mexico, and Cuba before

getting his chance in the Bigs in 1949 at 30 years old.

Irvin's father, an Alabama sharecropper, moved his family to New Jersey so his children could have opportunity. A four-sport athlete at East Orange High School, Irvin attended Lincoln University in Pennsylvania and played pro ball under the name Jimmy Nelson to preserve his amateur status. The easygoing, talented 19-year-old signed with the NNL Newark Eagles in 1938 and quickly became the team standout with his exceptional fielding, speed on the basepaths, and his ability to hit for both power and average. A lucrative salary offer convinced Irvin to jump to the Mexican League in 1942, where he excelled while enjoying an integrated lifestyle. His plans to return to Mexico for the 1943 season were canceled when he joined the Army Engineers and served in Europe until 1945. After rejoining the Newark Eagles in 1946, Irvin won the batting title with his .404 average and the Eagles beat the Kansas City Monarchs for the NNL World Series title.

Selected by the Giants to integrate the team in 1949, Irvin batted .299 in 1950, his first full season. He had a terrific 1951 season, batting .312 with 24 home runs, 174 hits, and a league-leading 121 RBI. Leo Durocher's "Miracle" Giants won the 1951 pennant but the Yankees took the Series. Irvin did his part though, batting .458 with a record-tying 11 hits and thrilled fans by stealing home in Game One of the contest. An All-Star in 1952, Irvin missed most of the season after fracturing his right ankle sliding into third base. He came back strong in

Mr. Murder

★ ★ ★ ★ ★ ★ ★ ★ ★ ★ ★

1953, batting .329 with 21 homers and, in 1954, he helped the Giants to the World Series title. After seven years in New York, Irvin played one year for the Cubs and retired after the 1956 season, at 37 years old, with a career .293 batting average and 731 hits compiled in eight MLB seasons.

In retirement, Monte Irvin was community relations director for Rheingold Brewery until his appointment in 1968 as assistant to the Commissioner of Major League Baseball, a post he held until 1984. Irvin became the fourth Negro League great to be elected to the Hall of Fame in 1973. He was chairperson of the Special Committee on the Negro Leagues for the Hall of Fame and later served on the Veterans Committee. Irvin was elected to Mexico's Salón de la Fama in 1971, the Cuban Baseball Hall of Fame in 1997, and the Giants retired his uniform number "20" in 2010. A true gentleman and ambassador of the game, Monte Irvin died in January 2016 at 96 years old.

The Ultimate Season:			Career:		
Year/Team: 1951 NYG			Years: 8		
G:	151	HR:	24	G:	764	HR:	99
AB:	558	RBI:	121	AB:	2499	RBI:	443
R:	94	SB:	12	R:	366	SB:	28
H:	174	BB:	89	H:	731	BB:	351
2B:	19	OPS:	.929	2B:	97	OPS:	.858
3B:	11	BA:	.312	3B:	31	BA:	.293

Irvin signed an endorsement contract with the bat company during his first season, which means the majority of the bats Irvin used had his facsimile signature on the barrel. While Irvin's primary uniform number was "20" with the New York Giants, he did wear number "7" briefly in 1949 and "39" during his last year with the Chicago Cubs in 1956. Since so few of his gamers are known at this time, there is little to study when it comes to player characteristics and knob marking tendencies. Irvin, one of the early African-American representatives in baseball and a Hall of Famer, is a name that resonates with collectors as a result of his historical importance to the game and the pure difficulty of his lumber.

Tales from Joe's Bat Rack

Along with lumber made for Sandy Koufax, Monte Irvin professional model bats rank near the very top of the list when it comes to rarity. With Koufax, the rarity of his bats is easily explained since such a small number of them were made to begin with. When it comes to Irvin, the reason behind the scarcity remains a mystery. Irvin did have a brief MLB career (1949–1956) after spending several years in the Negro Leagues, but that doesn't explain why only a small handful of Irvin bats are known today. According to the H&B records, Irvin had over 250 bats shipped to him while playing in the majors.

" *Monte was the best all-round player I have ever seen. As great as he was in 1951, he was twice that good 10 years earlier in the Negro Leagues.*"
– Roy Campanella

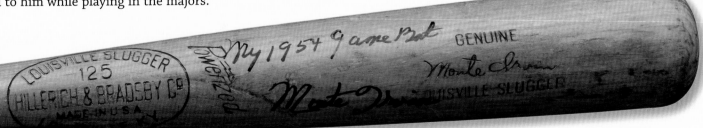

▲ *Monte Irvin's 1954 H&B bat.*

Reggie Jackson

★ ★ ★ ★ ★ ★ ★ ★ ★ ★ ★

moment on a baseball field was all about the number "3." Three pitchers, three pitches, three swings, three home runs. It was Game Six of the 1977 World Series, the renewal of the Yankees-Dodgers rivalry. The 1977 Yanks were a bickering bunch and acquiring Jackson was akin to adding gasoline to a brush fire. Graig Nettles hated Jackson. Jackson hated Thurman Munson. Billy Martin hated everyone. Earlier that season in Boston, Jackson and Martin nearly came to blows after Reggie was benched for dogging it in right field. Like Jackson's 1972, 1973, and 1974 Oakland A's world champions teams, the 1977 Yankees were a psychoanalyst's dream. In the locker room and in the press, it was utter mayhem, but on the field, it was Mozart.

In 1976, the Yanks were swept by Cincy's "Big Red Machine." Owner George Steinbrenner signed Jackson to assure that such October futility would not be repeated. And so it was that on October 18, 1977, "Mr. October," Reginald Martinez Jackson stepped to the plate. The Yanks held a 3–2 series lead over Los Angeles and could clinch their first crown since 1962 with a win. Dodgers starter Burt Hooton had walked Jackson in the second inning. In the fourth, the left-handed-hitting slugger drilled Hooton's first pitch into the right-field seats. The very next inning, against reliever Elias Sosa, Jackson cracked a two-run dinger off of Sosa's very first offering. The man who loved the limelight and craved the camera was utterly in his element. In the eighth inning, Jackson stepped to the plate against crafty knuckleballer Charlie Hough. Amid a deafening roar, he absolutely

In baseball arithmetic, the number "3" is most associated with a certain curse-starting, power-hitting legend named Babe Ruth, but that digit may be more appropriate for a latter-day Yankees slugger. While he wore number "31" with Kansas City, "9" with Oakland and Baltimore, and number "44" with the Yanks, Angels, and again with the A's, Reggie Jackson's seminal

★ ★ ★ ★ ★ ★ ★ ★ ★ ★ ★ ★ ★ ★ ★

"*A baseball swing is a very finely tuned instrument. It is repetition, and more repetition, then a little more after that.*" – Reggie Jackson

The Ultimate Season:			Career:		
Year/Team: 1969 OAK			Years: 21		
G:	152	HR: 47	G:	2820	HR: 563
AB:	549	RBI: 118	AB:	9864	RBI: 1702
R:	123	SB: 13	R:	1551	SB: 228
H:	151	BB: 114	H:	2584	BB: 1375
2B:	36	OPS: 1.018	2B:	463	OPS: .846
3B:	3	BA: .275	3B:	49	BA: .262

launched Hough's first pitch some 450 feet away into the center-field seats. It was bedlam in the Bronx.

Jackson hit 563 career home runs and led the American League in that category four times. He knocked in over 1,700 runs and slugged .490 in 21 big league seasons. His violent corkscrew swing was worth the price of admission even when he struck out, and he did so 2,597 times, tops all-time. On that night in 1977, however, Jackson did something never accomplished before or since. Three pitchers, three pitches, three swings, three home runs, and one undeniable legend named Reggie Jackson.

Tales from Joe's Bat Rack

Whether it's a product of his 563 home runs, his postseason performances, or his overall swagger, Reggie Jackson is a name that is hard to ignore if you collect the lumber of legends. When it comes to the slugger's bats, the demand can vary depending on the era of the bat. "Mr. October" moved around a bit during his career as he played for the Kansas City A's, Oakland A's (twice), Baltimore Orioles, New York Yankees, and California Angels. Bats that date to his Yankees days and first stop with the A's often sell for a premium. Exceptions to this general rule would include special event bats such as those used for and linked to a specific home run or milestone from the latter stages of his career.

In addition, Mr. October seemed to prefer H&B (endorsement contract) bats during the early stages of his career. He signed an endorsement contract with the company in 1966 prior to making his Major League debut one year later. Jackson gradually transitioned to Adirondacks (block letter) and seemed to prefer them from the late 1970s until the end of his career in 1987. While a number of his bats from the first half of his career were made with a natural-colored finish, Jackson did order quite a few hickory-finished (dark-colored) bats. These are seen with or without "sand handles"—ones without added color. Some of his gamers exhibit modest pine tar remnants along the handle, but Reggie did not typically use heavy amounts of the substance.

Most of the time, you can find Reggie gamers with his uniform number noted on the knob in marker. As a member of the A's and Orioles in the 1970s, his uniform number "9" would often be underlined in black marker. While his primary uniform number was "44" for most of his career, Jackson did wear "31" during his first season with the Kansas City A's.

▲ *Reggie Jackson's 1977 Adirondack bat.*

Al Kaline

★ ★ ★ ★ ★ ★ ★ ★ ★ ★ ★ ★ ★

Louis Requena/Major League Baseball Collection/Getty Images

One of the great outfielders of his generation, Kaline won 10 Gold Gloves and was voted an All-Star 18 times. His 22-year career spanned from 1953 to 1974, and in that time, he established himself as a terrific hits and doubles man. In that 1955 season, as a precocious 20-year-old, Kaline stroked 200 hits on the nose. He followed that up with totals of 194, 170 twice, and 167 the next four seasons. In 1961, he smashed 190 hits along with a league-leading 41 doubles and 19 home runs. Even late into his 30s, Kaline remained a consistent threat in that Tiger lineup. In 1971, at age 36, he batted .294 with 15 homers and 54 RBI in 133 games. More than consistency, Kaline was about class. He carried himself in a way that endeared him to fans everywhere. In 1973, he received the Roberto Clemente Award which "exemplifies the game of baseball, sportsmanship, community involvement and the individual's contribution to his team."

The Tigers' greatest team feat during Kaline's career encompassed his personal greatest moments. In the 1968 World Series against the defending champion St. Louis Cardinals, Kaline batted .379 with 11 hits in 29 at-bats. The seven-game series was a thrilling ride, and Kaline definitely drove the Tigers' bus. He had 2 home runs, 2 doubles, and 8 RBI in the Series while slugging .655 and posting an OBP of .400. The following year, Kaline was voted to the Greatest Tiger Team of All Time, and in 1970, a street adjacent to Tiger Stadium was named Kaline Drive in his honor. In one of those great baseball ironies, Kaline got his 3,000th hit on September 24, 1974, in his native Baltimore. In 1976, he began a new 26-year career as color commentator for the Tigers, and he was elected to the Hall of Fame in

The epitome of quiet grace and diligent work, Al Kaline was one of the greatest Detroit Tigers of all time. A smooth swinging outfielder, Kaline was the quintessential professional hitter and his consistency was second to none. The Baltimore native spent 22 years in Detroit, amassing 3,007 hits, 399 home runs, and 1,582 RBI. In his last two seasons, 1973 and 1974, Kaline batted .255 and .262, respectively, dipping his career batting average to .297. He was, however, a consistent .300 hitter throughout his career, topping the mark nine times, including a league-leading and career high .340 in 1955.

1980. Fittingly, Albert William Kaline remains the only man who answers to the name "Mr. Tiger."

The Ultimate Season:				Career:			
Year/Team: 1955 DET				Years: 22			
G:	152	HR:	27	G:	2834	HR:	399
AB:	588	RBI:	102	AB:	10116	RBI:	1582
R:	121	SB:	6	R:	1622	SB:	137
H:	200	BB:	82	H:	3007	BB:	1277
2B:	24	OPS:	.967	2B:	498	OPS:	.855
3B:	8	BA:	.340	3B:	75	BA:	.297

Tales from Joe's Bat Rack

The Detroit Tigers have a rich history when it comes to outstanding hitters, from Ty Cobb to Hank Greenberg to Miguel Cabrera. Along the line, during the 1950s through the mid-1970s, Al Kaline kept that tradition going. This 3,000 Hit Club member and 1955 American League batting champion was also popular with fans, which helps his gamers secure a spot in most comprehensive bat collections. Professional model bats of the Detroit legend remain a hot commodity and are fairly tough to locate compared to some of his contemporaries, such as those shipped to Harmon Killebrew and Brooks Robinson. In terms of weight, Kaline's bats are very much like the gamers that are used in the current game, often weighing in around 31–32 ounces.

" *I like to send him [Kaline] to the plate in the number two slot because he is the best there is at moving up the runner. He can bunt, hit the ball behind the runner to right, or belt it out of the park."* – Billy Martin

Kaline, who primarily used H&B bats throughout his career after signing an endorsement contract with the company in the spring of 1954, often applied a modest amount of pine tar to the handles of his gamers to enhance his grip. You will often see slightly concentrated tar on the upper-handle area, about eight inches or so up from the knob area. Keep in mind that Kaline did make his debut in 1953, prior to having signature models made, but the vast majority of his bats used during his 22-year career feature his facsimile signature.

In addition, Kaline bats are often marked on the knobs, but different variations do exist. One variation contains a large, more traditional-looking uniform number on the knob. In some instances, Kaline's primary uniform number "6" nearly covers the entire knob and is very distinct looking. In most cases, the "6" is underlined, but there are examples that feature the number without the line. Other styles may contain a much smaller "6" and his last name "Kaline" in print or his entire name "Al Kaline" in print without his uniform number. You can see the latter styles in a number of vintage photographs. It is important to note that Kaline did wear number "25" during his first season with Detroit.

▲ *Al Kaline's 1958-59 H&B bat.*

Willie Keeler

★ ★ ★ ★ ★ ★ ★ ★ ★ ★ ★

Bettmann/Bettmann Collection/Getty Images

Famous for the line, "Hit 'em where they ain't," Willie Keeler was a master of finding a hole in the defense. He sprayed the ball to all fields and was an expert baserunner. At 5-foot, 4-inches, and 140 pounds, he was a pesky gnat and a constant pain for opposing pitchers. After starting his career with the Giants, Keeler spent one season in Brooklyn, and then moved to the National League Baltimore Orioles where he blossomed as a

superstar. Over five seasons in Baltimore, he batted .388 with 1,097 hits. A dynasty in the final decade of the 1800s, the Orioles were a talented but bickering bunch. They won over 400 games between 1894 and 1898 and two Temple Cups, the prize for a year-end series between the National League's two best teams. The 1894 season was the first of eight straight 200-hit campaigns for Keeler. The mark lasted for over a century, until Ichiro Suzuki broke it in 2009. A Brooklyn native and son of Irish immigrants, Keeler played in his hometown for five seasons, batting .352 with 833 hits, but he was truly a Subway Series all to himself, having played for all of the New York teams—the New York Giants, Brooklyn Superbas, and New York Highlanders during his 19-year career.

For 17 consecutive seasons from 1892 to 1906, Willie Keeler hit over .300, including a mark of .424 in 1897, still the all-time high for a lefty batter. He opened that 1897 season with a 44-game hitting streak, a record that would reign until Joe DiMaggio's epic 56-game streak in 1941. A run-scoring machine, he topped the century mark every year from 1894 to 1901. Keeler won two batting crowns and three hits titles, but his 44-game hitting streak of 1897 stands out as his signature accomplishment. He actually posted a 45-game streak given that he hit safely in the final game of the 1896 season. When Pete Rose matched Keeler's 44-game streak in 1978, he did so with much media attention, but it was Wee Willie Keeler who set the pace.

Keeler had a career 2,932 hits, the majority of them singles. Upon his retirement in 1910, he was second all-time to Hall of Famer Cap Anson in career hits. In retirement, Keeler

★ ★ ★ ★ ★ ★ ★ ★ ★ ★ ★ ★

> "*Keeler could bunt any time he chose. If the third baseman came in for a tap, he invariably pushed the ball past the fielder. If he stayed back, he bunted. Also he had a trick of hitting a high hopper to an infielder. The ball would bounce so high that he was across the bag before he could be stopped.*" – Honus Wagner

The Ultimate Season:				Career:			
Year/Team: 1897 BLN				Years: 19			
G:	129	HR:	0	G:	2123	HR:	33
AB:	564	RBI:	74	AB:	8591	RBI:	810
R:	145	SB:	64	R:	1719	SB:	495
H:	239	BB:	35	H:	2932	BB:	524
2B:	27	OPS:	1.003	2B:	241	OPS:	.802
3B:	19	BA:	.424	3B:	145	BA:	.341

coached and went through some hard times. Ever popular, his teammates were always there to help him out with a job or a place to live. On New Year's Day 1923 Keeler died of heart disease at the age of 50. William Henry Keeler was inducted into the Hall of Fame in 1939 and remains a standard-bearer for consistency and production.

Tales from Joe's Bat Rack

As a result of Willie Keeler's wizardry with the bat during the late-nineteenth century and early-twentieth century, finishing his career with a .341 batting average, his professional model bats remain a key component to most comprehensive collections. Most players of the era have left the hobby with either very few or, in some cases, no known examples of their gamers. Keeler is no exception. As of the time of this writing, only a few Keeler bats have been verified. Keeler appeared to use a very short but heavy bat. The known examples measure under a mere 31 inches in length, but they usually weigh in the mid-to-high 30s in ounces.

Of the miniscule number that do exist, most were manufactured by Spalding. Hobby experts have concluded that Spalding Autograph Series and Gold Medal Autograph Series bats were used at the Major League level as a result of these bats being present in the vault at Louisville Slugger. Players would send the bats to Louisville Slugger, after using the Spalding bats, to have the company replicate and produce the exact model with their brand. These Spalding bats can be found bearing the signatures of period stars like Roger Bresnahan, Frank Chance, and Johnny Evers, in addition to Keeler.

While it is true that some of these Spalding bats were made available to the public, experts can distinguish them from the pro models by the characteristics located on the knob or barrel end. The retail models feature the Spalding trademark, which has a sharp, finished appearance. Bats that were made for professional use do not possess the trademark and showcase an unfinished knob, one that appears to have been hand turned. In many cases, the knobs also feature lathe marks and/or filed edges.

▲ *Willie Keeler's 1908-10 Spalding bat.*

Ralph Kiner

★ ★ ★ ★ ★ ★ ★ ★ ★ ★ ★

Bettmann/Bettmann Collection/Getty Images

joined the Pirates in 1947, he mentored the young Kiner on hitting and conducting himself like a professional. The short left-center field at Forbes Field was originally called "Greenberg Gardens," but it soon became known as "Kiner's Korner" for the prodigious blasts that Kiner launched over that short porch. The six-time All-Star led the league in home runs seven straight years from 1946 to 1952, becoming the first major leaguer to accomplish that feat. Kiner reached another MLB milestone when he hit home runs in four consecutive at-bats on two separate occasions. He was also the first National League player to hit 50 home runs twice. In 1949, Kiner's 54 homers fell just two short of the National League record held by Hack Wilson. In addition to his power numbers, Kiner led the league at various stages of his career in OPS, OBP, slugging, total bases, runs, walks, and RBI. Unfortunately, he developed severe back issues which curtailed his career when he was only 32 years old.

Ralph Kiner parlayed his successful baseball career into a lifelong job that lasted over 50 years. His "other" baseball career started in 1961 when he began broadcasting Chicago White Sox games. In 1962, he moved over to the National League to assume broadcasting duties for the New York Mets. The highlight of his career with the Mets was broadcasting the 1969 "Miracle Mets" season. Kiner ended up broadcasting for a total of 53 seasons, one of the longest tenures ever. His home run calls became famous in New York, "It is gone, goodbye!" was his battle cry. Also well-known for his connection with Hollywood personalities,

From 1946 through 1955, Ralph Kiner was one of the most feared power hitters in the National League. Playing primarily for the Pittsburgh Pirates and later the Chicago Cubs and Cleveland Indians, he was a beast at the plate. Kiner credits Hank Greenberg as his biggest influence. When the 36-year-old Greenberg

★ ★ ★ ★ ★ ★ ★ ★ ★ ★ ★ ★ ★

Kiner's friends included megastars in the music and movie industry. He was linked with several Hollywood starlets over the years, including Elizabeth Taylor, and it was not uncommon to see Kiner hanging with Sinatra or Bing Crosby. In 1951, Kiner married 22-year-old tennis star Nancy Chaffee. Although he never hit for a high average (lifetime .279), Kiner was elected to the Hall of Fame in 1975, getting in by one vote over the minimum. Had his career not been cut short by injury, he may have surpassed the 400-home run mark and 1,200 RBI total. Ralph McPherran Kiner continued his broadcast career until just before his death in 2014. He left the air waves at the young age of 91.

The Ultimate Season:				Career:			
Year/Team: 1949 PIT				Years: 10			
G:	152	HR:	54	G:	1472	HR:	369
AB:	549	RBI:	127	AB:	5205	RBI:	1015
R:	116	SB:	6	R:	971	SB:	22
H:	170	BB:	117	H:	1451	BB:	1011
2B:	19	OPS:	1.089	2B:	216	OPS:	.946
3B:	5	BA:	.310	3B:	39	BA:	.279

Tales from Joe's Bat Rack

The story of Ralph Kiner is one that needs to be shared with fans who never had the chance to see him play so that future generations of collectors can realize how great he was during his somewhat brief career. Unlike a number of the legendary names on most advanced bat collector lists, Kiner did not accumulate the career totals that cause people to stop in their tracks. What Kiner did during his first seven seasons, however, was incredible. Kiner led the National League in home runs in each of his first seven seasons, a feat that is hard to imagine ever being repeated or eclipsed. Kiner professional model bats are relatively tough since his career was cut short due to injury (chronic back issues) in 1955. Kiner signed an endorsement contract with H&B in the spring of 1946, which means virtually all of the bats the slugger used at the MLB level feature his facsimile signature.

Most of his career, Kiner wore the number "4," but he did briefly wear "43" in 1946 and "9" in 1955. You will find Kiner gamers with his uniform number in large black marker on the knob, but you might also see another notation. Kiner would occasionally have the weight of the bat placed on the knob as well. For example, in addition to a large "4," you might also see "37" on the knob, which represents the ounces. Speaking of weight, Kiner ordered some very heavy bats during his career, with several orders of bats tipping the scales at 38–42 ounces each. Other players, including Hall of Famers like Frank Robinson and Harmon Killebrew, would also identify the weight of the bat on the knob at different stages of their careers. This was done so a player could immediately identify the appropriate bat in the bat rack.

> "*Kiner can wipe out your lead with one swing.*" – Warren Spahn

▲ *Ralph Kiner's 1950 H&B bat.*

Roger Maris

★ ★ ★ ★ ★ ★ ★ ★ ★ ★ ★

stock, Mantle an Oklahoman and Maris from Minnesota. Basically the same height and weight, both men possessed the unique ability to hit a baseball out of the park. Maris broke into the Bigs in 1957 with Cleveland, slugging 14 home runs and adding 51 RBI. In 1958, he blossomed with 28 round-trippers and 80 RBI, but was traded to Kansas City where he was productive although prone to injury and inconsistency.

In December of 1959, Maris was dealt to the Yankees in a multi-player deal. The 1960 Yankees lost the World Series to Pittsburgh, but they were absolutely stacked, winning 97 games with players like Mantle, Bill Skowron, Tony Kubek, and Clete Boyer. The quiet Maris smashed 39 home runs and led the American League with 112 RBI. He made his second consecutive All-Star Game and was voted league MVP while winning a Gold Glove for his outfield play. In 1961, Roger Eugene Maris would experience one of the greatest, most wonderful, and agonizing seasons ever. He and Mantle exploded out of the gate bashing home runs at an alarming rate. Tabbed the "M & M Boys," they thrilled home and road audiences. For Maris, it was no thrill at all. First, he was chasing a record held by the most beloved Yankee ever, and second, the guy he was battling may have been number two on that list. Maris, introverted by nature, was hounded by the press and jeered by fans of Ruth and Mantle.

I n 1961, New York Yankees teammates Roger Maris and Mickey Mantle feverishly chased the hallowed milestone of a Yankee from yesteryear—Babe Ruth's single-season mark of 60 home runs set in 1927. Maris and Mantle were both from rural

As Mantle's injuries and nightlife derailed his home run pace, Maris was all alone, figuratively and literally. He experienced hair loss and horrible anxiety due to the stress. To add insult to injury, Commissioner Ford Frick, a longtime friend of Ruth, ruled that in order to be recognized, the record would

★ ★ ★ ★ ★ ★ ★ ★ ★ ★ ★ ★

> "*His swing was level and compact, and it wasted nothing. He seemed to leverage his entire body when he swung, in an almost perfect use of it as a physical instrument.*" – David Halberstam, ESPN columnist

The Ultimate Season:			Career:		
Year/Team: 1961 NYY			Years: 12		
G:	161	HR: 61	G:	1463	HR: 275
AB:	590	RBI: 141	AB:	5101	RBI: 850
R:	132	SB: 0	R:	826	SB: 21
H:	159	BB: 94	H:	1325	BB: 652
2B:	16	OPS: .993	2B:	195	OPS: .822
3B:	4	BA: .269	3B:	42	BA: .260

have to be broken within 154 games, the amount played in 1927, not the 162 games played in 1961. Maris persevered and tied Ruth's record on September 26. Five days later, he entered the final game of the season vs. Boston, one homer away from history. On October 1, 1961, Maris took Tracy Stallard deep in the fourth inning to break the record and secure his place in history, but the silent slugger was never the same. He would have a few more productive seasons in New York before ending his career with the Cardinals in 1967 and 1968. Always steadfast and focused on his craft, Roger Maris had immense talent but was an ordinary man tossed into extraordinary circumstances.

Tales from Joe's Bat Rack

Roger Maris professional model bats are amongst a small group of Non-Hall of Famer lumber that remain extremely desirable. With the exception of bats used by Shoeless Joe Jackson, and arguably Pete Rose, Maris bats rank near the top of the list for those not enshrined in Cooperstown. In fact, like the two aforementioned stars, Maris bats are actually more popular than bats used by many other players who are Hall of Fame members. When it comes to Maris gamers, there are a couple of characteristics to note.

To begin with, there are several different styles of knob notations seen on Maris gamers. In black marker, "Roger" or "Maris" notations on the knob can often be seen in a number of vintage photographs. It is believed that these notations were actually made by Maris himself and they have a very distinct look. On occasion, you can also find Maris gamers with an "RM" or his primary uniform number "9" underlined on the knob from his post-1959 career. It is important to remember that Maris wore different uniform numbers before settling on "9" in 1960. Maris wore "32" and "5" with the Cleveland Indians and "35" and "3" with the Kansas City Athletics.

Maris was an avid user of pine tar at certain points of his career and the placement of the tar is usually seen on the upper handle in a concentrated six-inch area—a pattern that is very similar to the one seen on some Mickey Mantle game-used bats from the 1960s. Furthermore, it is clear that Maris preferred H&B bats throughout his playing days. Yankee-era Maris bats are generally valued higher than bats used prior to 1960 or while playing for the St. Louis Cardinals at the end of his career.

▲ *Roger Maris' 1961 H&B bat used to hit home run #49 of the season.*

Paul O'Neill

★ ★ ★ ★ ★ ★ ★ ★ ★ ★ ★

Icon Sportswire

1981 amateur draft. After some seasoning in the minors, O'Neill played his first full Major League season in 1988 under manager Pete Rose. The Reds took second place that year and O'Neill batted a respectable .252 with 16 homers, 122 hits, and 73 RBI. After Rose was banned for gambling, Lou Piniella took the helm in 1990 and led Cincy to their first World Series win since the "Big Red Machine" did it in 1976.

After his 1993 trade to the Yankees, O'Neill's career took off. During that period, he batted .300 or better six consecutive seasons with a career-best .359 BA in 1994 for the American League batting title. He slammed 20-plus home runs seven seasons and had 100-plus RBI four consecutive seasons. O'Neill is remembered for his three-home run game on August 31, 1995, vs. the California Angels. Both O'Neill and the Yankees had slumped in August, but they had a chance for the AL Wild Card slot. In the first inning, with two men on base, O'Neill hammered Brian Anderson's offering for a three-run homer. In the bottom of the second, O'Neill came through with another three-run dinger, and he homered again in the fifth inning. The Yanks won 11–6 thanks to O'Neill's eight RBI. That proved to be the third of 25 late-season wins that clinched the Wild Card.

A fierce competitor, Paul O'Neill was that player you hated—unless he was on your team. He patrolled right field for most of his career and was a solid contributor to the Cincinnati Reds from 1985 to 1992 and the New York Yankees from 1993 to 2001. Paul Andrew O'Neill grew up in Columbus, Ohio, dreaming of playing for the Cincinnati Reds. That dream came true in the

Joe Torre came in as manager in 1996 and led the Yanks all the way to a World Series win—their first since 1978. They took three more Series titles (1998, 1999, 2000) and a pennant in 2001, O'Neill's final season. In his nine years with the Yankees, he batted .303 with 858 RBI, 1,426 hits, and 185 home runs. A fan favorite, O'Neill put everything he had into every game. He was known for his

★ ★ ★ ★ ★ ★ ★ ★ ★ ★ ★ ★

fiery outbursts, slamming his helmet and punching the water cooler, but also for joyously celebrating with teammates on the field. After 17 seasons, O'Neill retired in October 2001 with a career .288 BA, 281 homers, 2,105 hits, and 1,269 RBI. He has been a broadcast analyst for the Yankees since 2002, and in 2014, the Yankees honored him with a plaque in Monument Park which reads in part: "An intense competitor and team leader, O'Neill was beloved for his relentless pursuit of perfection."

The Ultimate Season:		Career:	
Year/Team: 1994 NYY		Years: 17	
G: 103	HR: 21	G: 2053	HR: 281
AB: 368	RBI: 83	AB: 7318	RBI: 1269
R: 68	SB: 5	R: 1041	SB: 141
H: 132	BB: 72	H: 2105	BB: 892
2B: 25	OPS: 1.064	2B: 451	OPS: .833
3B: 1	BA: .359	3B: 21	BA: .288

Tales from Joe's Bat Rack

Bats used by New York Yankees favorite Paul O'Neill are amongst the most collectible non-Hall of Famer bats in the hobby. O'Neill, who did have other bat brands shipped to him, such as Young and SAM, clearly preferred Louisville Slugger bats during his career. Collectors may encounter some pre-endorsement contract, block letter O'Neill bats from his early days with the Cincinnati Reds, but the majority of his gamers feature his facsimile signature.

The All-Star outfielder used a larger, heavier bat than most other players did during the era. Well-used O'Neill gamers are known for exhibiting outstanding character. O'Neill was known for applying a distinct pattern of tape along the handle in order to enhance his grip at the plate. The unique pattern, which has a crisscross appearance, usually starts at the base of the handle and stops right before the center brand. The application has very large gaps between the points where the tape crosses along the handle. O'Neill was known to use varying amounts of pine tar as well, but most of his gamers do not feature a heavy application.

In addition, O'Neill was known for pounding his cleats with the barrel of his bats. His well-used gamers can be found with clusters of deep cleat impressions along the back of the barrel. O'Neill wore the number "21" for his entire career with the Cincinnati Reds and New York Yankees. A fair number of his gamers can be found with his uniform number marked on the knob or barrel end, but many of O'Neill's bats do not. This is especially true of bats that date to his Yankees days.

" *Hitting is a lot more than just picking up a bat and swinging it. You've got to be observant, evaluate the situation, know the pitcher and his tendencies, and know yourself. If you want to be successful, you have to become a student." – Paul O'Neill*

▲ *Paul O'Neill's 1999 Louisville Slugger bat.*

Kirby Puckett

★ ★ ★ ★ ★ ★ ★ ★ ★ ★ ★

Mickey Pfleger/Sports Illustrated Collection/Getty Images

20 or more home runs six times with a career-best of 31 homers in 1986. The 1989 batting champ with .339 BA, Puckett led the American League in hits, RBI, total bases, and singles at various times in his career. On May 13, 1989, Puckett hit four doubles in one game to tie the MLB record. Built like a fireplug, his body type belied his speed, but he was a threat on the basepaths and in centerfield, making tremendous leaping catches to rob sure home runs. Puckett led the league in putouts, assists and double plays turned several times during his career.

With his engaging smile, outgoing personality, and great enthusiasm, Kirby Puckett's love of the game was infectious. Known for his free-swinging style at the plate, acrobatic catches in centerfield and speed on the basepaths, Puckett brought baseball fever back to Minneapolis. A Minnesota Twin for his entire 12-year career, Puckett was a first-round draft pick in 1982, made his debut in May of 1984, and became part of a new roster of Twins talent.

The stars were aligned in 1987. With new manager Tom Kelly, and Puckett, Kent Hrbek, Gary Gaetti, and Tom Brunansky to provide the power, the Twins notched their first World Series championship since moving the team to Minnesota in 1961. A 10-time All-Star and the 1993 All-Star MVP, Puckett garnered six Silver Slugger Awards and six Gold Gloves. He batted .300 or better eight seasons and slammed

After finishing in last place in 1990, the Twins amazingly won the World Series in 1991. Kirby Puckett is credited with two pivotal plays in Game Six of the Series vs. Atlanta. The Twins were down 3–2 going into the game on October 26, 1991, at the Metrodome. In the third inning Puckett leapt high on the fence for an improbable catch of Braves Ron Gant's sure-fire extra-base hit. In the bottom of the 11th inning, he launched a walk-off home run for the win. Game Seven was scoreless for nine innings but the Twins prevailed in the 10th to take home the title.

Sadly, in March of 1996, Puckett lost vision in one eye due to glaucoma, which abruptly ended his career. He officially retired in July of that year with a career .318 batting average, 207 home runs, 1,071 runs and 2,304 hits. Puckett's uniform number "34" was retired by the Twins in 1997 and he was inducted into the Hall of Fame in 2001, his first year of

★ ★ ★ ★ ★ ★ ★ ★ ★ ★ ★

> "*Kirby played the game the way it was meant to be played—with enthusiasm, with class, with all-out energy and most important, with a smile on his face. For Kirby, baseball was a joy and it made the game fun for everyone around him too.*"
> – George Brett

The Ultimate Season:				Career:			
Year/Team: 1988 MIN				Years: 12			
G:	158	HR:	24	G:	1783	HR:	207
AB:	657	RBI:	121	AB:	7244	RBI:	1085
R:	109	SB:	6	R:	1071	SB:	134
H:	234	BB:	23	H:	2304	BB:	450
2B:	42	OPS:	.920	2B:	414	OPS:	.837
3B:	5	BA:	.356	3B:	57	BA:	.318

eligibility. Just 10 years after retiring from the game, Kirby Puckett died after suffering a massive stroke in 2006 at the age of 45.

Tales from Joe's Bat Rack

While Kirby Puckett's career may have been cut short due to a sudden loss of vision in one eye, he was able to showcase his well-rounded talents with the bat prior to his retirement in 1996. There are a few keys to note about Kirby Puckett professional model bats. First, Puckett certainly preferred Louisville Slugger bats during his career. He ordered many natural-colored, black, and two-toned bats throughout his playing days, but the chosen brand stayed the same. Puckett signed an endorsement contract with the company towards

the very end of his rookie year, so it is possible to find gamers that feature his name in block letters from 1984. That year, Puckett had nearly 600 plate appearances.

Second, Puckett would occasionally tape the handles of his bats with a standard, spiral taping method or crisscross application along the lower half of the handle. Puckett did not utilize tape all the time to enhance his grip; however, he was a fairly avid user of pine tar throughout his career. The use of tar changed over time, from a more focused application on the upper handle to a more liberal use of tar later on. In addition to tape and tar, Puckett was known to shave the handles on some of his gamers, which was a fairly common practice in the 1980s and 1990s.

Finally, and perhaps the most unique characteristic about Puckett gamers, are the markings that can sometimes be found on the knob and barrel end. You can often find Puckett's uniform number "34" in black, silver, or gold marker, but it is the addition of motivational words like "Win" or "Hits" and even his nickname "Puck" that set his knob markings apart from those seen on other player bats. Puckett gamers have been found with several different words of this nature, beyond the few mentioned above.

▲ *Kirby Puckett's 1992 Louisville Slugger bat.*

Manny Ramirez

Icon Sportswire

seasons in Boston where he clowned and clouted his way to two World Series crowns, the 2004 World Series MVP award, and numerous instances of the now infamous phrase, "Manny being Manny." With his long dreadlocks and even longer tape measure blasts, Ramirez both endeared and enraged the Boston fans and media. The press questioned his injuries and bashed him for his slow jogs down the first base line and in left field. Ironically, teammates will aver that Ramirez was one of the hardest working hitters in the game. The Dominican Republic native nailed the 2002 batting title with his .349 average, owns nine Silver Slugger Awards and, as of this writing, he holds the record for most postseason home runs with 29.

Along with the likes of Kevin Millar, Johnny Damon, Trot Nixon, David Ortiz, and Pedro Martinez, Ramirez formed the guts of the 2004 Red Sox "Idiots" who ended the 86-year-old curse of the Bambino. Along the way, Ramirez and company became the first team to win an ALCS series after trailing three games to none, defeating the Yankees in historic fashion in the 2004 ALCS. A star long before his Red Sox rings, in 1999 with the Indians, Ramirez smacked 44 home runs and knocked in an amazing 165 runs, good for 14th on the all-time single season list. His career marks of 555 homers, 1,831 RBI, a .312 batting average, and 12 All-Star selections (11 straight between 1998 and 2008) would be beyond Hall of Fame worthy, except for, well, Manny being Manny. Ties to steroid use cloud Ramirez's legacy, but his outstanding production over a long period of time cannot be denied.

One of the most productive and lethal right-handed hitters of his generation, Manny Ramirez was in the media spotlight from his time in Cleveland as a precocious 23-year-old who clubbed 31 homers and 107 RBI in 1995 to his tumultuous seven-plus

In July 2008, Boston shipped Ramirez to the Dodgers. It is here, perhaps, that Ramirez experienced his shining moment as a ballplayer, albeit brief. That season he batted a whopping .396 with 17 home runs and 53 RBI in just 53 games. With his textbook stance—right knee slightly bent,

★ ★ ★ ★ ★ ★ ★ ★ ★ ★ ★ ★ ★

left leg straight, and bat cocked near his head—Ramirez knocked the ball to all fields, admired his home runs, cajoled fans, and became the biggest thing in Los Angeles since the Hollywood sign. In fact, the Dodgers named a section of left field seats after Ramirez, dubbing it "Mannywood." This California dream was short-lived however, and in 2011, after brief stints with the White Sox and Rays, he was out of baseball at age 38. Ramirez's personality quirks could be both entertaining and enraging, but they were never boring. The soap opera that was Manuel Aristides Ramirez is truly one for the baseball ages.

The Ultimate Season:			Career:		
Year/Team: 1999 CLE			Years: 19		
G:	147	HR: 44	G:	2302	HR: 555
AB:	522	RBI: 165	AB:	8244	RBI: 1831
R:	131	SB: 2	R:	1544	SB: 38
H:	174	BB: 96	H:	2574	BB: 1329
2B:	34	OPS: 1.105	2B:	547	OPS: .996
3B:	3	BA: .333	3B:	20	BA: .312

Tales from Joe's Bat Rack

Manny Ramirez ended his career with a bit of controversy as a result of his link to performance-enhancing drugs. However, his career offensive numbers place him in an elite group of all-time hitters. It remains to be seen how future generations will treat the 500 Home Run Club member in time, but the fact remains that his combination of power, plate coverage and average made Ramirez a very special offensive force. During his career, Ramirez used just about every bat brand manufactured during the era. This includes, but is not limited to, Diablo, Louisville Slugger, Marucci, Nokona, Rawlings/Adirondack, Sam, SSK, and X bats. This is just a sampling. Some players were loyal to one or two bat brands throughout their playing days. Not Manny. He may have gone up to the plate with a broomstick or a tree branch if MLB let him.

In addition, Ramirez employed various types of bat preparation, which changed throughout his playing days. Collectors may encounter well-used examples with different styles of taping along the handle and knob. Sometimes, Ramirez would apply a tape wrap around the knob alone. Other times, Ramirez would apply tape all the way up the handle to enhance his grip. Ramirez used many different techniques. In addition, you will often find a heavy layer of Mota stick and/or pine tar, especially on bats where no tape is present on the handle. Ramirez played for a few different teams during his career but only wore two different uniform numbers, "24" (Cleveland Indians, Boston Red Sox, and Tampa Bay Rays) and "99" (Los Angeles Dodgers and Chicago White Sox). It is important to note that only a portion of the bat knobs on Ramirez's gamers feature his uniform number.

> " *He's [Manny's] got a great work ethic, as far as his preparation... I know there's a lot of colorful anecdotes about him and whatnot, but when it comes to the work stuff, he's all business." – Joe Torre*

▲ *Manny Ramirez's 2004 Louisville Slugger bat.*

Jim Rice

Focus On Sport/Getty Images Sport Collection/Getty Images

nature and focused veneer only added to the distance. Ted Williams had an oil and water relationship with the media. Carl Yastrzemski regularly sidestepped silly questions from the press. These men, Rice's predecessors in Boston's hallowed left field, were deified, while Rice was ostracized.

In 1975, he put together a stellar rookie season with 22 home runs, 102 RBI, and a .309 batting average,

For many baseball fans, justice was served in 2009. After 15 years of being snubbed by the Baseball Writers Association of America, James Edward Rice took his much-deserved place in baseball's Hall of Fame. Many felt that Rice's delayed selection was a product of his frosty relationship with the media. At best, the Red Sox slugger was cordial to the press. At worst, he was impenetrable. In truth, Rice's only real crime was being silent. In a 1993 interview, Rice revealed why he seemed aloof. "I was very protective of my work habits," Rice said. "I didn't want anyone to know what I did to achieve the success I had."

Rice, an African-American from Anderson, South Carolina, came to Boston in 1974 at the height of racial unrest in the city. Almost from day one, he was overlooked and undervalued by the predominantly white media. His serious

but it was fellow rookie Fred Lynn who grabbed Boston's headlines and hearts; and Rice finished second to Lynn for Rookie of the Year honors. Dubbed "The Gold Dust Twins," Rice and Lynn batted third and fourth in the order, infusing new life into the Sox, driving them to the World Series. Perhaps the most memorable at-bat in the career of this star-crossed slugger was a negative experience. On September 21, 1975, Rice stepped to the plate against the Tigers Vern Ruhle. He settled into that quiet batting stance, feet shoulder-width apart, and bat nearly at a 90-degree angle. Ruhle delivered and hit Rice with a pitch that shattered his left hand and ended his season. Red Sox fans still imagine what might have been if Rice had played in that memorable 1975 World Series vs. the Reds. The entire course of baseball history might have been altered.

The Boston Strongboy

★ ★ ★ ★ ★ ★ ★ ★ ★ ★ ★ ★

"*I don't like to compare players, but I think the closest I've ever seen for sheer power to Jim Rice was Mickey Mantle.*" – Don Zimmer

The Ultimate Season: Year/Team: 1978 BOS				Career: Years: 16			
G:	163	HR:	46	G:	2089	HR:	382
AB:	677	RBI:	139	AB:	8225	RBI:	1451
R:	121	SB:	7	R:	1249	SB:	58
H:	213	BB:	58	H:	2452	BB:	670
2B:	25	OPS:	.970	2B:	373	OPS:	.854
3B:	15	BA:	.315	3B:	79	BA:	.298

In 1978, Rice hit .315 and led the league with 46 home runs, 139 RBI, 15 triples, and 406 total bases to win American League MVP honors. On that short list of baseball's best players from 1975 through 1986, he smacked 382 home runs with 1,451 RBI, and a .298 batting average in his 16-year career spent entirely with Boston. The eight-time All-Star's numbers dipped after 1986 due to injuries, but to his credit, Rice did not hang around just to chase the 400-home run and 1,500 RBI milestones. In retirement, Rice coached for the Red Sox and, believe it or not, became part of the Boston media that had so grossly mistreated him. His raw power and burning focus remain legendary in Red Sox lore and his retired number "14" sits in its rightful place high above Fenway Park.

1970s and 1980s, Rice's run came to a somewhat abrupt end in 1989. As a result, Rice's totals may not stack up against players that had longer careers, but his peak years were tremendous. During his playing days, Rice used various bat brands including Adirondack, Cooper, and Worth bats, but it was H&B/Louisville Slugger that the slugging outfielder seemed to prefer. Rice signed an endorsement contract with the company very early on.

Rice used varying amounts of pine tar to enhance his grip. While most well-used Rice gamers do not feature a very heavy application, some of his bats are absolutely caked in the substance. In addition, Rice would occasionally tape the handles of his bats using a crisscross formation or a spiral, overlapping taping pattern, but both types were relatively thin in nature. Some of the spiral patterns have slight gaps between the continuous strip of tape. A large number of Rice gamers do feature his uniform number "14" on the knob or the barrel end in black marker, the number which he wore his entire career with the Boston Red Sox.

Tales from Joe's Bat Rack

Jim Rice professional model bats are part of a small group of relatively affordable gamers from the Hall of Fame player group. Despite being one of the premier power hitters in the game during the

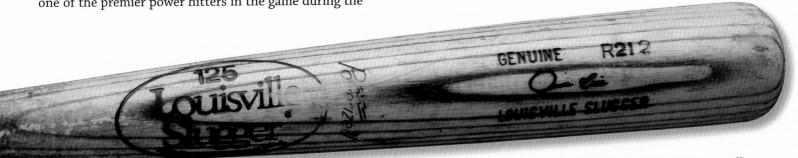

▲ *Jim Rice's 1981-83 Louisville Slugger bat.*

Frank Robinson

★ ★ ★ ★ ★ ★ ★ ★ ★ ★ ★ ★

Bettmann/Bettmann Collection/Getty Images

In December 1965, Robinson was shockingly traded to Baltimore. In a new league, Robinson found new life and delivered one of the best overall seasons in baseball history in 1966. He smacked 49 home runs and scored 122 runs, both league-highs. In addition, he paced the junior circuit in RBI, batting average, OBP, and slugging. They do not hand out a Sextuple Crown, so he had to settle for the Triple Crown and, oh yeah, the AL MVP Award. Moreover, his Orioles won the 1966 World Series with a four-game sweep of the Dodgers, and Robinson was named Series MVP, hitting .286 with 2 homers and 3 RBI. Robinson's greatest moment may have come in that inaugural Oriole season. Batting against Cleveland's Luis Tiant on May 8, 1966, in Baltimore, Robinson crushed an El Tiante offering high and deep to left field. It was gone—literally. The ball sailed up and completely out of the park. According to *The Baltimore Sun*, the crowd gave Robinson a standing ovation in appreciation of the only fair ball ever hit out of Memorial Stadium.

A **man of great pride, integrity,** and self-confidence, Frank Robinson was one of the most respected personalities in baseball as a player, manager, and executive. A focused talent, Robinson first made his name as a Cincinnati Red. He played in the Queen City for a decade and his numbers were remarkable: 324 home runs, 1,009 RBI, a .303 batting average, and six All-Star appearances. Overall, Robinson would be named an All-Star 12 times in his 21-year career (1956–1976). Cincy made it to the postseason just once in Robinson's 10 seasons, 1961, a year that saw Robinson bash 37 homers with 124 RBI and a .323 average. He won the National League MVP Award, but batted just .200 in the World Series as the Reds lost to the Yankees in five games.

In the kind of revenge that only baseball can provide, Baltimore defeated Cincinnati in the 1970 World Series. Robinson clouted two dingers against his former mates along the way to another ring. It would take the Reds another five seasons to finally win a World Series after several near misses. One can only imagine how powerful and dynastic the "Big Red Machine" would have been if Robinson had not been traded. A Texas native and product of the fertile Oakland, California, sports feeder system, Robinson would

remain a productive player well into his 30s. In fact, with the Angels and Indians in 1974 at the age of 38, he hit 22 home runs and knocked in 68 runs. Robinson went on to become the first African-American manager in both the American and National Leagues. He was inducted into the Hall of Fame in 1982 and ranks as one of the most driven and destructive hitters of his or any other generation.

The Ultimate Season:				Career:			
Year/Team: 1966 BAL				Years: 21			
G:	155	HR:	49	G:	2808	HR:	586
AB:	576	RBI:	122	AB:	10006	RBI:	1812
R:	122	SB:	8	R:	1829	SB:	204
H:	182	BB:	87	H:	2943	BB:	1420
2B:	34	OPS:	1.047	2B:	528	OPS:	.926
3B:	2	BA:	.316	3B:	72	BA:	.294

Tales from Joe's Bat Rack

The hobby is filled with a number of overlooked professional model bats, but one could argue that Frank Robinson gamers are the most underappreciated of the bunch based on his tremendous all-around ability. When it comes to Robinson bats, there are a few key characteristics to consider. For a time, Robinson gamers were marked on the knobs in a unique fashion. Notations can be found for both his uniform number and the approximate weight of the bat (ounces) in black marker.

For example, you will find bats that have both his primary uniform number "20" and "35" for the weight in similarly-sized black marker on the knob; however, you don't usually find Robinson knobs marked this way until the mid-1960s. Some Robinson gamers feature his uniform number marked on the barrel end as well, but the presence of his number in that location is less common.

It is important to note that Robinson did wear numbers "36" and "33" at different stages during his time with the Los Angeles Dodgers and Cleveland Indians, but those were short stints. You may also notice cleat marks and shoe polish along the barrel of many of his gamers, as Robinson would often bang his cleats at the plate. While you will see some well-used Robinson gamers with pine tar remnants along the handle, most of his gamers do not possess a heavy layer or any tar at all.

Robinson clearly preferred using H&B (endorsement contract) bats throughout his career after signing an endorsement contract with the company in 1955 prior to his Major League debut one year later. Finally, pre-1969 Robinson gamers are tougher to find than those made afterwards, with gamers that date to the 1950s rarely seen in the marketplace.

" *If you got him [Robinson] out with a pitch, he'd eventually hit that pitch, so you had to constantly change your pattern with him." – Jim Kaat*

▲ *Frank Robinson's 1966-68 H&B bat.*

Gary Sheffield

★ ★ ★ ★ ★ ★ ★ ★ ★ ★ ★

Icon Sportswire

In his 22 MLB seasons, Gary Sheffield hit 509 home runs with 1,676 RBI and a .292 lifetime batting average. He won a batting title in 1992 with a .330 average and knocked in 100 runs or more eight

times, including 132 in 2003. A nine-time All-Star, he won five Silver Slugger Awards and was a World Champion with the Marlins in 1997. On the flip side, Sheffield played during baseball's steroid controversy and his volatile personality created problems. He played for eight different teams, battling with managers, fans, and the media along the way. Gary Sheffield is both of these players.

A Tampa, Florida, native, Sheffield broke in with the Brewers at age 19 in 1988 and it did not take him long to get started. By age 23, he posted his first great season with 33 home runs and 100 RBI. He did so as a Padre, having been traded by the Brewers before the 1992 season. Sheffield would again be traded during the 1993 season, this time to the expansion Marlins where he would team with a bevy of high-priced superstars including Bobby Bonilla, Devon White, Moises Alou, Kevin Brown and Al Leiter to bring a world championship to the Marlins in 1997. Sheffield batted .556 in the NLDS vs. the Giants and .292 in the memorable seven-game Fall Classic vs. Cleveland. His three postseason home runs propelled Florida to the crown.

The nephew of former Mets phenom Dwight Gooden, Sheffield would face similar off-field challenges as his celebrated uncle. The ongoing drama that was his personal life was a distraction, but Sheffield put up consistently great stats moving from Florida to the Dodgers, Braves, Yankees, Tigers, and Mets. In three-plus seasons in Los Angeles, he hit 129 homers and knocked in 367 runs while batting .312. On contending teams with the Braves and the Yanks, he was outstanding, smashing 140 home runs, 485 RBI, and batting .304 between 2002 and 2006. While with the Tigers, Sheffield reached an historic MLB milestone. The 13th grand slam of his career, blasted on September 8, 2008, was recorded as the official 250,000th

★ ★ ★ ★ ★ ★ ★ ★ ★ ★ ★

> *"You talk about adding a bat to your ballclub and then you talk about adding Gary Sheffield. It's a whole different scenario. This is one of the ultimate bats in baseball and one of the ultimate people in baseball."*
> – Jim Leyland

The Ultimate Season:				Career:			
Year/Team: 1996 FLA				Years: 22			
G:	161	HR:	42	G:	2576	HR:	509
AB:	519	RBI:	120	AB:	9217	RBI:	1676
R:	118	SB:	16	R:	1636	SB:	253
H:	163	BB:	142	H:	2689	BB:	1475
2B:	33	OPS:	1.090	2B:	467	OPS:	.907
3B:	1	BA:	.314	3B:	27	BA:	.292

home run in MLB history. After being cut by Detroit in spring training, the 40-year-old Sheffield joined the Mets for the 2009 season. As pinch-hitter on April 17, 2009, Sheffield got his first hit as a Met, which just happened to be the 500th home run of his career. He was the 25th member to join the elite 500 Home Run Club, and the fourth oldest player in history to reach the 500 mark, behind Willie McCovey, Eddie Murray, and Ted Williams. Throughout his career, Gary Antonian Sheffield was traded for Hall of Famers and no-names but, through it all, he took his cuts, was a versatile performer, and played the game with a ferocity that made him worth watching for more than two decades.

Tales from Joe's Bat Rack

For collectors of professional model bats used by members of the 500 Home Run Club, Gary Sheffield gamers are a must. Sheffield used a variety of bat brands during his playing days, including Louisville Slugger, Rawlings/Adirondack, Cooper, Worth, Old Hickory, and SAM bats to name a few. In addition to varying degrees of pine tar remnants along the handle, collectors may encounter many Sheffield gamers with a distinct tape application located near the lower handle and knob area, and this is especially true of bats used during the second half of the slugger's career. Notably, the application is somewhat similar to tape jobs seen on well-used Jim Thome bats, a contemporary of Sheffield.

The tape is often padded underneath and very pronounced. As a result, you may not be able to see what knob notations—if any—exist. Other Sheffield gamers exhibit a more traditional-looking tape application, which was spiral in nature and fairly thick, covering a large surface area of the handle. For a good portion of his career, especially early on, Sheffield was known for hitting with the label facing downward, causing most of the contact marks to appear on the right barrel. Sheffield bats are often found with his uniform number marked either on the knob or barrel end. Keep in mind that Sheffield's number changed during his career. His two primary numbers were "10" and "11" (which he wore with several teams), but he also wore "1" (debut and rookie season), "5" (Los Angeles Dodgers), and "3" (Detroit Tigers).

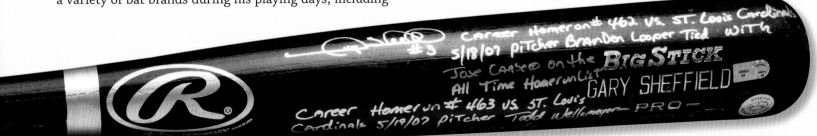

▲ *Gary Sheffield's 2007 Rawlings bat used to hit career home run #s 462 and 463.*

Al Simmons

out 2,927 hits over his 20-year career. In later years, Simmons groused that he could have reached the magical 3,000-hit plateau if he had not missed games because of a hangover or nagging injury.

Simmons became the toast of the town after joining Connie Mack's Philadelphia Athletics in 1924. One of the American League's most fearsome right-handed hitters, he loved the nightlife, fine clothes, and the attention from female fans that came along with success. With the Athletics, Simmons played on two World Series Champions, and was a two-time batting champ. Although a favorite of Connie Mack, Simmons was jettisoned like his highly-paid teammates when Mack dismantled the team for monetary reasons. He was traded to the White Sox in 1933 and became a three-time All-Star while in Chicago.

With many memorable moments over his great career, a doubleheader that took place between the A's and Washington Senators on May 30, 1930, particularly stands out. The A's were down 6–3 going into the bottom of the ninth when Simmons homered with two out, and two on base, to tie the game. He singled to center field in the 11th inning and did not score. In the 13th, Simmons doubled, and scored the winning run on an Eric McNair single, but strained his knee. In the second contest of the day, Simmons was benched because of his knee injury. With the A's down 7–5 and the bases loaded in the fourth, he entered the game as a pinch hitter and promptly hit a grand slam, which eventually won the game—not a bad day's work.

Nicknamed "Bucketfoot" for his unusual batting stance in which he stepped toward third base rather than the pitcher, Simmons was a fierce competitor who backed it all up with his stick. Born Aloys Szymanski to Polish immigrants in Milwaukee, Wisconsin, he soon tired of announcers mispronouncing his name and changed it while playing in the minors. Tough, surly, intense, and self-confidant, Simmons put together a .334 lifetime average, socked 307 home runs, and banged

Simmons always remained close to his mentor, Connie Mack. He returned to Mack's A's as coach from 1944 to 1949, and retired after coaching the Cleveland Indians for one season. Bucketfoot Al was elected to the Hall of Fame in 1953. Sadly, on May 26, 1956, Simmons collapsed and died of a massive heart attack at the fairly young age of 54. *The Sporting News*

★ ★ ★ ★ ★ ★ ★ ★ ★ ★ ★ ★ ★

ranks Simmons 43rd on the all-time greatest players list. With his great offensive stats, including six 200-hits seasons, who can argue?

The Ultimate Season:				Career:			
Year/Team: 1930 PHA				Years: 20			
G:	138	HR:	36	G:	2215	HR:	307
AB:	554	RBI:	165	AB:	8759	RBI:	1828
R:	152	SB:	9	R:	1507	SB:	88
H:	211	BB:	39	H:	2927	BB:	615
2B:	41	OPS:	1.130	2B:	539	OPS:	.915
3B:	16	BA:	.381	3B:	149	BA:	.334

Tales from Joe's Bat Rack

Along with fellow Hall of Famers Mickey Cochrane and Jimmie Foxx, Al Simmons provided a potent bat in the middle of the powerful Philadelphia Athletics lineup in the 1920s and 1930s. As a result of his key role on that legendary team, his two American League batting titles, and his lifetime .334 batting average, professional model Simmons bats have always garnered solid interest. Simmons signed an endorsement contract with H&B in the summer of 1924. This was his first season in the majors, so most of the bats made for Simmons featured his facsimile signature on the barrel, but there was a small window for block letter bats to be produced during the first half of his rookie year.

Perhaps the most interesting aspect of Simmons' gamers is the fact that he ordered the longest professional model bats in the history of H&B. Some of his bats nearly measured 39 inches in length! These Simmons gamers look more like a pole than a baseball bat. So, you might be wondering why a player would want to swing a bat that big. Despite being one of the greatest hitters of all time, Simmons had a poor habit that plagues so many hitters who struggle at the plate. Simmons had a tendency of "stepping in the bucket" as they say, which means his lead foot was positioned more towards third base than directly towards the pitcher. Some players would tease him by calling him "Bucketfoot Al." To cover

the outside portion of the plate and compensate for his bad habit, Simmons ordered gigantic pieces of lumber.

While Simmons bats are not quite as scarce as the ultra-rare Cochrane gamers, they are considered tougher to find than those ordered by his powerful teammate Jimmie Foxx. Bats that date to his first stop with the Athletics tend to sell for a premium compared to bats that date to his later years with the Chicago White Sox, Detroit Tigers, Washington Senators, Boston Bees, Cincinnati Reds, Boston Red Sox, and his last two pit stops with the Athletics again in 1940–1941 and 1944.

> "*I've studied movies of myself batting. Although my left foot stabbed out toward third base, the rest of me, from the belt up, especially my wrists, arms, and shoulders, was swinging in a proper line over the plate.*" – Al Simmons

▲ *Al Simmons' early-1930s H&B bat, factory side-written to 1937.*

Duke Snider

★ ★ ★ ★ ★ ★ ★ ★ ★ ★ ★ ★

40 home runs in five consecutive seasons, from 1953 to 1957, and led the National League with 43 homers in 1956. The eight-time All-Star played in six World Series and won two championships. A clutch hitter, he still holds the National League record for World Series home runs, and he hit four homers in both the 1952 and 1955 Series.

With three teams in New York at the time, it is not surprising that Snider would be compared to rival center fielders Willie Mays of the Giants and Mickey Mantle of the Yankees. Although Snider was just a notch below the two superstars, he was the piston that drove the Brooklyn Dodgers to their first World Series win in 1955. That year, "The Duke of Flatbush" received *The Sporting News* Major League Player of the Year award, but in a close and very controversial vote, Snider lost the National League MVP award to teammate Roy Campanella. Some sportswriters believed Snider was too temperamental and, apparently, one writer voted for Campanella twice, leaving Snider off the ballot.

Considering Snider still holds the overall Dodgers record for home runs (389), RBI (1,271), and extra base hits (814), it is fitting that he was the last player to hit a home run at Ebbets Field. The Los Angeles native stayed with the Dodgers when they moved to California in 1958, but the aging Los Angeles Coliseum was not conducive to Snider's power hitting. Although he did not see the success he attained at Ebbets Field in Brooklyn, Snider had a few solid years in LA and continued to be a very good outfielder.

When it comes to the great Hall of Famers, Duke Snider falls somewhere in the middle of the pack. The power guy for the famed Brooklyn Dodgers teams of the 1950s, Snider carved out an illustrious career and, along with teammates Jackie Robinson, Pee Wee Reese, Roy Campanella, and Preacher Roe, "Dem Bums" were pretty hard to beat. Snider hit at least

Sold to the hapless New York Mets in 1963, the 36-year-old Snider was reunited with some Brooklyn Dodgers teammates, including Gil Hodges. The Mets hoped to draw Brooklyn fans

★ ★ ★ ★ ★ ★ ★ ★ ★ ★ ★ ★

who were still mourning the Dodgers' move to California. Unfortunately, the team was awful. Snider did reach some career milestones that year, hitting his 400th home run, and reaching his 2,000th hit as a Met but, after one season, he asked to be traded to a contender. Snider spent 1964 with the San Francisco Giants, and after they finished in fourth place, he decided to hang up the cleats. He became a broadcaster and batting instructor for the San Diego Padres and, later, the Montreal Expos. Snider developed a reputation as a steady color guy and analyst. Edwin Donald Snider was elected to the Hall of Fame in 1980. He passed away in 2011, at the age of 84.

The Ultimate Season:			Career:		
Year/Team: 1954 BRO			Years: 18		
G:	149	HR: 40	G:	2143	HR: 407
AB:	584	RBI: 130	AB:	7161	RBI: 1333
R:	120	SB: 6	R:	1259	SB: 99
H:	199	BB: 84	H:	2116	BB: 971
2B:	39	OPS: 1.071	2B:	358	OPS: .919
3B:	10	BA: .341	3B:	85	BA: .295

Tales from Joe's Bat Rack

Duke Snider was not only the most prolific home run hitter of the 1950s and a key member of the Brooklyn Dodgers, but his professional model bats can possess terrific character. Snider, who clearly preferred H&B bats throughout his career, signed an endorsement contract with the company near the end of his debut season in 1947. When it comes to gamers used by "The Silver Fox," there is one obvious trait that sticks out above all else. Snider would often apply a layer of tape in a crisscross pattern along the handle to enhance his grip. This taping method is documented in many vintage photos, which capture Snider during his playing days. Not only does the presence of the tape add excellent eye appeal, but it also helps place the bat in Snider's hands.

While some of the surviving examples showcase the tape completely intact, others are found with the tape removed,

leaving remnants along the handle. As long as evidence of the tape remains, it clearly helps connect the bat to game use by Snider. Most advanced collectors look for Snider gamers with evidence of this distinct handle preparation. With the exception of Snider bats that date to the early portion of his career, well-used gamers are usually found with his uniform number written on the knob in black marker. Keep in mind that while Snider wore number "4" for the majority of his career, he also wore "11" in his first season with the New York Mets and "28" with the San Francisco Giants.

> " *We wept, Brooklyn was a lovely place to hit. If you got a ball in the air, you had a chance to get it out. When they tore down Ebbets Field, they tore down a little piece of me.*"
> – Duke Snider

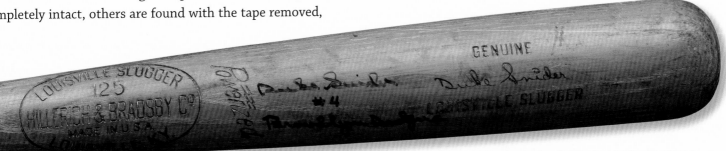

▲ *Duke Snider's 1956-57 H&B bat.*

Sammy Sosa

★ ★ ★ ★ ★ ★ ★ ★ ★ ★ ★

Icon Sportswire

Sammy Sosa might be the only baseball player in history whose career is tied to a United States president. A free agent signee with the Rangers in 1985, Samuel Peralta Sosa debuted with Texas in 1989 at age 20, hitting one home run and batting .238. After appearing in just 25 games, he was traded to the White Sox. The owner of the Rangers at the time was future president,

George W. Bush. Sosa would achieve fame in Chicago, but not with the White Sox. In his three seasons with the Pale Hose, he had a pedestrian 28 home runs and 113 RBI, along with an anemic .227 batting average. It was not until 1993 that Sosa, with the cross-town rival Cubs, would begin his road to baseball stardom. His career arc and rise to power were remarkable. Sosa smacked 33 home runs that season, the first time he had hit more than 15 in any season. He also drove in 93 runs and posted a .261 batting average. That was merely an opening act. For the next 11 seasons, Sosa would be a headliner and superstar. His power numbers exploded as he posted home run totals of 36, 40, and 36 from 1995 to 1997, and made his first All-Star team in 1995.

In 1998, Sammy Sosa's numbers moved from impressive to immortal. Along with Mark McGwire of St. Louis, Sosa eagerly chased Roger Maris' single-season home run record of 61 set in 1961. The baseball world was smitten with his personality and mannerisms. He kissed his hands and touched his heart, sprinted out to his position in right field at Wrigley, gleefully hopped after each home run swing, and joyously interacted with the fans. The Dominican Republic native was loved as much for his outlook as his output. Sosa finished his career with 609 home runs, one of only eight players to surpass 600 and good for eighth place all-time.

His greatest moment was his most historic, albeit short-lived. In 1998, McGwire surpassed Maris' 61 homers on September 8. Sosa would eventually do the same on September 13. Twelve days later, Sammy Sosa would, for a moment, become the all-time single season home run leader. On September 25 in Houston, he smashed a fourth-inning Jose Lima pitch deep to left for his 66th home run, passing McGwire. That would be Sosa's final round-tripper of the

★ ★ ★ ★ ★ ★ ★ ★ ★ ★ ★

"*A wildly popular player among younger fans, Sosa was known for flamboyant on-field antics such as his exaggerated skip after belting a ball over the fence.*" – Alex Reimer, Forbes.com contributor

The Ultimate Season: Year/Team: 1998 CHC				Career: Years: 18			
G:	159	HR:	66	G:	2354	HR:	609
AB:	643	RBI:	158	AB:	8813	RBI:	1667
R:	134	SB:	18	R:	1475	SB:	234
H:	198	BB:	73	H:	2408	BB:	929
2B:	20	OPS:	1.024	2B:	379	OPS:	.878
3B:	0	BA:	.308	3B:	45	BA:	.273

season, while McGwire would reach 70, setting a new record. That same year, Sosa added 158 RBI and the National League MVP award while leading the Cubs to the playoffs. Like Mark McGwire, Sosa would eventually be embroiled in baseball's steroid controversy, limiting his chances at Hall of Fame induction. Nevertheless, Sammy Sosa's passion and pure love of the game were matched by few in history.

Tales from Joe's Bat Rack

Sammy Sosa, along with Mark McGwire, took baseball by storm during their epic home run battle in 1998. Sosa's home run barrage continued for several seasons, pushing him past 600 home runs before his career was over. While the controversy surrounding Sosa and some other sluggers during that time has changed the way some fans and collectors view them, many bat collectors still have a soft spot for their gamers. Sosa ordered various bat brands towards the end of his career, but he used both Louisville Sluggers (block letter) and

Rawlings/Adirondack (signature contract) bats for most of it, preferring the latter more. Perhaps the most interesting aspect to Sosa gamers is his unique tape application to the knobs of his bats. Sosa would pad and tape the knobs of many of his bats in very dramatic fashion. This was done so the slugger could comfortably wrap his bottom hand as low on the bat as possible.

In most cases, the application would cover the entire underside of the knob, but you can find bats with his primary uniform number "21" marked and still visible. Sosa's number may also appear on the barrel end. Keep in mind that Sosa did wear numbers "17" (Texas Rangers) and "25" (Chicago White Sox) earlier in his career. You will also notice that many of his well-used gamers have some remnants of pine tar along the handle, but most of them do not feature a heavy application. For a time, Sosa provided game-used bats directly to the public. This included autographed, documented home run bats amongst other items. These bats can be found with a specially-designed Sosa sticker and LOA.

Sosa gamers that date to his home run binge during the 1998–2002 period tend to sell for a premium.

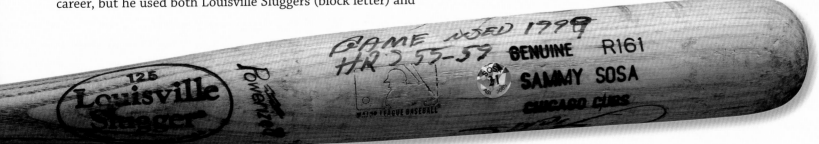

▲ *Sammy Sosa's 1999 Louisville Slugger bat used to hit home run #s 55–59 of the season.*

Tris Speaker

★ ★ ★ ★ ★ ★ ★ ★ ★ ★ ★ ★

1915 and was a fan favorite in Boston. He broke out in 1909, batting over .300 for the first of 18 seasons. Speaker led the American League with 53 doubles, 10 homers, and an OBP of .464 while delivering 222 hits in 1912 to win the Chalmers Award for Most Valuable Player; and he batted over .380, a feat he would repeat four times. The Sox won the World Series that season and again in 1915. Defensively, Speaker was famous for playing a shallow outfield, and it worked as he is still baseball's all-time leader in assists and double plays for an outfielder. In both 1909 and 1912, he led the American League with 35 assists at outfield.

After numerous battles with teammates and Red Sox president Joe Lannin, Speaker was traded to the Cleveland Indians in 1916 for Sam Jones, Fred Thomas, and cash. While Speaker's time in Boston is legendary, his most satisfying hitting display may have come in that first year with the Indians. As if to send a message to the Red Sox, he was magnificent, posting 211 hits, 41 doubles, a .386 batting average, and .470 OBP—all league highs. Speaker seemingly got better with age. In 1923, at age 35, he had 218 hits, 59 doubles, 130 RBI, and a .380 batting average. Two years later, he hit .389 with a .479 OBP.

A fine leader, Speaker served as player-manager in Cleveland from 1919 to 1926, posting a 617–520 record over eight seasons. In 1920 he hit .388 with 107 RBI and 214 hits to lead his Indians to their first World Series championship. After 11 years in Cleveland, Speaker had stops with the Senators and Athletics before retiring after the 1928 season. Overall, Speaker led the American League in doubles eight times and is still the all-time MLB leader with 792. His career 3,514

"The Grey Eagle"—has there ever been a more appropriate nickname in baseball history? Tristram E. Speaker played the outfield with the grace of an eagle and, when he stepped to the plate, he was as ominous as an eagle hovering overhead. Born in Hubbard, Texas, Speaker played for the Red Sox from 1907 to

hits rank fifth all time and his lifetime batting average of .345 is sixth all time.

Speaker remained active in the game as a broadcaster, minor league manager, and instructor. He also formed Tris Speaker, Inc., made numerous speaking appearances, and worked in the liquor and steel industries. Immortalized in baseball's 1937 Hall of Fame class, Tris Speaker died of a coronary occlusion at age 70 in December 1958. He rivaled some of the greatest players ever, including Ty Cobb. The pair had a truly mutual respect as they battled for batting titles and American League supremacy. Even today, we can imagine The Grey Eagle soaring toward a fly ball or swooping into second base with a double—a true legend.

Tales from Joe's Bat Rack

As an elite hitter, all-time doubles leader and member of the 3,000 Hit Club, Tris Speaker's professional model bats are certainly desirable. However, high-quality examples can be very tough to find. Speaker signed an endorsement contract with H&B near the end of the 1912 season, which was several years after making his debut in 1907 with the Boston Red Sox. Most of the existing Speaker gamers, however, date to the 1920s during the second half of his career when he primarily spent time with the Cleveland Indians and had brief stints with the Washington Senators and Philadelphia Athletics. It was a career that spanned 22 years.

Speaker bats that exhibit evidence of tape along the handle, much like some Ty Cobb gamers from the same era, do exist.

The Ultimate Season:				Career:			
Year/Team: 1923 CLE				Years: 22			
G:	150	HR:	17	G:	2789	HR:	117
AB:	574	RBI:	130	AB:	10195	RBI:	1531
R:	133	SB:	8	R:	1882	SB:	436
H:	218	BB:	93	H:	3514	BB:	1381
2B:	59	OPS:	1.079	2B:	792	OPS:	.928
3B:	11	BA:	.380	3B:	222	BA:	.345

That said, this was certainly not the norm, and finding the tape still intact has been a futile endeavor for high-end bat collectors. None are known to exist in that condition at the present time. Also like Cobb, Speaker did order some hefty pieces of wood at times according to the shipping records—bats which usually weighed in at 37–44 ounces. Despite Speaker's historical importance, his professional model bats can currently be obtained for a reasonable price in relation to the mega-stars of the period who overshadowed "The Grey Eagle," such as Cobb and, later on, Babe Ruth.

"*I have no rule for batting. I keep my eye on the ball and when it nears me make ready to swing. I cut my drives between the first baseman and the line and that is my favorite alley for my doubles.*" – Tris Speaker

▲ *Tris Speaker's 1912–15 J. F. Hillerich & Son bat.*

Willie Stargell

★ ★ ★ ★ ★ ★ ★ ★ ★ ★ ★

Focus On Sport/Focus On Sport Collection/Getty Images

Known for his tape measure blasts, Willie Stargell was a force to be reckoned with. Stargell's powerful swing and amazing bat speed, made him a fan favorite in any ballpark that he played in. A career Pirate, Stargell had success at the cavernous

Forbes Field, hitting more home runs out of that ballpark than anyone, but after the move to Three Rivers Stadium in 1970, his production really took off. Montreal's Olympic Stadium in 1978 was the setting for a prodigious Stargell blast that sailed 538 feet and landed in an upper-deck seat, which has since been painted gold to mark the occasion.

Born in Earlsboro, Oklahoma, Stargell had a difficult childhood, abandoned by his father and raised for several years by an abusive aunt before moving as a teen to Alameda, California, to live with his mother. At 18 years old, Wilver Dornel Stargell was signed by Pittsburg and sent to the minors in 1958. The young, strapping left fielder got called up in 1962, but his career really began to take off in 1964. That was the first of 13 consecutive 20-plus home run seasons, and when he changed to a heavier, 38-ounce bat in 1969, he became one of the premier power hitters of the 1970s. The colorful Stargell liked to intimidate pitchers by warming up in the on-deck circle with a sledgehammer.

Stargell crushed a league-leading 48 homers in 1971 and brought the Pirates to their first World Series championship since 1960. In 1979, the 39-year-old Stargell became "Pops" of the "We Are Family" Pirates team, handing out "Stargell Stars" to teammates who performed well. A leader in the clubhouse and on the field, "Pops" hit .455 with two homers in the 1979 NLCS and batted .400 with three home runs in the Series. His blast in the sixth inning of Game Seven was a major factor in the Pirates' win. He was named World Series MVP, NL MVP, and 1979 Major League Player of the Year.

The seven-time All-Star switched to first base and battled injuries in his last few seasons before finally retiring in 1982 with 475 career home runs and a .282 batting average.

★ ★ ★ ★ ★ ★ ★ ★ ★ ★ ★

> *"I never saw anything like it. He [Stargell] doesn't just hit pitchers, he takes away their dignity."*
> *– Don Sutton*

The Ultimate Season:				Career:			
Year/Team: 1973 PIT				Years: 21			
G:	148	HR:	44	G:	2360	HR:	475
AB:	522	RBI:	119	AB:	7927	RBI:	1540
R:	106	SB:	0	R:	1194	SB:	17
H:	156	BB:	80	H:	2232	BB:	937
2B:	43	OPS:	1.038	2B:	423	OPS:	.889
3B:	3	BA:	.299	3B:	55	BA:	.282

Among his many awards are the 1974 Lou Gehrig Memorial Award, 1974 Roberto Clemente Award, 1978 Comeback Player of the Year, and the 1979 NL Babe Ruth Award. It's not surprising that Stargell was inducted into the Hall of Fame in 1988, his first year of eligibility, with 82.4% of the vote. Although he coached for the Pirates and Braves for several years, Stargell struggled with health issues in retirement and passed away in 2001 at the age of 61, on the day of the first game at Pittsburg's new PNC Park.

Tales from Joe's Bat Rack

Willie Stargell professional model bats are among the most affordable, and perhaps underrated, Hall of Famer bats from the era in which this powerful slugger played. There is no question that narrowly missing entry into the 500 Home Run Club suppresses the value of his gamers, but 500 home runs or not, Stargell was undoubtedly one of the most formidable hitters of his generation. Stargell preferred H&B (endorsement contract) bats during his career and signed with the company before making his MLB debut in 1962,

but the Pittsburgh powerhouse occasionally used Adirondack (block letter) bats as well.

When it comes to Stargell gamers, there are two key characteristics to note. First, Stargell employed two different ways of marking the knobs of his bats. Many Stargell gamers are found with his uniform number "8" in large black marker. This was the only number Stargell wore his entire career. Some of his bats, however, feature his uniform number in Roman numerals (VIII) instead. In some cases, you will encounter Stargell bats that also have his uniform number marked on the barrel end.

Second, to provide extra grip, Stargell would at times use tape along the handle. It was one continuous strip of tape, and the strip itself was extremely thin—the thinnest tape application you will ever see on a professional model bat. Stargell did use pine tar every now and then, with slightly caked applications found on the upper handle, but it wasn't a regular practice. While Stargell used natural-colored bats for most of his career, collectors are likely to see his bats with darker finishes starting in the late 1970s to the end of his playing days. Finally, Stargell bats that date to the 1960s are much tougher to find than those from the 1970s onward.

▲ *Willie Stargell's 1969-72 H&B bat.*

Ichiro Suzuki

★ ★ ★ ★ ★ ★ ★ ★ ★ ★ ★

VJ Lov/Icon Sportswire

Suzuki came to America at the age of 27 to pursue his Major League Baseball dream. While new to the United States and his freshly-minted home city of Seattle, Ichiro was no baseball neophyte. He had established himself as one of the most exciting and popular players in Japan, playing for Orix in the Pacific League. With the Mariners' ownership controlled by the joysticks of the Nintendo Corporation and a large Asian population in metropolitan Seattle, it was a match made in international baseball heaven. Ichiro Suzuki became an instant sensation. His quiet confidence, lethal bat, and rocket arm in the outfield helped him become the first Japanese-born non-pitcher to earn an everyday starting position in Major League Baseball.

During his rookie season of 2001, Suzuki became the team catalyst helping the Mariners achieve a record 116 wins while leading the league in hits (242), batting average (.350), and stolen bases (56). His historic campaign was capped off by winning both the AL Rookie of the Year and MVP awards, a feat that had not been accomplished since Boston Red Sox outfielder Fred Lynn did it in 1975. He was elected to 10 straight All-Star Games and garnered 10 straight Gold Gloves from 2001 to 2010. In that time frame, Suzuki delivered 200-plus hits per season and led the league in hits seven times. A superstar of the highest caliber, he won batting crowns in 2001 and 2004, batted .350 or better in 2001, 2007, and 2009; but saved his best for 2004, batting .372. On October 1 of that year, Suzuki had his finest moment at the plate, surpassing the hallowed record for most hits in a single season, 257, set by Hall of Famer George Sisler in 1920. Suzuki finished the 2004 season with a record 262 hits. It was an incredible milestone that helped define his incredible career.

Becoming a star in Major League Baseball usually takes years of continued perseverance. Mr. Ichiro Suzuki of Nichi Kasugai-gun, Aichi, Japan, proved to be the exception to this rule. After spending the early portion of his career playing in Japan,

★ ★ ★ ★ ★ ★ ★ ★ ★ ★ ★

On August 7, 2016, the 42-year-old Suzuki joined MLB's elite 3,000 Hit Club, and if you count his 1,278 hits in Japan's Professional Baseball League, he blew by Pete Rose's all-time hits record of 4,256 in June 2016. The combination of his speed and lightning-quick swing made Suzuki one of the most dangerous hitters of his era. A frightening sight for opponents at the plate, on the bases, and in the field, Ichiro Suzuki will long be remembered not merely as the greatest Japanese-born player ever, but as one of the greatest hitters ever to grab a bat.

The Ultimate Season: Year/Team: 2004 SEA		Career To Date: Years: 16	
G: 161	HR: 8	G: 2500	HR: 114
AB: 704	RBI: 60	AB: 9689	RBI: 760
R: 101	SB: 36	R: 1396	SB: 508
H: 262	BB: 49	H: 3030	BB: 626
2B: 24	OPS: .869	2B: 356	OPS: .761
3B: 5	BA: .372	3B: 96	BA: .313

Tales from Joe's Bat Rack

Since the beginning of Ichiro Suzuki's MLB career in 2001, professional model bats used by the Japanese-born star have been amongst the most desirable of the post-2000 era. Ichiro has always used a specially-designed (or labeled) Mizuno bat that includes his name on the barrel and his uniform number imprinted on the knob. The vast majority of these feature a dark finish, but Ichiro did use some blonde bats, most notably in 2015. Keep in mind that Ichiro wore number "51" for his entire stay with the Seattle Mariners, but changed his uniform number to "31" with the New York Yankees in 2012. He then returned to "51" after joining the Miami Marlins in 2015. Ichiro has been very protective about his equipment, so the market has not been flooded with professional model bats used by the perennial All-Star.

Even the Ichiro bats that do enter the market do not often showcase heavy use. Ichiro has a reputation for changing bats more often than the average player, much like past superstar Roberto Clemente. As a result, many of his gamers have a relatively clean look overall, other than ball contact marks along the hitting surface or moderate amounts of Mota stick or pine tar on the handle. The only exception would be bats used during the last few years, which occasionally exhibit a slightly heavier application.

Ichiro bats are amongst the toughest gamers to acquire from the era in which he played. Since the supply has been relatively low and the demand is high in the United States and Japan, where Ichiro has a very strong following, his bats often sell for much more than bats used by contemporary stars. Collectors may encounter signed and inscribed Ichiro gamers that are accompanied by a hologram from Mill Creek Sports, a hobby company the star has worked with for many years.

> " *Any pitch, any time, any place, any situation—you throw it, Ichiro will hit it.*" – Leigh Montville, Sports Illustrated

▲ Ichiro Suzuki's 2013 Mizuno bat.

Mike Trout

★ ★ ★ ★ ★ ★ ★ ★ ★ ★ ★ ★ ★

Icon Sportswire

The "Millville Meteor" hits for average, hits with power, is a very good outfielder, runs like gazelle, and appears to be on the road to baseball immortality.

The New Jersey native and Millville High School star was the youngest-ever AL Rookie of the Year, leading the league with 129 runs and 49 stolen bases, and was also an All-Star in 2012. Named *The Sporting News* Rookie of the Year, Trout was selected by Baseball America as both Rookie of the Year and Major League Player of the Year. In August 2012, he became the youngest player to hit 20 home runs and steal at least 40 bases, and by September he was the youngest to join the 30-30 club. Also that year, he became the first player in MLB history to hit 30 home runs, steal 45 bases and score 125 runs in a season.

In 2013, Trout became the youngest player to hit for the cycle. He was AL MVP in 2014, leading the league with 111 RBI and 115 runs; and in 2015, at 23 years old, he was the youngest player to join the 100-100 club. A five-time All-Star and two-time All-Star MVP in just six seasons, Trout garnered four Silver Slugger Awards, the Hank Aaron Award in 2014, the 2015 ESPY award for Best MLB Player, and the 2016 AL MVP Award. The comparisons with Mickey Mantle are impossible to ignore. Both players have similar physical make ups, similar swings, and played similar defense.

At this point in his career, the analytical website *Fangraphs* rates Trout as one of the best players in baseball history. Maybe that's a little ambitious, but he is definitely on the radar. A 2009 first-round draft pick by the Anaheim Angels, Trout has been the model of consistency for LA, delivering roughly 180 hits, 95 RBI, and 35 home runs a season since 2012. Off the field, Trout is involved in charitable endeavors, donating time and money to help sick kids and inner-city youth at risk. When

It may be premature to declare Mike Trout the Mickey Mantle of the new millennium, but he is off to one heck of a start. A legitimate five-tool player, Michael Nelson Trout is currently the best player in baseball.

Millville Meteor

★ ★ ★ ★ ★ ★ ★ ★ ★ ★ ★

all is said and done, it will be interesting to see if Mike Trout finishes his career the way most are predicting. If he does, move over Mantle, the kid from New Jersey will be sitting right next to you.

The Ultimate Season:				Career To Date:			
Year/Team: 2013 LAA				Years: 6			
G:	157	HR:	27	G:	811	HR:	168
AB:	589	RBI:	97	AB:	2997	RBI:	497
R:	109	SB:	33	R:	600	SB:	143
H:	190	BB:	110	H:	917	BB:	477
2B:	39	OPS:	.988	2B:	175	OPS:	.963
3B:	9	BA:	.323	3B:	37	BA:	.306

Tales from Joe's Bat Rack

When compiling a list of the top 100 bats, I usually would never consider a player as young as Mike Trout, but what he has done in his first several seasons is simply remarkable. Mike Trout connected with the manufacturer Old Hickory on a bat deal early on in his career. Trout bats used in the minor leagues exclusively will be those that are the solid-blonde variety. Trout began using two-toned Old Hickory bats most of the time in 2011, when he split the season between the minors and his debut season with the Angels. During that year, Rawlings/Adirondack did attempt to convert Trout to a bat deal, sending him several bats to try. So, a few of these gamers were used in the majors in 2011, though Trout did not end up switching over permanently.

For his 2012 rookie season, Trout only used two-tone (black barrel with blonde handle) Old Hickory bats. There were, allegedly, only about 50 total bats ordered by Trout during that entire year, which is about one-fifth of the average total ordered by most Major Leaguers, making them tough to locate by comparison.

Many Trout professional model bats were often prepared with a twisted wrap of tape around the knob end, which extends about 3–4 inches up the handle. In addition, you will find well-used gamers with a heavy coat of Mota Stick, typically with a very red or brownish tint, extending from the bottom handle and up about 7–8 inches. The longer the bat is used, the heavier the coat, with a lighter coat transfer located near the center brand. In recent times, Trout has been applying Lizard Skins tape to more of his bats, which has become popular with many current players. Most Trout bats are made with a cupped end and, while some of his early gamers do, many of his bats do not exhibit Trout's uniform number "27" on the knob. Instead, they often have his initials "MT" notated in pencil.

Through a hobby representative, Trout has produced autographed, game-used equipment during his first few seasons, which includes documented bats used for specific home runs.

> " *I just keep thinking about putting up good numbers, playing hard and winning games.*" – Mike Trout

▲ Mike Trout's 2012 Old Hickory rookie year bat used to hit home run #16 of the season.

Billy Williams

★ ★ ★ ★ ★ ★ ★ ★ ★ ★ ★

League but nearly packed it in because of the discrimination he encountered. He attributed his success to the hometown support from his family, teachers, and coaches who were responsible for shaping what would be a great career that never involved controversy. There he learned a mantra he lived by, "Good, better, best. Never let it rest, until the good is better and the better is best."

Coached and mentored by Rogers Hornsby while in the minors, Williams blossomed into a feared hitter almost immediately. In 1961, he won the coveted National League Rookie of the Year Award, whacked 25 home runs and batted .278 to go along with 147 hits and 86 RBI. He became a steady, reliable leader in the Cubs' clubhouse, and even greats like Ernie Banks, Ron Santo, and Fergie Jenkins deferred to the soft-spoken Williams to lead by example. A consistent contributor, Williams hit 20 or more home runs for 13 consecutive seasons. In 1970, he led the NL with 137 runs and 205 hits while blasting a career-high 42 homers. The six-time All-Star won the National League batting crown in 1972 with a .333 batting average to go along with 37 home runs and 122 RBI, and was named MLB Player of the Year.

Perhaps his greatest achievement was setting a new National League record for consecutive games played. The dependable Williams played every game for seven years, from September 1963 to September 1970, posting 1,117 consecutive games played and breaking Stan Musial's record. Williams' own record was eventually broken by Steve Garvey. In 1974, he was traded to Oakland. With the Athletics, although in the twilight of his career, Williams

Quiet and unassuming, "Sweet Swingin'" Billy Williams was a player who led by example. With a distinguished 18-year career played mostly for a Chicago Cubs team that never got a whiff of the postseason, Williams went about his business as an offensive force on the field and role model off the field. The Whistler, Alabama, native came up through the Texas

Sweet Swingin' Billy

★ ★ ★ ★ ★ ★ ★ ★ ★ ★ ★ ★

> "When I get into the box, the only thing I look at is the hand and the ball. I try to pick up the ball as close to the hand as possible. If I'm lucky, halfway to the plate I should know what the pitch is going to be, by the spin, by the arch." – Billy Williams

The Ultimate Season:		Career:	
Year/Team: 1972 CHC		Years: 18	
G: 150	HR: 37	G: 2488	HR: 426
AB: 574	RBI: 122	AB: 9350	RBI: 1475
R: 95	SB: 3	R: 1410	SB: 90
H: 191	BB: 62	H: 2711	BB: 1045
2B: 34	OPS: 1.005	2B: 434	OPS: .853
3B: 6	BA: .333	3B: 88	BA: .290

smacked 23 home runs and posted 81 RBI to help the A's to the 1975 American League West championship. In October 1976, at 38 years old, Billy Leo Williams retired with a .290 lifetime batting average, 2,711 hits, 426 home runs, and 1,475 runs batted in. He coached for the Cubs, A's, and Indians for 19 years, and currently works in an advisory capacity for the Cubs. Billy Williams was elected to the Hall of Fame in 1987 and became a member of the Hall of Fame Veterans Committee in 2011. Still beloved in Chicago, his uniform number "26" was retired by the Cubs in 1987, and a statue of Williams was placed at Wrigley Field in 2010.

Tales from Joe's Bat Rack

Billy Williams is one of those players who fell short of some magical milestones in his career, which helps keep the price of his bats in a more affordable range compared to some of his

contemporaries like Roberto Clemente or Willie Mays. That said, his offensive excellence with the bat was abundantly clear. Williams, who played most of his Hall of Fame career for the Chicago Cubs, wore several different uniform numbers during his playing days. In addition to "26," the number he made famous as a member of the Cubbies, Williams also wore "4" and "41" (Cubs) and "7" and "28" (Oakland A's). His uniform number is often found on the knobs of his Cubs-era gamers in relatively small numerals, as was the norm for that team.

Yosh Kawano, the Chicago equipment manager during the 1960s and 1970s, would often mark the barrels with the model number and sometimes the length of Cubs bats. These barrel notations have become known as "Yosh" marks in the hobby and are desired by hobbyists. Williams was also an avid user of pine tar. On well-used Williams gamers, you will often find a concentrated application or remnants on the upper handle area. It is similar to the pattern seen on Joe Morgan gamers from the same era (1960s/1970s). Finally, it is clear that Williams preferred H&B bats throughout his career. Williams signed an endorsement contract with the company very early on, producing a signature model, prior to his first full season in 1961.

▲ *Billy Williams' 1965-68 H&B bat.*

Hack Wilson

★ ★ ★ ★ ★ ★ ★ ★ ★ ★ ★ ★

During that fabulous run with the Chicago Cubs, Wilson was a four-time National League home run leader and two-time RBI leader. Although his career spanned only 12 years, Wilson certainly left his mark, most significantly in 1930. That year Wilson had one of the best seasons in Major League history, batting .356 with .454 OBP and .723 slugging percentage. He went yard 56 times, a National League record that stood until Mark McGwire slammed 70 in 1998. Wilson drove in 191 runs in that stellar season, a MLB record that still stands and may never be broken.

The son of alcoholic parents, Wilson left school after sixth grade to work as a laborer. Signed by the New York Giants in 1923, baseball became Wilson's ticket out of a life of poverty but his fame and fortune were short lived. At the height of his career, it was not uncommon for Wilson to blast a home run during a game, stay out partying with the boys most of the night, and come back hung over the next day to do it all over again. Unfortunately, burning the candle at both ends eventually caught up with Wilson and cut short his tenure in Major League baseball. A few fights with fans and sports writers did not help his cause, and in December 1931 he was traded to the Cardinals who, in turn, almost immediately traded him to the Brooklyn Dodgers. Wilson batted .297 with 23 home runs and 123 RBI for Brooklyn in 1932 but his offensive capabilities quickly deteriorated and by 1934 he was out of baseball.

Excessive drinking and bad business investments forced

With a penchant for imbibing, fighting, and playing hard, Lewis Robert "Hack" Wilson is certainly considered one of the most colorful characters to ever wear a baseball uniform. At 5-foot, 6-inches, and 190 pounds, with small hands and feet, Wilson was built like a beer keg but was one of the most feared hitters in Major League baseball from 1926 to 1930.

★ ★ ★ ★ ★ ★ ★ ★ ★ ★ ★

" *Under Joe McCarthy's wing with the Cubs, Wilson's rise in the majors was little short of spectacular."* – New York Times, *November 24, 1948*

The Ultimate Season:			Career:		
Year/Team: 1930 CHC			Years: 12		
G:	155	HR: 56	G:	1348	HR: 244
AB:	585	RBI: 191	AB:	4760	RBI: 1063
R:	146	SB: 3	R:	884	SB: 52
H:	208	BB: 105	H:	1461	BB: 674
2B:	35	OPS: 1.177	2B:	266	OPS: .940
3B:	6	BA: .356	3B:	67	BA: .307

Wilson to take on menial jobs and he was virtually penniless when he died from a series of medical complications on November 23, 1948, at the age of 48. MLB covered the cost of his funeral. Just a week before he died, Wilson appeared on *We, The People* radio program and said, "There are many kids in and out of baseball who think that just because they have some natural talent, they have the world by the tail. It isn't so. In life, you need many more things besides talent. Things like good advice and common sense." Like a meteor, Hack Wilson rocketed across the baseball sky only to burn out much too early. The fact remains, however, that he was a great hitter during those few memorable Cubby seasons. Wilson was voted into the Hall of Fame by the Veterans Committee in 1979.

Tales from Joe's Bat Rack

Hack Wilson professional model bats are as coveted for the style of the bats themselves as they are for the intriguing character behind the lumber. Wilson, who still holds the seemingly unbreakable single-season record for RBI with 191 in 1930, was a compact 5-foot, 6-inches tall and weighed close to 200 pounds. At the plate, he was an explosion waiting to happen.

When it comes to Wilson gamers, they are not only very unique in design, but also very scarce. Using an ultra-thin handle for the era, the barrel-chested Wilson was able to generate great bat speed. The thin handle extends upward from a small but protruding knob, unlike a flare handle and certainly more dramatic than a Hornsby-style knob, which became popular in the 1920s and 1930s.

In fact, later in his career, Babe Ruth experimented by ordering bats with Wilson-style handles as the iconic slugger learned more about the science of the swing. Wilson's bat construction and appearance is frequently referred to as a "broomstick" handle in the hobby. The notes in Wilson's ordering records indicate that the slugger requested the factory to "shave a little near knob" in order to create the desired shape. Wilson signed an endorsement contract with H&B in 1924, just one year following his brief debut in 1923 when the mini-powerhouse had 10 plate appearances.

▲ *Hack Wilson's 1932-33 H&B bat.*

Dave Winfield

★ ★ ★ ★ ★ ★ ★ ★ ★ ★ ★ ★

Focus On Sport/Getty Images Sport Collection/Getty Images

Winfield declared the incident a complete accident and there was no intent to harm the bird, the charges were eventually dropped. Although this is an interesting little tidbit in the professional life of Dave Winfield, we cannot shortchange the great career of this incredible athlete.

The powerful 6-foot, 6-inch, and 220-pound St. Paul native was drafted out of the University of Minnesota by professional basketball, baseball, and football. He chose baseball, signing with the San Diego Padres who sent him up to the majors right away. Winfield was the complete package. Over his 22-year career from 1973 to 1995, Winfield made 12 All-Star appearances, had over 3,000 hits, won six Silver Slugger awards, hit 465 home runs, and won seven Gold Gloves. It was no surprise Winfield was a first ballot inductee to the Hall of Fame in 2001.

In a scene right out of a Hitchcock movie, on August 4, 1983, at Exhibition Stadium in Toronto, a man was taken into custody for what was either manslaughter or accidental death. There, on the field, the deceased was covered by a blanket. The man in custody was New York Yankee Dave Winfield. The victim was a seagull. In a very bizarre twist of fate, Winfield was warming up in the fifth inning of a Yankees vs. Blue Jays game when the seagull intercepted his throw and was sent to bird heaven. A police officer working the game thought Winfield hit the seagull deliberately and arrested him. Winfield was actually booked on animal cruelty charges at police headquarters but was released after posting bail. Because

After eight years as a Padre, Winfield became one of the most highly paid athletes of the era when he was signed by George Steinbrenner's Yankees as a free agent. Winfield donned the pinstripes in 1981, and while an All-Star each year, Steinbrenner was disappointed he did not produce in the 1981 World Series, dubbing him "Mr. May." Thus began a contentious relationship that lasted throughout Winfield's nine years in New York. Ironically, Winfield returned to Toronto as a member of the Blue Jays 1992 World Series Championship team. At age 40, he clinched that title for

★ ★ ★ ★ ★ ★ ★ ★ ★ ★ ★

Toronto with his 11th-inning, two-out double in Game Six, forever erasing the "Mr. May" moniker.

Besides his heroics on the field, David Mark Winfield is a hero off the field. His Dave Winfield Foundation provides food, meals, scholarships, and healthcare to the needy, and he has established programs to combat drug abuse. A successful businessman and savvy investor, Winfield is on the board of many organizations. Still an ambassador for the game, Winfield has been recognized for his charitable work with numerous awards including the Roberto Clemente Award, the Josh Gibson Leadership Award, the Brian Piccolo Award for humanitarian service, and the Branch Rickey Community Service Award.

Tales from Joe's Bat Rack

Dave Winfield was known for using a few different professional model bat brands during his career. H&B/Louisville Slugger, Rawlings/Adirondack, and Cooper seem to be the primary brands Winfield brought to the plate over his long 22-year career. Winfield did sign an endorsement contract with H&B during his first season in July of 1973. The big, athletic star ordered bats with a variety of models and finishes during his playing days, including a number of two-toned bats. As far as player characteristics are concerned, Winfield was known to occasionally apply a spiral tape application to the handle of his bats. The tape would often extend well up the handle, covering a large surface area.

Winfield was also known to use varying amounts of pine tar as well, whether he taped the handle or not. For a post-1970s

The Ultimate Season:			Career:		
Year/Team: 1979 SDP			Years: 22		
G:	159	HR: 34	G:	2973	HR: 465
AB:	597	RBI: 118	AB:	11003	RBI: 1833
R:	97	SB: 15	R:	1669	SB: 223
H:	184	BB: 85	H:	3110	BB: 1216
2B:	27	OPS: .953	2B:	540	OPS: .827
3B:	10	BA: .308	3B:	88	BA: .283

player, Winfield did seem a little inconsistent about applying his uniform number on the knobs of his bats. Therefore, you will often see plenty of his gamers with or without his uniform number in large black marker, which changed from "31" to "32" and back to "31" before the end of his career. Bats that date to the pre-1980 period are noticeably tougher to find than those shipped afterwards, and gamers that specifically date to his time with the New York Yankees (1981–1988) tend to sell for a premium.

" *Good hitters don't just go up and swing. They always have a plan. Call it an educated deduction. You visualize. You're like a good negotiator. You know what you have, you know what he has, then you try to work it out"* – Dave Winfield

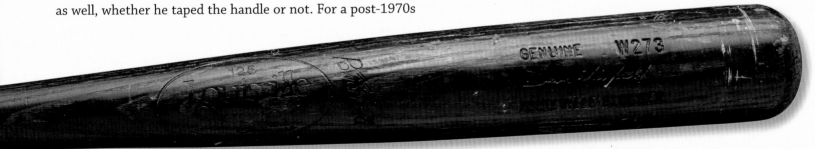

▲ *Dave Winfield's 1984 Louisville Slugger bat.*

Carl Yastrzemski

★ ★ ★ ★ ★ ★ ★ ★ ★ ★ ★

Focus On Sport/Getty Images Sport Collection/Getty Images

As a 21-year-old rookie, Carl Michael Yastrzemski had the difficult task of replacing Ted Williams, possibly the greatest hitter in baseball history. Yaz rose to the occasion for the Red

Sox, and over his 23 brilliant years with Boston, the team captain participated in 18 All-Star games, amassed 3,419 hits, 452 home runs, and knocked in 1,844 runs. Captain Carl was the American League batting champ three times, and won seven Gold Gloves. No one could play the famous left-field wall known as "The Green Monster," better than Yaz.

In 1967, Yaz did everything except sell hot dogs and mow the lawn at Fenway Park. That magical year, he won the Triple Crown bashing 44 home runs to go along with 121 RBI and a .326 batting average. Named AL MVP and the 1967 Major League Player of the Year, Yastrzemski led "The Impossible Dream" Red Sox all the way to the seventh game of the World Series, only to lose to the Cardinals. Yaz did his part, batting .400 in the Series with three home runs. The word "clutch" comes to mind when describing Yastrzemski's great 1967 season, as there were countless times he did it with either his bat or his glove.

Opening day, April 14, 1967, Red Sox vs. Yankees at Yankee Stadium, was rookie Boston pitcher Billy Rohr's Major League debut. In an incredible outing, Rohr mowed down Yankee after Yankee, with a no-hitter going into the ninth inning. With the Sox up 3–0 in the bottom of ninth, Yankee Tom Tresh caught every inch of Rohr's pitch, hitting a bullet to left field. As soon as the ball hit the bat, Yaz was on his horse furiously attempting to save the no-hitter. At full speed, Yastrzemski leaped into the air, caught the ball over his shoulder, hit the ground in a somersault, lost his cap, and jumped up with the ball in his hand. It was such a spectacular catch that Yankees fans gave him a standing ovation. Unfortunately, after Joe Pepitone flied out, Elston Howard stroked a single to break up the no-hitter, but that Yaz catch was a taste of what would come during that glorious 1967 season.

★ ★ ★ ★ ★ ★ ★ ★ ★ ★ ★

> "*Yaz hit 44 homers that year, and 43 of them meant something big for the team. It seemed like every time we needed a big play, the man stepped up and got it done.*" – George Scott, Red Sox teammate

The Ultimate Season:				Career:			
Year/Team: 1967 BOS				Years: 23			
G:	161	HR:	44	G:	3308	HR:	452
AB:	579	RBI:	121	AB:	11988	RBI:	1844
R:	112	SB:	10	R:	1816	SB:	168
H:	189	BB:	91	H:	3419	BB:	1845
2B:	31	OPS:	1.040	2B:	646	OPS:	.841
3B:	4	BA:	.326	3B:	59	BA:	.285

Known for his unusual batting stance in which he held the bat high over his shoulder, when he retired in 1983, Carl Yastrzemski was the only American League player to achieve both 3,000 hits and 400 home runs. He was elected to the Hall of Fame in 1989, his first year of eligibility. A hero in Boston, the Red Sox retired his uniform number "8" in 1989, and erected a statue of Yaz at Fenway Park in 2013.

Tales from Joe's Bat Rack

Carl Yastrzemski professional model bats have always been popular with collectors. Not only was "Yaz" a staple in Boston, but his well-used gamers often showcase great character. When it comes to specific characteristics, there are two key elements to look for on Yastrzemski bats. You will often find Yastrzemski's uniform number "8" on the knob or barrel end in large black marker. This was the only number he wore during his MLB career. The style of most "8"s is best described as two circles placed on top of one another, which is somewhat similar to the "8" seen on the knobs of some Yogi Berra gamers.

You may also find the word "Game" written on the knob of his bats, referring to the bat that was reserved for game action and not batting practice. In some instances, collectors will encounter Yastrzemski gamers that have the weight of the bat, in ounces, marked on the barrel end.

Furthermore, Yastrzemski occasionally applied a very distinct taping method along the handle. The tape was spiral in nature but with gaps between the continuous strip of tape, extending towards the center brand. It was a very thin application of tape, since only one layer was used. In addition to the distinct tape pattern, you will notice gamers with varying degrees of pine tar along the handle and near the center brand area. While the presence of pine tar is not uncommon, Yastrzemski rarely used heavy amounts on his bats.

The Boston slugger used bats with a variety of finishes, from natural-colored ash bats to ones with a hickory finish, which are dark brown in color. Finally, his bat brand of choice was clearly H&B/Louisville Slugger (endorsement contract) after signing with the company in the spring of 1959, prior to making his debut two years later. Early examples, dating to the 1960s, have been far more difficult to locate than examples from the 1970s and 1980s.

▲ *Carl Yastrzemski's 1977–79 H&B bat.*

Index

★ ★ ★ ★ ★ ★ ★ ★ ★ ★

About the Authors and Contributors

★ ★ ★ ★ ★ ★ ★ ★ ★ ★ ★ ★ ★ ★ ★ ★ ★ ★ ★ ★

Joe Orlando is president of Professional Sports Authenticator and PSA/DNA Authentication Services, the largest trading card and sports memorabilia authentication service in the hobby. Editor of the nationally distributed *Sports Market Report* (SMR), a Juris Doctor, and an advanced collector, Orlando has authored several collecting guides and dozens of articles for Collectors Universe, Inc. He is the author of *The Top 200 Sportscards in the Hobby* (2002) and *Collecting Sports Legends (2008),* and he contributed to the award-winning *The T206 Collection: The Players & Their Stories* (2010), *The Cracker Jack Collection: Baseball's Prized Players* (2013) and *The 100 Greatest Baseball Autographs* (2016). As a hobby expert, Orlando has appeared as featured guest on numerous radio and television programs, including ESPN's *Outside the Lines,* HBO's *Real Sports,* and on the Fox Business Network.

Tom Zappala is a businessman in the greater Boston area who is passionate about maintaining the traditions and historical significance of our National Pastime. He is co-author of the award-winning books *The T206 Collection: The Players & Their Stories, The Cracker Jack Collection: Baseball's Prized Players*, and *The 100 Greatest Baseball Autographs.* In addition to co-hosting a popular Boston area radio talk show, Zappala co-hosts *The Great American Collectibles Show* which airs nationally every week. As co-owner of ATS Communications, a multimedia and consulting company, he handles publicity and personal appearances for several authors and a variety of artists in the entertainment field. He enjoys collecting vintage baseball and boxing memorabilia using the simple philosophy of collecting for the love of the sport. Proud of his Italian heritage, Zappala recently authored *Bless Me Sister*, a humorous book about his experience attending an Italian parochial school.

Ellen Zappala is president of ATS Communications, a multimedia marketing and consulting company. Co-author of the award-winning books *The T206 Collection: The Players & Their Stories, The Cracker Jack Collection: Baseball's Prized Players*, and *The 100 Greatest Baseball Autographs,* Zappala also worked with former welterweight boxing champ Tony DeMarco on his autobiography *Nardo: Memoirs of a Boxing Champion.* Zappala was publisher of a group of six newspapers in Massachusetts and New Hampshire for many years and served as president of the New England Press Association. She works closely with various publishing companies on behalf other authors, and handles publicity in both print and electronic media. She especially enjoys bringing the stories of the Deadball Era and Golden Age players to life.

John Molori is a columnist for *Boston Baseball Magazine, Patriots Football Weekly*, and *New England Golf Monthly*. He contributed to the award-winning books, *The Cracker Jack Collection: Baseball's Prized Players* and *The 100 Greatest Baseball Autographs*. Molori has also written for ESPNW.com, *Boston Metro, Providence Journal, Lowell Sun*, and *The Eagle-Tribune*. His radio and TV credits include: ESPN, SiriusXM, Fox, Comcast, NESN, and NECN. A writing and media professor at Lasell College, Molori has lectured at Emerson College, Boston University, and Curry College. His awards include: New England Emmy Award, CableACE, Beacon Award, and the New Hampshire Association of Broadcasters Award. For his contributions as a sports journalist, Molori was inducted to the Methuen, MA, Athletic Hall of Fame in 2011, along with 1987 Cy Young Award winner Steve Bedrosian.

Vince Malta is a recognized Professional Model Bat expert and author of *Louisville Slugger Professional Player Bats—A Complete Reference Guide*, the primary reference for countless collectors, auction houses, and baseball museums, including the Baseball Hall of Fame in Cooperstown, New York. A great ambassador to the bat-collecting hobby, Malta is known as a person very willing to share his extensive expertise with others. He currently works with fellow bat expert, John Taube, on providing authentication services for PSA/DNA.

John Taube, owner of J.T. Sports, is the lead Professional Model Bat expert for PSA/DNA Authentication Services. With over 25 years of experience, Taube's dedication to the study of physical attributes and bat dating have pinned him as one of the world's leading experts in the field. Taube, in conjunction with Vince Malta, has helped standardize bat authentication and grading in the sports collectibles industry. Together, they have an ongoing commitment to expand the existing knowledge of professional model bats.

Tony Dube is president of White Point Imaging in Windsor, Connecticut. One of the first to embrace digital photography, he has extensive knowledge of leading-edge equipment and techniques. His images depicted in *The T206 Collection: The Players & Their Stories The Cracker Jack Collection: Baseball's Prized Players,* and *The 100 Greatest Baseball Autographs* received critical acclaim for set design, styling, and lighting. In addition to product and collectibles photography, Dube works on lifestyle and model photography, as well as non-professional subjects. He also enjoys coaching baseball, playing racquetball, inventing products, and working on his photographic series called "Collectographs™," the art of collecting.